THE SLEEPER MUST AWAKEN

Jean Erasmus

Llumina Press

© 2007 Jean Erasmus

All rights reserved. No part of this publication may be reproduced or transmitted in any form or by any means electronic or mechanical, including photocopy, recording, or any information storage and retrieval system, without permission in writing from both the copyright owner and the publisher.

Requests for permission to make copies of any part of this work should be mailed to Permissions Department, Llumina Press, PO Box 772246, Coral Springs, FL 33077-2246

ISBN: 978-1-59526-782-5 (PB)
       978-1-59526-783-2 (Ebook)

Printed in the United States of America by Llumina Press

Library of Congress Control Number: 2007901720

Contents

Acknowledgments	i
Author's Note	iii
Introduction	v

ACT I — 1
    Of Heroes and Journeys — 3
    The Ordinary World — 12
    Beware: Threshold Guardians and Shape Shifters Ahead — 16
    Crossing the Threshold — 23

ACT II — 25

The Mentor — 27
    Question Everything — 27
    Open Your Eyes: Life as a Box — 33
    Eyes Opening — 37
    Opening Wider — 37
    Life as a Box: Breaking Free — 41
    The Universe Within — 42
    Eyes Open, but Not Yet Focusing — 45
    Focusing — 49
    Starting to See — 53
    See and Understand — 53

Deconstructing Illusion — 61
    Time as an Illusion — 61
    Space as an Illusion — 62

Reality Check — 65
    Tantra — 65
    Kabbalah — 67

Understanding	70
Applying the Tools to Our Lives	74
The Obstacles Ahead	83
Approaching the Point of No Return	86

Our Allies — 89
Your Best Friend	89
Confessions of Spirit Existence	94
Mind the Mind	96
The Body Re-Viewed	97
Now What?	103

Body — 105
Maintenance: An Introduction	105
Maintenance: Energy in = Energy out	106
Maintenance: You Are What You Eat	109
Maintenance: Crystal Clear Water	115
Maintenance: Exercise	116
Maintenance: Supplements	117
Health as Wealth	118
The Mind-Body Tango	118
Body, Mind and Health	120

Mind — 124
Repairing the Bridge	124
The Difference Between Religion and Spirituality	126

Spirit — 133
The Glass Elevator	133
Remember Slumberland	135
Conclusion	139

Obstacles — 142
Ego	143
The Holy Grail Called Happiness	147
Relationships	151

Relationship with You	152
Sex and Sexuality	153
A Message for Men	158
A Message for Women	161
Sexuality: A Final Thought	164
Relationships Continued	165
Partners/Spouses	169
Children	172
A Short Note on "Teenagers"	177
Friends and Family	178
Difficult and Nasty Ones	178
Work	179
Money and Wealth	180
The "Want a Lots"	182
The "Have a Lots"	184
Villains	**186**
Puppet Masters	186
Social Services	192
Private Services	194
Moving into Act III	195
ACT III	**197**
Faust Syndrome and Its Created Obstacles	199
Recognizing the True Root of "Evil"	209
Easier Said Than Done, but…	217
World of Wonder	222
How to Save GAIA and Ourselves	**224**
Vibratory Savvy	224
Environmental Savvy	225
Beware of Consumerism Sands	226
Ideas for a Brighter Future	228
Artificial Intelligence or AI	230

Signs: The Call to Awaken	235
Ancient Fingers	237
Modern Fingers	249
Now What?	262
…Ordinary World into World of Wonder	265
References and Recommended Reading	269

Acknowledgments

Although they were not directly involved or physically present during the writing of this book, I would still like to thank the great thinkers and writers of this century who dared to break out of the dogmatic and mental as well as spiritual prison of the present human condition. Their works have inspired me tremendously, and I have mentioned them throughout the book.

I would also like to thank my friends and family members for their support through the years—it is always appreciated.

And then, I would like to thank my wife—my muse and soul mate—for her tremendous support and love. Without her, this book would never have been written.

Author's Note

The reader will notice that the book is divided into three acts, which might seem strange for a nonfiction book. But the reason for this will become apparent in the first part of the book.

It is also worth mentioning that the first part of act 2 contains some pages with technical details that might seem daunting to some readers. I have presented it in the easiest way possible, as it shapes one of the cornerstones of most concepts in this book and life in general. It is a small but very important part of the book, so please don't skip it, no matter how tempted you feel. The perseverance through this small section will pay off to reveal a much easier and hopefully very enjoyable journey.

Good fortune!

Introduction

Strange is this thing we call life. We live it everyday: getting up in the morning, feeding the kids, surviving rush hour, working, loathing the narcissistic boss, rush hour yet again, feeding the kids (yet again), the nagging wife when you drink with the buddies, the slob snoring after sex, sexual desire for people other than your spouse or partner (that burns you with guilt), debt, the crappy trailer after a hard day's emotional slavery for an "idiot" of a director, lazy "diva" actors, tax, bigger-getting butt, and then those other "little" things like the war in the Middle East (where is this Iraq exactly?) and some kind of weird virus killing dozens (as long as it doesn't come here)…life in a nutshell.

Most of us never stop and think what this "life" really is all about. We often treat it as though it were nothing special, getting the blues, often thinking or saying, "I wish I was dead." And then one day, when life threatens to leave us, we cling to it with knuckles white as bone. Why?

For a moment step back from your own life and look at the world as objectively as you can. On the positive side, there are things like love (that often "hurts"), family (whom you love and loathe, depending on the day), friends (love and loathe like family), good food, beaches, café latte, internet, books, films, art, music, parks with dogs, running streams, theater, children's laughter, the embrace of a loved one…

Then on the negative side, there's war (the reason always obscure), people dying of hunger, ethnic cleansing, shrinking rain forests, species going into extinction, global climate change, terrorism…

You find yourself center stage, with all of this playing out around you, and wonder: "What is the meaning of it all? What is my part in it?"

It must be the oldest question by humanity: "What is the meaning of life?"

Is it happiness? Seems to be, as everyone desperately searches for happiness, even the newly invented gods called celebrities—one day smiles and marriage, tears and lawsuits the next. Yes, we are all searching for that "Holy Grail" called happiness. We look for it in religion or neo-religion (leading us into war, killing millions over millennia), psychiatrists (who have psychiatrists themselves), self-help books that help for a week or so, alcohol, drugs, weird sex, diets, plastic surgery...the list is endless. But the happiness eludes us like a phantom in the night.

But what if happiness per se, is not the thing we are really looking for? What if happiness is only the reward we feel as a by-product when we accidentally and lightly touch the thing we are unknowingly looking for, tricking us into thinking it to be the Holy Grail? It would then be like mistaking a sweet taste for sugar, honey, strawberry, chocolate or the kiss of a loved one, forever pursuing the shadow instead of the shadow-caster itself. What if our world, or "reality" as we perceive and believe it to be, is the way it is because we have forgotten the secret of life, ignorant of the true meaning of it, and maybe even kept away from deliberately? Let me paint a quick picture.

Once upon a time, there was a lonely ship battered by a merciless midnight storm. As it shipwrecked near a desolate island, only the children and a few elders survived. Some weeks had passed when suddenly the elders contracted a strange fever and died, leaving the children armed with only a sparse knowledge of written and spoken language.

After a few days of escalating hunger, the law of survival surfaced from the children's primate subconscious minds, as they started competing heavily for food and shelter; fight after fight occurred until death befell one of the meekest. It was at this precise moment that the strongest became the leaders of the pack and the meekest the followers.

But there were some of those meek ones, who while waiting on the side for their scraps after the feast, sat and looked over the sunset seascape, dreaming of faraway places, somehow feeling connected to what lay beyond. Day after day, sunset after sunset, the dreamers gazed upon the horizon and the strange rusty iron structure that vaguely reminded them of the night of the storm, until one day, years later, one of the dreamers leaped into the sea, swimming out to the iron structure with all his might.

He swam against the tide,
he swam against the shark,
and blindly broke through the cunning webbing of the dark.

Exhausted, he reached the brown iron skeleton of the desolate ship, catching his breath as he looked back at the faraway shore with waving miniature figures bobbing up and down, their vocal noises drowned by the raging ocean below.

After catching his breath, he started exploring the vessel inch by inch. After some time, he found skeletons of "giants," their front limbs sprawled out upon tables with strange pictures and rectangular objects. He opened one of the rectangular objects and remembered the sound "book" in his mind. Yes, this thing in his hands was a book! And books contain information! He paged through all the books, remembering some of the words here and there. But it was the pictures that interested him most, pictures of magic places with rectangular mountains in which people dwelled. He kept paging, book after book, until he reached one that was filled with pictures of people he vaguely remembered. He kept staring at their faces—the man, woman and child smiling benevolently at him from the page—until he suddenly felt a warm current rushing from his heart, welling up his eyes with tears. Fond, forgotten memories started flooding his mind as he fully remembered those smiles, the smiles of his beloved family.

We are not unlike those children. We are stranded here in "Life on Planet Earth," the Why completely forgotten. While most of us merely fight to survive day after day through primate habit, even though it is in designer suits and high heels, there are those who, like the children on the sides waiting for the scraps, sense the lost and forgotten connectedness that needs to be found.

The "fighters"—the rich and powerful corporate and world leaders—have become so accustomed to and so good at surviving that they are delusional, believing themselves to be the ultimate invincible rulers of "their" little island, mistaken for the universe. But the archetypal picture of the top dog with the dream house and car, programmed into us since childbirth to be the Holy Grail of happiness, eventually fails all of us dreadfully. We are chasing after the illusory shadow, and not the shadow-caster. Ironically this illusion (and delusion) does not only lead to unhappiness, but will eventually lead to the loss of everything, our quest for happiness through our consumerist fever burning everything we hold dear to a cinder.

This sad knowledge is subconsciously known by all of us. This basically divides us into the "fighters" and the "dreamers." The fighters deny and suppress this knowledge and try escaping it by fighting even harder. They are like a panic-stricken animal caught in a pit of quicksand—the more they fight to survive, the more they sink into the depths of it, taking everything with them, including the would-be helpers. Unfortunately, they don't realize this, as they sink very slowly, feeling the false comfort of the hugging warm death trap.

The dreamers, on the other hand, acknowledge this feeling in their hearts, and set themselves on a quest to find the forgotten path, leading away from the cave of quicksand.

But many a dreamer who tried to break free from this illusion, seeking the forgotten knowledge beyond the distant horizon, failed due to the cunning of some fighters who lured them into these very caves in order to use them as an escape or last meal ticket before the ultimate doom. This per se has created mainly three groups of dreamers:

Firstly, those who blindly follow any possible glimpse of light to relieve the pain of everyday "suffering," not realizing that the light at the end of the tunnel could be an approaching train, so desperate they are to find the answers to the burning questions.

Secondly, the ones on the opposite side, so accustomed to the way of humanity and so filled with cynicism and subconscious fear that they will resist anything out of the "norm," even if it can help them. There are so many false prophets out there leading the first group into desolate caves, who blames them?

Thirdly, the minority group who stand in the middle, unsure of which side to take. To them, both sides seem to be a lose-lose situation, as neither of the first two groups succeeds in finding the path that leads from the caves.

Seems like a very depressing scenario, but there is a way out of the death caves. It is indeed the third group of dreamers who are the most likely ones to find the answer, as they are in the most objective position of all. They are on the fine balance of, "shall I or shan't I?" The problem for the rest is that they are so caught up in the detail of what they are busy with—be it fighting to the bone to survive, desperately chasing after illusory answers cunningly spun by the fighters or sitting on the other side being fear-filled and cynical—that they don't stand back and see the bigger picture. It is in the bigger, objective picture that the answer lies.

On this point I can say that this book was not meant to be another cheap and cheerful, quick buck-making self-help book. In my humble opinion, there are enough of those out there addressing only a minute part of the human condition. Frankly, there is no more time for this kind of selfish "change your life in a jiffy" indulgence trickery. Things are getting hot under the cover of our world, and the time has come to make a change, starting with ourselves. Luckily, there are numerous books written on this very subject. Most of them either fall in the quantum physics category, or the "New Age" category, dividing our dreamers in the process. With this book, I have tried to unify concepts ranging from religion to modern physics in a clear and understandable manner, and to use this unification to help the reader help him- or herself before helping others. It is my intention to bring people together; thus I wrote this book to act as a bridge, unifying everyone, from saint to sinner, pavement sweeper to world leader.

This book is a gentle nudge to the sleeper on the bench, taking an afternoon nap in the park. It is the wake-up call to the dreamer, for the time to wake up is at hand, as night falls on the park…

ACT I

All the world's a stage,
And all the men and women merely players;
They have their exits and their entrances,
And one man in his time plays many parts,

William Shakespeare

Of Heroes and Journeys

The human race is a magnificent species despite all of its errors. We are the primates that in the gray past one day, decided to stand up to our predators. We stood up to the big brown bear that came for our families, and the hunted became the hunter. We made fire by stone and wood, and with the blackened charcoal, skillfully mixed with iron red mud, drew our history on the walls of cavernous halls.

As far as those who can tell, humans in this form we possess today have been around for more than one hundred thousand years. In the last thirty to forty thousand years, we started telling our stories on the walls of caves by rock painting: tales of the victorious hunt and bizarre humanoid creatures from our dreams. We didn't just dream like most animals do (if REM sleep equals dreaming), but we told our dreams to each other. We shared our experiences in the form of the story, the story that remained with us through the ages, interwoven into the very fabric of our existence as a species.

We all love a good story. It is the flame to the moth as we get blindly drawn into the adventures of another, filled with pleasures and peril. It is this flame of the story that we find burning in every aspect of our lives, from bedtime stories as a child to the daily relaxing soap opera after work. From adventure film in cinema sublime to a game of football on the television, or better yet, at the stadium. Think sports are not stories? Then how about this: "Once upon a time, there were two great nations, and as the stars aligned, they would gather on the sacred green field, and fight for glory." You will find "once upon a time" in every sport, TV show, film and book with heroes, their goals, their villains and their obstacles. Sometimes they will be victorious, and sometimes they won't. Look deeper and you will find that life is a "once upon a time," and we are all obliviously living our stories in the greater story of humanity. "Once upon a time, there was a great species called Humanity living on the only living planet in the known universe. They were a magnificent species, capable of love and tenderness, prose, poetry and music. They built the most fascinating structures and devised machines that could fly at supersonic speeds. But there was also darkness in their hearts, a darkness that erupted from the depths of despair and threatened them with the extinction of their very existence. The blue pearl in black velvet sky was in mortal danger."

Stories go much deeper than we think. They are the threads that bind the magic carpet of our existence. They've been with us all along, defining in a sense our uniqueness as a species. They are the essential two-way mirrors in which our lives are reflected. Each and every one of us is living our own unique story, and in denial of these "boring" stories we live, we focus our attention on other "better" and more exciting stories. They range from fictional soap operas, movies and sports to the daily local and international news, to our cheap tabloids telling us the "secret" lives of our man-made gods—celebrities. Just as long as the story is more interesting than our own, lived obliviously in denial. But it is this denial and oblivion that lead us, the hero in our own story, into the forest of doom, the forest of boredom, of love lost and everyday slavery to pay the never-ending expenditures. I once read somewhere that, if one does not control one's own destiny, someone else will. Thus, if you are not telling your own story the way you want to hear, see, feel and live it, then someone or something else will gladly do it for you. We must take the courage to tell our stories the way we want to live them. But before we can do this, we need to know something more about the machinery of a story.

Think of your favorite story in a book or film. In this story you will find a setting and a central character that will create a story as he or she moves through this setting. The character will

The Sleeper Must Awaken

make us laugh and cry, and when he or she is in danger, we will fear for him or her. We will follow the ups and downs with this character until the very end, and be awash with a sea of emotion and wonder. While most of us just lose ourselves in the escapism of our favorite stories, others have wondered about the nature of the stories, the mystery behind them, and the power they hold over us.

It was in recent years that Swiss psychologist Carl Jung familiarized us with the term "archetype." Archetypes are those recurring symbols, metaphors and characters in everything we see, from "real" life to myths, legends and especially dreams. We will see good and evil, heroes, friends and foes. We will see messianic figures arising from every culture you can think of. We will dream of snakes and spiders, or of that strange but yet familiar house. And when we wake up, we feel that it should somehow mean something—like Joseph understanding the symbols of the Egyptian Pharaoh's dream, depicting the seven years of famine that would arise. They are the introvert and extrovert that Jung popularized—the follower and the leader, the oppressed and the oppressor. It was these archetypes of which Jung spoke that inspired Joseph Campbell, an American writer who studied comparative mythology, to dig deeper into the mysteries of the story and flesh out the fabric from which it was made. He wrote a highly influential book called *The Hero with a Thousand Faces* based on his years of comparison of worldwide mythical structure, in which he revealed the "cracked code" of myth and storytelling. He realized that myths, or stories, consist of recurring key elements, characters and archetypes that interact with each other in a certain pattern, shaping the likes of a quest or journey—the Hero's Journey.

This book had a profound influence on writers and filmmakers who used it as a rough template on which completely new and highly successful stories could be built. Christopher Vogler wrote a wonderful book called *The Writer's Journey*, based on the works of Campbell, to give a practical guide to writers in helping them polish their storytelling craft. He simplified and merged the Hero's Journey with the already used theatrical script pattern, infusing it with useful archetypes or ancient recurring characters. The classic script is broken down into three acts something like this:

ACT I: we find ourselves immersed in the Hero's world, the Ordinary World, where our hero lives an ordinary life (no matter how strange it may seem to us). We are introduced to the Hero, going about his or her daily routine. Then, something changes the circumstances of the Hero. It could be something subtle, like the Heroine realizing that she has a drinking problem ruining her life, or an out loud adventurous happening, like our Hero's wife being kidnapped by aliens. This happening is the Calling of the Hero to change, the so-called Herald. It challenges the Hero to leave behind the comfortable and familiar lifestyle and beliefs, and Cross the Threshold into a new way of life or an adventure. But the Threshold Guardians are there to keep our Hero from accepting the call, resulting in the Refusal of the call. It could be disbelief in our Heroine, enforced by her disbelieving parents and peers saying she will never be able to quit drinking, or our Hero fearing the aliens that took his wife. This hesitation makes us go, "come on, you can do it" in our hearts. And then, as if by magic, something pushes our Hero over the Threshold into the first steps of his or her adventure.

ACT II: It is here that our Hero will start on the journey that will manifest itself both externally and internally. There will be physical as well as mental perils and countless obstacles that our Hero needs to overcome in order to grow as a character. It is this growth that appeals to us. We love our Heroes to fight for their lives and their honor. Think how absolutely boring it would be if the Hero never struggled, if everything was just plain sailing. No, we want that tension and excitement. It is this that gives rise to drama and keeps us glued to the journey. And there must be other characters to make our Hero's Journey more interesting as well. They are the Hero's Mentor or wise old man or woman, the Hero's Allies or friends, the Shape Shifters or false friends, and then the Villain or ultimate foe. The Mentor will teach the Hero how to travel the journey the best he or she can; the Allies will assist the Hero in his or her quest; the Shape Shifters deceive our Hero; and the Villain will guard the ultimate prize for which our hero must fight in Act III.

It is in ACT III that our Hero will confront his or her inner as well as outer demons in order to reach the goal of the story—the so-called "elixir." This journey might have a happy or a tragic ending, but either way, there will be change and hopefully growth experienced by our Hero as well as the observers. This change and growth are the ultimate goal of any story, something to learn from before returning home with the elixir.

On reading Campbell's and Vogler's fascinating books, something profound dawned upon me, something that we all intuitively knew, but forgot—we are all heroes in our own stories, and archetypes to others' stories. From the less thought of cleaner in a small town, to a president of a country to humanity itself, we are all characters in each other's stories.

Let me explain and augment my point:

Act I: You are fast asleep in your warm bed, dreaming the most wonderful dream—The Ordinary World.

Then you hear this annoying and repeating sound pulling you from your slumber. You realize it is the alarm—The Herald.

You silence it and think you just can't face this day—Refusal to the call, the warm bed and the discontent for the awaiting working day being the Threshold Guardian.

You hear the sounds of your hungry child scrambling about in the kitchen, and you get out of bed, answering the call.

Act II: You are taking a shower, and the water is cold (boiler broke)—obstacle number one.

You burn the toast, and the kid has a tummy bug—obstacle number two.

At long last you get on the metro on your way to the job you hate, and look at all the sad faces around you. The person next to you suddenly starts a conversation you're not really ready to accept (second Refusal?), but after a while, you realize that he listens to you intensely, and gives you advice on how to think about life in better terms—The Mentor.

You're late for work, the narcissist boss giving you a warning—meeting the Villain.

Switching on your PC, you realize you forgot to save your work of the previous day, and your heart sinks into your boots—obstacle number three.

A friend comes over, gives you a disk and tells you they saved your work on the system before you left, relief—Ally.

As you get coffee on your break, you overhear another "friend" gossiping behind your back about you—Shape Shifter.

After lunch, your nasty boss starts bullying one of the introverted workers you have a soft spot for. Having a shitty day so far, you lose your head, stand up against the boss, telling him exactly what you think of him—challenging the Villain.

The boss finds a way to fire you.

Act III: You sit on the metro train, realizing that you just lost your job for standing up for the meek and mild. You are filled with fear for the unknown future. Being a single parent, you don't have any idea how you will be able to support your child.

But then you remember the conversation with the Mentor, and you realize you've always hated the job and secretly waited for something to push you into finishing that novel you've always wanted to write. The fear slowly dissolves as the train comes out into the open, the sun washing over your face. You realize you've just had a new and exciting calling, a calling to face the wicked world of "publish or perish," and you're feeling ready for the challenge.

The Sleeper Must Awaken

And so follows another exciting episode in the story of You.

And so you can apply the Hero's Journey to every aspect of your life. With every court case, patient, operation, client, film, album, book, new and current relationship—everything in your life is built upon the blueprint of the story. It is because the story is a reflection of life, and life is a reflection of the story.

We are Heroes in our own journeys, and the Mentors, Shape Shifters, Allies and Villains in others' stories. Just think about it. How many times have you had an argument with your spouse, children, boss or workers? To them, you are the Villain, as they are to you. How many times have you given someone small but effective advice, as others have you? That's being the Mentor. Defending your friends makes you an Ally, and betraying them, a Shape Shifter. Think you've never betrayed anyone? What about that promise you made that you couldn't keep? Even if it wasn't your fault (like running out of time or money), you still disappointed your friend or child, hoping for the best, then being disillusioned by you.

This happens on a larger scale as well. Think of two nations at war, both thinking the other one to be the enemy or Villain that needs to be destroyed. On a larger scale still, we look at ourselves as humanity, our greatest Villain being ourselves. The story of humanity has always been an interesting one, but looking to the future, I wonder if it will have a happy ending in Act III (which may just be upon us if one looks at the current state of things).

Now what makes a story good? What makes it exciting? The answer is conflict. Conflict, arriving from the reaction to other archetypes and obstacles, drives the drama. As Alfred Hitchcock once remarked, "Drama is life with all the boring bits cut out." Can you imagine how boring a story would be if the Hero was perfect, had all the money in the world, had a wonderful relationship with everyone around him or her, had no obstacles or conflicts and just did the day-to-day things until the story ended? There would be no character growth, no lesson learned and no drama. Some might argue and say that is exactly the story they want to read or see. But maybe this is because they need escapism from their own drama-filled stories. Our lives — our stories — are filled with obstacles and conflicts, from our character flaws (internal conflict) to our villains and day-to-day trivia (external conflicts). They are there to make our stories interesting and to provide purpose in a world seemingly there by chance; for all sentient beings need purpose.

Looking at this Hero's Journey and story concept and the way it so closely resembles our lives, one can't help but to wonder which was first: life or the story. What I mean by this is, are we here by mere chance and we just invented stories for entertainment, or are stories a gift, given to us by the ancient ones in order to remind us that it is a reflection of our own story that runs much deeper in the fabric of existence? Do we really exist, or are we, like my wife once remarked, just very realistic dreams of a super being? It reminds me of a dream I once had when I studied medicine. I was about twenty-three, unmarried with no kids (being a kid myself) and at that stage, mostly interested in passing my exams and going out in the evenings with friends. But then one night, I dreamed I was much older, in my dream coming home from work. As I entered the kitchen, I could hear my wife speaking to my child, telling him that he must go and look in the kitchen, daddy's home. Then in came running this beautiful, fair-haired, blue-eyed boy of roughly five years old, arms open toward me. I remember so distinctively when I picked him up and held him, the smell of his hair, and the love we shared for each other. I woke up, and that realistic world I found myself in was gone, leaving me feeling very down. That child, my child, was gone. It was as if he died, and I missed him severely for months after that. I still catch myself thinking about him, and writing about him now makes me a bit sad. From this dream, I wondered — what if he really does exist in some form or another? What if dreams are more real than we think? Maybe our minds create worlds and characters when we sleep just as

The Sleeper Must Awaken

God or some form of Super Being is dreaming us. Maybe we are dreaming each other while the Super Being is dreaming us and we are dreaming Him, thus creating and recreating each other's stories.

It is at this stage impossible to know, but that the story structure does apply to our lives is almost unquestionable. Our lives are stories; we are the Heroes in our own, and characters in others' stories, from friend to foe. Once we know this, we can realize that we are actually telling our own stories by making choices with each archetypal encounter and each obstacle. Why most of us live dead-end stories is because we don't know that we are living one. It is with our choices that we shape our own stories. Where you are today, is determined by those millions of choices you made after reacting to all those archetypes and obstacles in your passing life (story) so far. You are married to that person in your life because you said "yes." You are in that job because you chose it. It was the only job because you didn't look far enough, or found it easier to blame others afterward if something should go wrong. You are a very well-paid and respected actor, coming from the direst background, because you chose to persist until you found your dream. We all have our own Hero characteristics, our own strengths and weaknesses and our own obstacles and archetypal encounters. What looks as easy obstacles to one might be extremely difficult for another. We must learn to focus on our own stories, build on our strengths, improve our weaknesses and make the right choices when obstacles arise, for they always do.

We must recognize the Call to the Journey, cross the Threshold Guardian, and look for our Mentors, Allies, Shape Shifters and Villains, and live and tell more interesting and satisfying stories. We can then also as a community, a nation and a species, learn to tell a good story with a happy ending.

The Ordinary World

I lightly touched on our world we live in today in the Introduction. From the worst of humanity — war, genocide, pollution, greed, exploitation of developing countries and the cause for extinction of thousands of species — to the best of humanity — love, family, hugs and kisses, ice cream on a hot summer day, strolls in the park, watching a sunset at your favorite beach, Bach, Beethoven, The Beatles, popcorn at the cinemas, flowers from a loved one...

The Ordinary World.
Filled with an information overload in our modern day-to-day living, with broadcast giants delivering the "morning show" with breakfast, filled with dire news from all over the world. The same dire news seeps into our beings from the "newspaper of the year" or the radio on the metro trains or buses on the way to work. In between, mixed with the "who's who in the zoo" celebrity pages depicting our self-made gods as fallen heroes with their pimples and cellulite (that we all have), with mass bombardment by retail companies on what we should wear to be cool this summer, while our MP3 players are blasting away in our ears, creating a small but private space in an overcrowded world.

Our Ordinary World.
Work you hate, boredom (feeling guilty about it), unhappy relationships, desire for more _____ (fill in anything you like), chronic fatigue, that cold you just can't shake, the everlasting weight problem and of course, the self-help books that only work for about a week. The plastic surgery hype (makes one part look artificially great, only to overemphasize some other spot,

back under the knife you go), the bizarre fashion trends, not to mention the bizarre way of getting kicks (only to get caught with your pants down, literally).

Not enough money (although owning a private jet), too much money, not the right money, not the right house, neighborhood, state, city, country, husband, wife, kids, parents nor the right God.

Damn Ordinary World

Luckily, you now know that the Ordinary World is only a part of the story that you find yourself in, and that we are all characters playing our little roles in it. So now knowing that you are the Hero in your story, ever wondered who or what is telling yours? Is it God, or society, or chance as some empiricists might prefer it? Or is it you?

Looking at the many stories of creation we find in religious literature, it would seem that we chose to become the "masters" of our own destiny. We wanted to know the answer to the everlasting why, and the price we paid was free will. Free will in a world or stage if you will, without the crystal clear knowledge of why precisely we made the choice to have free will, and what to do with it. We lack the understanding of the greatest gift in the universe, and therefore use it to play out these little pop dramas of ours on a finite stage, while God or Chance is watching. And the name of this stage play is: "How to take happiness from others and have it all for yourself."

Happiness seems to be the most important relic, or Holy Grail, that everyone is thirsting for, deliciously eluding us in an eternal smash-and-grab game. Happiness is reflected in the likes of love, sex, money, status and health, hence our obsession with things connected to it—millions of books on the art of love and sex, sex toys and funny little garments to take the boredom out of it, plastic surgery, cosmetics, fashion following, slaving away for your (the bank's) perfect house and happy family portraits that get broken in a hard night's fight.

The happiness is there for a brief moment, but then like a soft dream fades away as you wake up to another day of slave labor, "unsupported" by your family and friends (as they themselves are struggling with the same dilemma).

Why, if happiness is so important, does it keep on being exchanged for its complete opposite? Is happiness then this sacred relic we are looking for, or is it a mere distraction from the real quest in our lives? Are we confusing the taste of sweet with all those things that can mimic it? And when it comes to unhappiness, aren't we confusing the cause for it with our own apathy to remove ourselves from the cause? In other words, why are we moaning about our burning hand but not removing it from the fire?

What if our Ordinary World is an illusion we ourselves have created, the fact forgotten? What if we have been lost in our own story, like going into a labyrinth for fun or other reasons, and by day six, forgot all about it, struggling from day to day by chopping up parts of the labyrinth for firewood and living off the occasional passing mouse? In this world, surely happiness would mean the hottest fire and the biggest mouse, wouldn't it?

But one day, some would pluck the courage to look up and see the sky above the labyrinth, filled with stars and a sun passing from "east" to "west," feeling that there must be more to this restrictive labyrinth world. They would use the sun and stars, and with other "believers" follow the clues out of the labyrinth. Of course they would be ridiculed by the nonbelievers, how else? It's a story, and our Heroes need Threshold Guardians, Shape Shifters and Villains for a fulfilling story.

The Herald is calling. It is saying that there is more to life than this Ordinary World we experience everyday. It is pointing to the sky, and only the fool stares at the finger pointing at the sky. In essence, do you want to be one of the actors acting out the age-old story of "How to take happiness from others, and have it all for yourself"? Or do you want to write and direct your own story in a company with others who aspire to greater stories?

Cross that Threshold if you dare. Seek out the new story that awaits you.

Beware: Threshold Guardians and Shape Shifters Ahead!

Never mind the boogie man, watch out for that Threshold Guardian—the voice of denial that says, "no, it's impossible, it can't be" or as I like to call him, the Bullshit Man or BS man for short.

The BS man in your life can be anything from your parents and peers saying that you're not able to do something, to cultural and religious beliefs that keep you from achieving your dreams. In this day and age, especially in the western world, religion and science can be the mouthpiece of the culprit. These two factors could just never stay free from politics, and have been abused so many times in human history to gain and maintain power by manipulation of the masses.

Religion and science in the ideal world would be wonderful, where religion is the bringer of comfort in difficult times, and also the source of social interaction, while science is the bringer of knowledge and novelty. But alas, we don't live in a perfect world, and these two elements are the most commonly worn masks by the shape-shifting Threshold Guardians. They are used as pillars to support the illusion of Western Civilization, which almost everyone accepts as the only reality.

But first, what are religion and science exactly? How did they come to be in the first place, and why do they have such a profound power in our lives?

Let's have a look at religion first. The origin of religion is a bit elusive, as it has been with the human race since the beginning. Strong traces of it can be seen, depicted in the rock paintings of Upper Paleolithic Europe and South Africa dating as far back as thirty to forty thousand years. When looking at all religious beliefs, a common theme is noticed—there is a strong belief and study of the origin of our universe, what happens before and after this life, the belief in supernatural beings from beneficial to malign and the influence these factors have on our daily lives. There is always a reference to a world beyond our own, where these supernatural beings reside, and where we return to after life or visit during shamanist ritual. Religion has shown to be beneficial, contrary to the beliefs of Sigmund Freud, who coined it mass neurosis and wish-fulfillment. It proves to aid the health of individuals, especially mental health and addictions, and acts as a strong social support system. But unfortunately, because of its strong influence on people, especially those in need and despair, it can become a tool to control, like Karl Marx said, "Religion is the sigh of the oppressed and the opium of the people." It can cause "us versus them" syndrome, and has been the cause as well as the excuse to make war. When one looks at the history of mankind and its religions using critical theory, one can clearly see how there never was neutrality in the forwarding of religious knowledge. It has always been used, abused and corrupted by powerful key players as a means to an end, especially in the obsession of land acquiring and colonialism, state power, politics and capitalism. Also, looking at the different kinds of religion—Christianity, Islam, Judaism, Buddhism, Hinduism, Jainism, Sikhism, Zoroastrianism and other indigenous beliefs—how can we tell which one is right? Obviously yours would be, but that is just because you grew up with it, or changed faith due to a profound "spiritual" experience (which is still regarded as hocus-pocus by reductionists). You will be greatly surprised by the profound coinciding similarities among all religions when closely studied (which we will look into a bit later). This said, it is then sad to see the three Abrahamic religions—Christianity, Islam and Judaism—which share the same ancient scriptures (apart from some, like the New Testament, Zohar and Holy Qur'an) and essentially believe in the same God, the God of Abraham, to have been locked into war for so many centuries.

Christianity alone has shattered into so many pieces, from Roman Catholic to Anglican to Protestant to Methodist, Dutch-Reformed, Baptist, Seventh-day-Adventist, New Apostolic, Old Apostolic, Rhema, Christian Revival—the list is endless. Which of those Christians are right? Which one of those will be saved and taken in by God? The irony of Christianity is that Jesus Christ didn't just come for Christians. There were no Christians before his arrival. He came for everyone, resisting politicized religion of the day and age with teachings of peace and love, coming up for the meek and discriminating against no one. After his death, powerful key players took his peaceful teachings and turned them into an exclusive and torture-loving religion, as can be seen with early Catholicism. This religious abuse can also be seen in the hatred between the Islamic groups, such as the Sunni and Shi'a. Furthermore, if we look at the history of religion, we will see that the two most common and probably the most powerful and influential (especially in a negative way with wars, land acquisition, looting, inquisition and—in this century—fundamentalist politics in both Christian and Muslim countries) are also two of the very young religions, with Islam being the younger of the two. It is then ironic to see that older religions like Buddhism, Jainism and Taoism are the more peaceful ones (with exceptions of course).

Now don't get me wrong. I am not an atheist nor opposed to religion. I'm merely saying that because of religion's strong influence on the human psyche, it is a tool of control, and has been used and abused for centuries by the powerful. It has been used to alienate people from one another and to oppress, torture and defeat the meek and the mild, hence the term "divide and conquer." Even in our modern and "enlightened" age, powerful nations are using the mask of religion to guard the threshold of acceptance, understanding and forgiveness that can give rise to eternal peace. We must guard against the abuse of religion. Leaving the matter at that, I can bring together religion and the Threshold Guardian on this point: Today's heretic is tomorrow's prophet and messiah.

Secondly, science, meaning knowledge (*scientia* in Latin), is based on acquiring knowledge by experimentation and observation of nature or empiricism. What can't be seen, observed or experimentally proven is deemed unscientific and even false. Science, a broad term for things ranging from politics to society and nature, was, according to our western history, born in ancient Greece and Rome, the fathers being Galileo Galilei, Archimedes and Leonardo da Vinci to name but a few. As a matter of fact, scientific concepts like cosmogenesis, astronomy and alchemy (chemistry) have long before CE (common era) European science existed in the east in the form of Tantra (which will be discussed later) and other ancient texts. But it is on western science that I want to focus as the modern day Threshold Guardian.

Over the centuries, as free thinkers and scientists were seen as a threat and thus oppressed by the Roman Catholic Inquisition (especially in the case of Galileo), science ironically changed into another kind of religion with the slogan, "I'll believe it when I see it." Where religion (especially Christianity in the forming western world) tried to blindly force down the existence of its view of God, science unknowingly started to try and prove or disprove it in reaction to the harsh and painful methods of religion in the latter centuries. It came to the sum of everything had to be proven, otherwise not believed nor practiced. The irony in this way of thought and general approach to life lies in the fact that this itself causes a very limiting philosophy, as can be seen in the history of science. The expert of the day will have established his name in "proving" his theory, which will be blindly believed. Then, when a younger free thinker comes with a bright new idea, challenging the old ones, he will be ridiculed and spat at, until years later, he (or she) gets "proven right." Even then the older "expert" will try and disprove the newcomer's concept to save him or herself embarrassment.

Let me tell you about the backbiting science industry, which can even be seen in day-to-day medicine, where aspiring consultants fight and ridicule each other like school boys, manipulating their "research projects" to gain that "Holy Grail" consultant post. There are some sad tales told of how scientists stabbed each other in the back for fame, fortune and mere pride and prejudice. Yes, the BS man and the Ego devil have had their fair share of causing tears and heartache in the science community. Lots of these tales can be found — from Edison trying to keep Nikola Tesla from gifting the world with the now widely used alternate current (AC) in electricity, to Fred Hoyle clinging to his steady state universe against the now "accepted" Big Bang theory, to "professional" French archaeologists belittling a Spanish "amateur" by the name of Marcelino Sanz de Sautuola, who made one of the most significant rock art findings in Europe and then was not acknowledged until his death with his lifelong bullies taking the credit. And then there's the scientific scandal of the century (as Arthur C. Clarke put it), how Big Bucks "hot fusion" university buffs spit on the finds of "cold fusion" by two "nobodies" (whose findings have been recreated numerous times by other independents), because it made them look bad in terms of economics, as their project cost millions of taxpayer dollars, and the nobodies' almost nothing.

How many times have we heard: "Scientists have found that…." or "scientists claim to have…" and "according to the latest scientific evidence…"? Have you ever thought that these scientists are mere academic men with frailties? I leave out women, because it is only recently that these same "scientists" consisting of men only have accepted women to study and sit exams to become scientists themselves. It was only in the nineteen seventies that Oxford University fully opened its doors to the female gender. Yes, for centuries, the minds of these "men of science" were clogged by the BS man and most importantly by their Egos.

Science of today, with its narrow-minded outlook of, "I'll believe it when I see it," limits the human race severely. It's like looking for your car keys. How many times have you found them at the least thought of place? It was because of your subconscious thought, "It surely can't be there," and then it was. We can also look at it this way — can we hear radio waves or see infrared light? No. But it doesn't mean they don't exist. How many times have new and groundbreaking ideas been laughed at, only to be "proven" later? As St. Augustine remarked, "Miracles do not happen in opposition to nature, but in opposition to what we know of nature." Supernatural phenomena are coined by "real scientists" as nonsense, and the study of these phenomena looked down upon as "pseudo-science." This just holds us back, keeps us from discovering and sometimes rediscovering things earlier. Worse yet is today's pharmaceutical industries, clawing at each other in the competitive market of today, selling their products after "scientifically proving" the beneficial effects, only to be caught out years later with new evidence suggesting that this "beneficial" product does more harm than good. Easily withdrawn from the market, because profits were made, they will sell their new "better and improved" product.

If we want science to be totally democratic and free, we need to adapt our view of science and change the slogan of, "It can't be, it's nonsense" to "It could be, let's investigate from all possible angles." But before that happens, don't just blindly accept the scientific Threshold Guardian's voice. Investigate for yourself by using intuition and various points of view.

I can end science as a Threshold Guardian on this point: Today's ridiculed pseudo-scientist, is tomorrow's genius.

There are a lot of Threshold Guardians and BS men out there to stop you from your continuing journey and self-discovery, more than often in the shape of a friend, thus a Shape Shifter. Critique from parents, teachers, peers, buried in your subconscious mind, cultural belief systems, religion and science — all that could be beneficial, but equally harming.

You are the Hero in your journey who needs to discover the path, learn the secrets of the path, and then walk the path to retell your story and change your destiny.

If you are ready, you can accept this calling and cross the Threshold to your new journey. But beware—for every new discovery on your path will have a Threshold Guardian lurking in the shadows of your mind—the BS man can be listened to, but then must be weighed against other points of view. The truth resides inside the Hero, inside you, and must be found.

Crossing the Threshold

It's crowded, the air loaded with the smell of smoke and bodies as people around you enjoy the party, chatting and laughing like chickens in a den. But somehow you feel alone amongst all these friends and strangers surrounding you. You take a look around the room at the furniture and interior decorating that somehow seems fake. You look up and see stage lights, and you realize that you are on a stage with everyone around you oblivious to the fact while they smoke and laugh, relishing in lame pickup lines and cheap humor. You feel claustrophobic, the need for fresh air burning inside you as you start looking for the exit. But it seems almost impossible to find your way out of the mass of sneering faces surrounding you.

You feel someone lightly touching your arm, and as you turn around you look into the eyes of heaven. A being in the likes of a human looks at you, and a benevolent smile and twinkle in his or her eyes fill your heart with warmth you haven't experienced since you were born. "Looking for some fresh air, are you?" the being asks. You nod almost sheepishly. The being points in a direction, saying, "over there you will find an old rusty door that will lead to what you are looking for." Somehow the crowd disperses slightly in the line of pointed direction, and you vaguely make out a door in the distance. You feel a bit fearful, but the being reassures you. You decide to make your way over to the door, hiding behind dark velvet curtains. As you stop in front of it, touching the old rusty doorknob, you can't help but feel the fear suffocating you again. The old red door, flaky and sinister looking, makes you think it could be a trap. Isn't red supposed to be the color of danger?

You turn around, the being still looking at you with radiance. Suddenly you can hear the being's voice in your head, "don't be afraid. Isn't red the color of a sunset? Isn't red the color of a rose you give or receive when in love? Not the color of the blood in your veins keeping you alive day by day? Don't listen to the external voice of fear. Listen to your own inner voice that urges you to seek what you shall find."

The words comfort you, and you turn around, touching the rusty knob. As the door opens, a bright light and the freshest smelling air push in against your face. You take a deep breath and open the door some more. What you see amazes you. On the other side of the door is a path, leading to a faraway forest over a beautiful meadow, a tangerine sun shining brightly on the swaying emerald grass. You look back once more, the sweaty bodies going about their business. The being's voice rings clear in your head again, "you can always come back. Just find the old rusty red door."

You smile, the excitement lifting your heart from the depths of years-long sedation and apathy. You turn around and take your first step. After all, you can always come back to this fake, stuffy old stage room.

As you walk over the meadow toward your forest, the sun and breeze washing away the stench of the stage, you can feel the being's presence in everything around you. It is very subtle, but you can feel it. The feeling telling you that your journey won't be easy. How can it be? No Hero's Journey has ever been easy. It will be filled with pleasures and perils alike, ready to be discovered. And the being of benevolence will be there to help, hidden in the fabric of the journey in the shape of coincidence, dreams and gut feel. It will be the bread crumbs and white rabbit. It will be the stars at night, guiding your ship out of the confusing labyrinth you have mistaken for real life.

ACT II

"The truth, as always, will be far stranger."

Arthur C. Clarke

The Mentor

You walk over the meadow as the sun shines warmly on your skin, a breeze gently playing with the grass around your feet. The beautiful forest is coming closer and closer, and excitement fills your heart. You come to a standstill right in front of the forest entrance, the coolness of its interior pushing against your face. You look around once more at the red door afar, and then enter the cool forest with the sun throwing a leafy glade on your face.

You hear a waterfall just around the corner, and quickening your pace, find it within a few minutes' walk. It is beautiful, a large waterfall of crystal clear waters cascading into a lovely emerald pool, surrounded by your favorite flowers. You notice flat rocks forming a path that leads to the area behind the waterfall, and you instinctively start your way there. The waterfall's soft, cool mist embraces you as you walk behind it, and you find a cave opening to your amazement. You first feel reluctant to enter, but then the inside starts to illuminate in a soft colorful glow that you find very familiar and comforting.

As you enter the cave, you realize that it is yours and yours alone. In here you can feel free to think what you want and imagine what you want without being judged by anyone, and it will be here where the Mentor will tell you interesting stories next to a warm and comforting fire.

Question Everything

In the cave you see a heap of wooden logs, neatly placed. You imagine the wood to catch flame and sure enough, a warm and cozy fire erupts. Now make yourself comfortable on the large cushion in front of the fire and open your mind to new ideas. Ready? Here we go.

I would like you to think how you did what you've done so far. I wrote a few words, describing a scene, and you created it faithfully in your mind. In fact, you are reading these words in your own cave in front of your log fire right now. You created your cave in your forest in your world in your mind. If you ever thought of being just ordinary, you couldn't have been farther from the truth. To be able to create such a world in your mind is absolutely amazing, and it is this amazing mind of yours that I would feel privileged to help free from restriction.

The first thing to help you free that stallion in your head is to ask questions. Never accept something blindly, and never take anything for granted. Questions are the dominoes of life. One leads to another and then another, until you have a kaleidoscope of questions, playing out in front of your eyes, making you follow the rabbit to wonderland. Ask questions, and the answers will eventually find their way to you.

The coming arguments that will follow in the first part of Act II, is your Mentor (you being the Hero on a journey to self-discovery). It is there to break away those restrictive habitual thoughts we have day in and day out before advancing to the next level of meeting your allies and then confronting the obstacles and ultimately the Villains. For those who find it technical, please battle through. I promise you, it will be rewarded. For those who find it boring because you understand the field, join the kindergarten bus, and you might be surprised how it connects to other things you haven't thought of. And for those of you who think it to be nonsense, try and think out of the Threshold Guardian box.

Okay, here we go…

Most of my patients in South Africa used to come for minor ailments or follow-ups for things like blood pressure and so on. Mostly I think patients come to a GP's office to talk about stuff, stuff that bothers them at work or at home. The other ailments were a secondary thing. If they find the GP in front of them approachable, they will start to lightly throw hints that they want to talk about their "stuff," and when the GP takes the bait, they fire away.

I used to be one of those bait-takers, and in the beginning I always regretted sitting and listening to their troubles. Mostly it would be things they brought on themselves, and I could only shake my head at the things I heard. After a while though, I decided to try and share some of the things I found on my quest to see if I could make a difference, as I usually saw the same patients again. It usually started with a simple question that threw most of the patients off guard. One such case was a lady who dropped out of school early because of a teenage pregnancy. She was stuck at home for years looking after her child and tending to a tired husband who was working his butt off for peanuts. It went something like this:

"...and he just doesn't care about me anymore doc," she said, tears welling up in her eyes.

"Why do you think the sky is blue?" I asked.

She looked at me as if I were mad. "Doctor, here I am telling you about my bastard of a husband who doesn't care about me, and you go and ask such a stupid question."

"Go ahead and try to answer the stupid question, you'll see why" I said.

Her tears dried up a bit, eyes rolling in her face. "Well, uh, I don't really know."

"You never thought about it?"

"No, not really."

"Why not?"

She frowned. "Why are you asking me this?"

"Because thinking about things outside the normal frame of your ordinary life is good for you. Gives you perspective on life again," I said.

She sat for a while, and then asked, "so, why is it blue then?"

"First another question that will in due time answer the first question. How many colors are there in the world?"

She snorted, then smiled and said, "I don't know, maybe seven or eight?"

"How about millions?" I said.

"Now doctor, I think you're pushing it a bit."

"OK," I said, "count how many shades of red you can find on your jersey," pointing to her jersey with all the shades of red you could dream of.

She looked at it foolishly, blushing a bit.

"And your blush is another shade," I said.

Her blush deepened, and she giggled a bit.

"Now that's only red."

"OK doc, now tell me how that will answer the question about the blue sky."

"What do you think causes stuff to have a color in the first place?"

"Oh no, another question."

"Yes, another one."

"I don't know," she said, sounding a bit annoyed.

"OK, what causes there to be light on earth?"

She smiled, as she knew the answer, and said, "the sun, of course."

"Yes, and what color is the sun's light?"

"Well," she said, "it depends on what time of day it is. Sometimes white, and sometimes orange or yellow."

"Absolutely. And why do you think that is?"

"Uh, maybe because…I don't know," she said, looking annoyed again.

"Have you ever seen the sun shining through a heavy-bottomed glass, throwing a rainbow of colors on the table?"

"Oh, yes plenty of times."

"Now the reason for that is because white light is a conglomerate of all the other colors you can think of. The moment you shine white light through a glass or prism, it breaks all the colors apart from each other, and then you can see them separately."

"Mmm, and why does a glass do that?" she asked.

My heart skipped with joy. She asked a question! She wanted to know more.

"Because every different color vibrates at its own individual frequency. The glass will separate these frequencies because it is denser than air, and then the colors split apart."

"Mmm" she said again, "then what causes objects to have color?"

I wanted to jump out of my skin now. In front of me was a woman who a few moments ago moaned and wailed about her husband, and was now asking questions about the nature of things.

"The answer lies in the different colors of light. Try to work it out for yourself."

She thought for a while, and then shook her head. "No, I can't."

"OK," I said. "Imagine you are in a pitch dark room with a flash light."

"The thought makes me uncomfortable. What's in the room with me?"

Ah, she had an imagination. She could scare herself just by imaging what else could be there in the room with her. Nice.

"You are alone in there, with various ornaments hanging on the walls."

"OK."

"You shine the flashlight onto a mirror. What happens?"

Her eyes looked into her own mind, and she said, "Well, the light reflects back to me."

"What color is it?"

She smiled. "White."

"OK, now you're shining it on a blue paper hanging on the wall. What do you see?"

"Blue paper, nothing else."

She frowned a bit with a smile. I could see she was trying to figure it out.

"The paper has a pigment that absorbs all the colors of white light, except that particular shade of blue. That which is not absorbed…"

"Is reflected!" she said with a smile. "Is that why the sky is blue?"

"No, it's more like in the case of the glass prism. The air that we breathe, our atmosphere, acts like a glass prism, and at certain times of the day, the sun's rays will be at different angles, causing different colors."

"Ah," she said, "makes sense." She sat for a few moments thinking about all this.

"For a moment there you forgot about all your worries and thought of more interesting things other than your own troubles," I said.

Her mood dipped a bit, and I could have kicked myself for saying that, but then she smiled.

"Yes, actually it was quite pleasant to think about some other things. I even think I know something more than the bully at home."

"Maybe. Now I want you to start thinking of things other than your own troubles, and go look for the answers. Question things, don't just accept them. Always question everything and then look for the answer."

She nodded like a little girl, and off she went.

I felt like a million dollars. I felt that I made a tiny little difference that day. I started doing it more on less busy days, or just ignoring my tea breaks, and chat to someone who I thought could be open-minded. At this point I would like to ask you, on what you see everyday, what it really is you see. Come to think of it, how does one see? How does the whole process work? I have thought about this so many times, and it is an absolute miracle. It starts with the sun of our solar system believe it or not. The sun (which is a ball of hydrogen and helium fusing continuously, making up ninety-nine percent of our solar system's weight) emits energy we call "light." It travels thousands of miles through space, and enters the earth's atmosphere. Here on earth, the "light" strikes all objects and then partially or completely reflects from it (depending on whether some of the object's particles absorb some of the colors or not), then enters our eyes. Our eyes in turn have a very complicated "sensor" called the retina, connected to our brains via nerves. These "sensors" or retinas, transform this "light" energy into electrochemical energy, and transfer the "message" to the visual cortex in the brain that will translate this message and send it to the higher cortex of your brain, so that you can see a sealandscape for example. See what I mean? A miracle, which in turn must make you think about other stuff, like hearing or feeling or dreaming. I hope you see what I mean that thinking about your "ordinary" world in these terms must make you think differently about the whole thing. Life is very far from ordinary. It is only ordinary when you think it is. Let's see how extraordinary you and your world really are.

Open Your Eyes: Life as a Box

I sometimes see us sitting in our own little boxes in a larger "humanitarian" box. On the inside walls of our boxes, we can see pictures of life as painted by our parents, teachers, peers and all other humans, as interpreted by the pictures on the inside of their boxes painted by their predecessors. As we grow up, we erase some of those pictures and paint our own, but they're almost always based on the pictures we see on others' boxes and the global box of humanity. What we never realize, and are never taught (even misled into thinking) is that this box doesn't have a roof or some opening. In fact, it is open above our heads. But we never look up or even dare to take a peep over the edge of it. This is exactly what we should do. We keep on looking at pictures of life instead of seeing and living it for ourselves. We can look and then move beyond the box if we start getting perspective on our realities, and see it for what it really is. Once we do this, we can acquire the tools that would enable us to tell our stories the way we were meant to.

Place yourself outside your cave, and into the place you first started reading the book today. Is it on the beach? Is it in your room on the bed, or in a car somewhere waiting for someone to return? Become aware of your surroundings—look at the detail around you, and get a sense of "being." Now, slowly drift away from yourself, becoming aware of a wider area around you—the street, parks or buildings. Up and up you go, till you can see miles around yourself and then the district or state, country, continent and eventually the beautiful planet earth, glimmering like a sapphire in black velvet. In the distance you can "sense" planets Mercury and Venus circling the sun, and as you turn around, you see the moon drifting by. Further afield, you see the red planet, Mars, approaching. Then the asteroid field, Jupiter, Saturn and her magnificent rings, the turquoise Uranus, Neptune the blue and last but not least, Pluto. You are now an average of 3,000 million miles from our sun. If you could travel at the speed of light, which is roughly 186 thousand miles per second or just over 300 thousand kilometers per second (which is the fastest anything can travel according to our current understanding of physics), it would still take a few hours to reach the earth again. Quite a distance we traveled. And this is nothing. If you travel further still, let's say at the speed of light, it will take you plus or minus 24,000 years to reach the center of our galaxy, because we are relatively "close" to the center. In turn, our galaxy is roughly 400,000 light-years across. That means it will take you 400,000 years to travel from one side to the other if you move at the speed of light. Better yet, our galaxy, the Milky Way galaxy, is only one of billions in the known universe. Gives you some perspective of how small we are compared to the universe.

Now, back in your normal surroundings, get your wits together for another journey. This time, let's travel inward.

Become aware of yourself and your surroundings again. Have a look at your arm, and study the detail of your skin. Look at the creases, the fine hair and the tonal value. Now, in your mind, slowly approach your arm's skin like a space ship would approach a massive asteroid. Slowly you come closer and closer, until the hair on your arm looks like giant trees, and your sweat pores like deep caves. You move closer and start to make out what your skin is made of — the cells of your skin — packed tightly like irregularly shaped bricks in a wall. As you move closer and closer, the cells become larger and larger, and out of the millions of cells, you pick one and move closer still. The one cell you picked is quite close, and you can see the structure of its hydrophobic cell membrane (made from microscopic fats and proteins), almost like an ocean filled with millions of balls, moving slowly to and fro. You notice one of the "transport proteins" bobbing in this "ocean of balls" like a buoy with smaller structures coming in and out of the transport protein like spaceships in a spaceport. You head for the transport protein and enter the cell through its cavernous entrance.

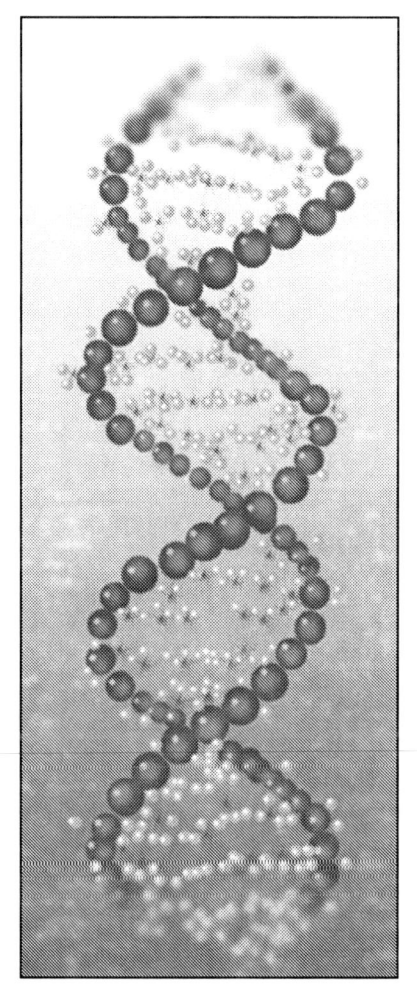

Inside, you are amazed at the size of it, with microscopic water molecules and other elements like potassium and sodium drifting in it like a fog. You notice a few organelles, but then your eyes fix on a massive ball-like structure. You are looking at the nucleus of the cell, the control center of this microscopic "city." As you move closer to the nucleus, you become aware of H-like structures inside it, and decide to have a closer look. Closer still, and you see the H-like structures being composed of very tightly woven spiral staircase structures. You are looking at your DNA spirals in your genes. Your DNA, or deoxyribonucleic acid, is you. It is the microscopic mirror image of yourself. This very complex combination molecule, two nanometers wide and almost two meters long and so tightly woven into genes that it fits into a microscopic cell, contains all the information to build a complete new you by a technique you know as cloning

You move closer still and see one of the genes unwinding its DNA contents, revealing the perfect spiral staircase. The DNA staircase suddenly splits in two, like an unzipped zipper, and another DNA-like molecule is coming closer to fit on one side like a puzzle piece. This other DNA-like molecule, is DNA's partner, called RNA which will code a piece of your DNA and then create an amino acid and other proteins necessary for a healthy life. Closer still you move to the DNA molecule and see what it's made of. You make out sugar molecules and protein molecules, combined to make the now massive looking DNA spiral. You move closer to the sugar molecule, making out the carbon, hydrogen and oxygen atoms, so arranged to make a sugar molecule. You decide to move into the hydrogen atom.

At first it appears to be a complete sphere, but as you get closer, you realize that the outer "shell" is a foglike "shield" created by the rapidly "spinning" electron around the proton at the center of the hydrogen atom. To get the right perspective of the atom, if one could assume the proton was the size of a golf ball, the closest electron would probably circulate the proton at a radius of approximately the size of two to three football stadiums — A lot of empty space in between. And so we can travel into electrons and protons to find smaller and smaller worlds.

Find yourself back with your book in your hands. Looking outward and inward is an equally daunting experience. You find yourself somewhere in the middle of a very large cascade. From a universal perspective, we are mere specs of dust in eternity, negligible little teardrops in an endless ocean. But equally, we ourselves are universes containing billions and billions of atoms, just as the universe contains billions of galaxies. Thus, outward and inward, we are right in the "middle" of eternity. This begs the question — what the hell are we doing in the middle of nowhere, or better yet, everywhere?

Eyes Opening

Before we come to that, let me remind you of the backbiting and controversial nature of the science community as stated in Act I. Remember that scientists' words can't just always be accepted as gospel, as they themselves are mere men (and women these days) with flaws, mainly due to prejudice. People will fight to the death for their beliefs, and science is no exception. The Ego is a cruel master, and will whisper deceptive little words in the ears of it's slave with a possible Nobel Prize winning theory under threat. This, however, doesn't mean that there are no decent scientists out there, fighting to find the truth in an unbiased manner. On the contrary. But never just believe things because everyone else believes it. Don't always follow the leader blindly, whether it be scientific, political or religious, as we've been deceived so many times by so many elements over such a long period of time.

Thus, yet again, question everything. Beware of the Shape Shifters as well as the Threshold Guardians. Look at different points of view. Break yourself free from indoctrinated childhood dogma, and let the "inner voice" speak the truth. There is a wise note in the Bible in 1 Thessalonians 5 that states: "test all things and keep that which is good."

Now we are ready to continue.

Opening Wider

In order to do something, one always needs to do something beforehand. It's a fact of life. Before we can be born, we need to be conceived. Before we can walk, we need to learn how to crawl. To learn new things, we need to learn how to read and comprehend first. The same applies to one's life. Before you can tell your story the way you want to, you need to know what this story is all about. You need to know what you are, and what this world you find yourself in is, and how it works.

Some will argue that it's not necessary. They will argue, "who needs to know how electricity and all that stuff works in order to switch on a light?" Okay, now what if something went wrong? It always does, being a natural fact. How else? The Hero needs his or her obstacles for a satisfying story. So, what if you knew nothing about lights, electricity and switches, and one day when you tried to switch on the light, it failed to repel the darkness? Would you call your friendly electrician at three in the morning, or would you try and fix it yourself? And if you didn't know how, would you rather wait patiently in the darkness till the break of dawn, only to hear that the electrician will be busy for another two weeks?

Now let's say you knew exactly how this simple system worked. You switch on the light, and darkness remains. You start from your fingertip, and work your way through the whole system until you find the problem.

Did you push the switch hard enough? Is there a connection problem between the switch and the lightbulb? Has the lightbulb blown? Is the trip switch for this particular room in order? Is there a power failure, or did you forget to pay the bill? If all these fail to correct the problem, you can even contemplate having had a stroke, and be suffering from instantaneous blindness!

I know this is a crude example, but you get the picture. There are many things that can make something work, or not. Personal computers are one of the many. Just one little hiccup somewhere, and your day will be ruined. Better still, it's a nightmare to find someone who will "quickly" fix your problem.

The same applies to our lives or our stories, from an individual level, all the way up to the global level. Most of us are living our lives absolutely oblivious of what we are, who we are, what this "reality" around us really is and why we are here. We know nothing about our "switches" nor "lightbulbs." We just use them without thought, but when they fail us, then we fail ourselves by bitching and moaning about it, and blaming external factors instead of simply understanding the problem and correcting it in a few simple (and sometimes difficult) steps.

We need to know, or at least try to understand what we are and what this reality around us really is. We need to open our eyes, and see the real world. If we do, we can then free our minds, and tell our stories the way we want to.

But most will fall into the Threshold Guardian trap again. "I am not clever enough...my grades were always too low...I lack the brain power," or something similar. Always an excuse to do the right thing. Don't despair, it's part of the Hero and his or her journey to refuse the call again. But let me tell you something about you and your brain.

The average human has a brain consisting of more than 10 billion interconnected brain cells, or neurons as they are called. Each of these cells has around 20,000 to 25,000 interconnections with neighboring brain cells. That means that each human has brain cell connections of universal proportions, and it is in this connection capability that the power lies. We all have powerful thinking tools in our skulls, but why is it then that some are "clever" and others are not? Let me put it this way—apart from people with serious learning disabilities due to labor trauma or abnormal genes, the average human being was born with a Porsche or Lamborghini, but rides it like a bicycle, or better yet, uses it only as a dumping zone for trash of various nature.

Take me, for example. As a child, I had a bad case of meningitis and possibly cerebellar encephalitis that left me with coordination problems for a while. Furthermore, growing up in South Africa and gaining my first impressions of the world via the Protestant church and strict Afrikaans schools, I experienced a world of restrictions. I grew up thinking I was stupid and that I would never excel in anything. But as I grew older, I realized that I was doing great in music, that my grades were actually pretty good, and that I had various other talents that popped up as life went on. I remember when I was about nine or ten, when we had our swimming pool built, there was a particular area that didn't want to dry up, and hence, couldn't be filled with water, hence, delaying me swimming. This annoyed me so much that I thought of ways to correct this little problem. I learned from books that white reflects the sun's heat, and black attracts and absorbs heat. Watching my mother cook, I used to be fascinated by how water would "disappear" when heated. Thus I thought, maybe I can heat that area in the swimming pool and thus make it dry quicker. So I cut a piece of black refuse bag, and placed it over the area. Days went by with no effect. The area was hot all right, but dryer? No. I spoke to my dad about this, and he talked about a "new" term called evaporation. "Ah," I thought, that wetness must escape, and the refuse bag is keeping that water from doing so. Thus, I cut small holes in the black refuse bag, and voila! Within two days the patch was dry. Not too bad for a ten-year old-encephalitis, bad coordination cretin.

But I went on with my life, always believing that I was a bit dimmer than my classmates, as my mathematics was terrible. In our schools, only the ones good with math were clever and went to classes for the "gifted" after school. But I must say, I hated math. I never could understand the significance of it. $2b+c=z$, what the hell does it mean? I always had some teacher who was never interested in telling me the significance of it, other than that of, "it's the only way you will get into medical school." And yes, I wanted to study medicine badly. So I continued struggling on with it without understanding it. My other subjects were good, and my music and languages great, but those subjects were for so-called "dimwits." I even had one teacher say to me, "if you become a doctor one day, I will eat my hat!"

Then came the crunch at the end of high school, when I lost my acceptance to medical school due to a bad grade in math. Devastated, I applied to get acceptance into medical school via studying for a baccalaureate in science. Yet again, that old faithful Villain of mine was there. You guessed it—math! Yet again the other subjects were fine, from chemistry to physics, but the Villain had me by the throat. Then came one of the angels in my life, as our regular math lecturer departed and was replaced by a lady. She was very approachable, and I went to her one day after class, begging her to help me understand math. She looked at me and said, "if you can speak, read and write, you can do math, because math is a language." I frowned, and she answered, "It is the language of everything. With mathematics, you can describe from the simplest fall of an apple to the movement of galaxies."

That was it. My eyes opened for the first time. Someone explained to me the significance of math, and with some effort, my mathematics became great. I learned to love it, and even helped my sister with her high school math!

And so I was eventually accepted by the medical school, and I became a doctor. I realized that if you just put your mind and your heart into something, you could achieve anything. Now if you look closely, you will notice the Hero's Journey in this little episode of mine, the Villains being the teachers, the Mentor being the lady lecturer, the obstacles and the eventual turning of the tide—all there. And I know of someone who still needs to eat his hat.

There are countless stories of "geniuses" who were thought dim-witted in school, and then became what they became. But as Edison said, "Genius is one percent inspiration and ninety-nine percent perspiration." Wise words. How many of you could be dormant geniuses because you lack the belief in yourself? And not only does potency in science make you a "genius." What about everything else—music, art, filmmaking, business, invention, design, sport and being a mum?

Stop thinking that you can't. It's only the BS man talking. And even if you fail several times, numerous successful people will always tell you that failure is one step closer to success. On being asked how he could persist continuing to research ways to create a lightbulb after he failed so many times, Edison replied that he didn't fail those times, but only learned how not to create a lightbulb. Now remember this, and free that powerful mind of yours.

Life as a Box—Breaking Free

We return to the idea of us being in our own little boxes in a larger box of humanity. These boxes are the way we see ourselves, our family and friends and even our foes. The pictures tell us what to think and how to act. It is all we know. We see ourselves as made from flesh and blood, fragile and perishable and worst of all, limited. We see the world around us as a conglomerate of random things, happening according to fate. Life to us is dangerous and scary, with a lot of enemies who want to harm us (and indeed there are, as they themselves feel threatened and decide it's better to become a predator before becoming a victim). But they are only boxes with pictures of life. It is not the real world and the real you. If we could simply look up, see the opening of our box above us, and take a peep at to what is out there, we would be astounded. We and these lives we live are much more than flesh and blood, friends and foes.

Let me help you look up and get the strength to stand up and take a peep. We will do this firstly by returning to the world within, the world of the infinitely small. Now this is where things can get a bit tough, but please don't skip it. Gradually work your way through the few technical pages ahead, and in the end, you will be rewarded.

The Universe Within

As I mentioned before, the building blocks of everything we know — from Joe Simple to a cat, a tree, a rock or an entire galaxy — is made from atoms.

But what are atoms really? So far we know them as those ball thingies flying around other ball thingies as taught to us in high school. As a matter of fact, that was just a scientific model of understanding atoms, which is rapidly changing into a more modern model of what the atom really is. Let me briefly take you through the evolution of understanding the building blocks of life.

The word atom came from the original Greek word meaning indivisible, as it was believed in the past to be the smallest indivisible thing one can find in nature. It turned out to be incorrect, and we now know that atoms are made from smaller "parts." An atom resembles a solar system. Just like the sun is the massive

The Sleeper Must Awaken

center of our solar system, and the planets orbit the sun, so do the proton and neutron resemble the sun at the center of the atom, and electrons orbit this center or nucleus like the planets do the sun. An eerie similarity, which is also found in our own solar system and billions of others, "orbiting" the center of the Milky Way galaxy. Reminds me of the words, "as above, so below" by the great and legendary teacher, Hermes Trismegistus.

Okay, so the atom has a nucleus made out of heavy "parts" called protons and neutrons, orbited by smaller "parts" at a comparatively great distance. The protons are positively charged, the neutrons are neutral, and the electrons are negatively charged. Now the interesting thing about atoms is that if you change the amount of protons, neutrons and electrons in each atom, you change the nature of the atom completely. For instance, if we take the simplest atom, hydrogen, we have one proton, no neutron and one electron. A lot of these atoms will form hydrogen gas, which explodes when in contact with fire. If we add a proton, two neutrons and electrons accordingly, we will get a complete new atom or element called helium. Helium is the gas used in balloons and dive mixtures that makes you sound like Mickey Mouse when inhaled. And so, adding more protons, neutrons and electrons, we get a different atom or element with completely different properties. They can be seen as "Lego blocks" with the difference that each different combination of building blocks shapes completely different things. Now if one takes two hydrogen atoms and one oxygen atom and combines or fuses them, we get a molecule we know as water, H_2O. Yet again, a completely different thing. Hydrogen and oxygen, both gasses that make flames go berserk, turn into a liquid that will tame a fire — fascinating.

Now a few of these elements are very important. They are hydrogen (H_1), oxygen (O_8), nitrogen (N_7) and carbon (C_6) With these four atoms, we can do so much. Let's take a look.

Oxygen and nitrogen in a <u>mixed</u> (not fused) amount of a rough ratio of 1:4 gives us the air that we breathe. Hydrogen and oxygen

<u>fused</u> together in the ratio of 2:1 gives us water. Carbon, hydrogen and oxygen fused together in various ratios will give us various forms of sugar molecules — the fuel of our bodies and the structure of plants. If we take carbon, hydrogen and nitrogen, we can shape various kinds of amino acids, which in turn form the proteins of our bodies, the basic building blocks of our tissue. Now if we take all four — carbon, hydrogen, oxygen and nitrogen — with a little bit of help from phosphorous (that stuff that glows in the dark), we can build the complex molecular system we know as DNA — the blueprint of life in all living creatures. So with only these four atoms, used in clever combinations, we get life as we know it, and of course, you sitting there reading this book.

Just for a moment, try to think of all this in a free way. Look at yourself and your surroundings. Try to look beyond the "obvious" and see an endless ocean of vibrant "little balls," from your "flesh" to the chair you're in to our planet orbiting the sun and our sun orbiting the center of the galaxy; all interacting with each other in various combinations. Weird, isn't it? But let's take this weirdness a bit further, and turn their "ball" like nature into a more appropriate model.

Classic Model of Helium Atom

Eyes Open, but Not Yet Focusing

If we look at the history of science, we notice that our models of science describing nature and her wonders keep changing as our understanding changes—from the early thoughts of earth being the center of the galaxy (changed by Copernicus and Galileo) to the still-used classical physics of action equals reaction by Newton. Then, after some plain sailing in the physics world, came the storm caused by Einstein when he came up with his Theory of Relativity, which boils down to everything being relative to the observer. Time and space are not fixed universal elements, but are entirely relative to the observer and his or her position and speed at which he or she travels. Then after some years of cooling off, the theory was accepted and widely used, with physicists feeling more at ease. Then quantum physics, or the study of the subatomic world, entered the stage, completely blowing physicists' hats off. As Richard Feynman, a quantum physicist and famous lecturer on the topic once stated, "I can safely say that no one understands quantum mechanics." It seemed that quantum physics, which in its own right completely worked, was in some ways opposed to classical physics and relativity, which also in their own right worked. How was it then possible that the large and seen world can be opposite to the small and unseen world? It would seem that more answers would be met by more questions, and bizarre questions at that. Let's have a look at the quantum or subatomic universe, the world of our bodies and universe's building "blocks."

Our current model of understanding the subatomic world is the Standard Model in Quantum Mechanics, developed about thirty years ago. Atomic and subatomic "particles" (as they are called, but will change due to reasons later stated), thus the building blocks of us and our universe, are categorized as bosons and fermions. Bosons are "particles" with integer or symmetrical spin, which have a positive ground state and almost act as "carriers" or "transmitters" of energy with electromagnetism (by photons) and weak nuclear force (by W & Z bosons), as an example. Fermions are "particles" with half-integer or asymmetrical spin, have a negative ground state and make up the "ordinary matter" of our universe. Electrons and quarks (building blocks of protons and neutrons) are examples of fermions. Protons and neutrons will be shaped from three grouped fermionic quarks depending on their up or down spin.

So you and I, Joe Ordinary, the trees and rocks are basically made from fermions—electrons, protons and neutrons (thus quark combinations) that obey the "exclusion principle of Pauli." This principle states that no two fermions can share the same quantum state. This is the reason why "matter" seems stable and can form different atoms or elements from hydrogen to carbon. It is also the reason why we cannot walk through walls. No two fermions can occupy the same "space" so to speak. Light, on the other hand, consisting of photons (from the symmetrical spin group, bosons), does not obey the exclusion principle, and thus can share quantum states. This is why light beams do not "crash" into each other.

The reason why fermions (or us lot made from atoms) obey the exclusion principle, is because of the half integer spin, which basically means that our "matter" has asymmetrical wave properties. Light, with its integer spin, has symmetrical wave properties.

The term "wave property" is the key on which we will build. Thus:

A wave is a change of one state to another in a certain time span, in plain English, a vibration. These waves or vibrations are everywhere—in the sea, in sound, light and even looking at a playground swing, swinging to and fro.

It was noted by quantum physicists that particles like electrons had a wave property, that is, acted like a wave, or was indeed a wave, being at all possible places around the atom's nucleus till observed, when it suddenly "changed" into a particle at a certain position. This meant that an electron (or any other particle for that matter) is a wave or a vibration and can be anywhere (exist in an infinite amount of quantum states called the Uncertainty Principle of Heisenberg), till it is observed, when it "becomes" a particle due to the Observer Effect. This then basically boils down to things not existing as definite "things," but being in a state of infinite possibility until observed by consciousness. This gives rise to a lot of difficult philosophical questions. Does this mean that the universe has to be observed by an omnipotent presence to exist in a certain form, or do we as conscious beings create the universe as it exists around us by observing it? And by being part of these waves turning into particles, thus matter, who is changing us from wave into matter by observing us, and who or what is observing that? Are we then dreaming the dream, or is the dream dreaming us?

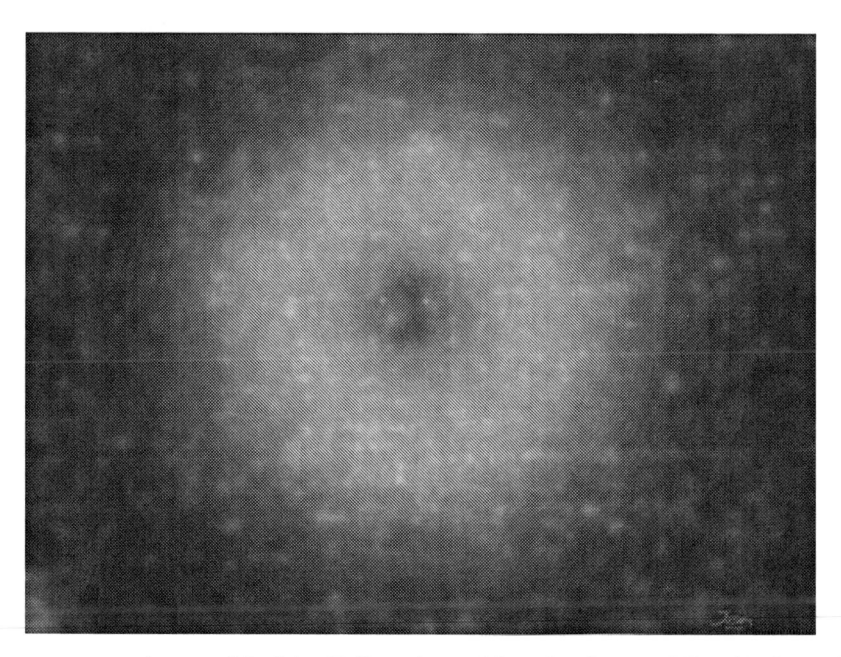

A more appropriate model of the Helium Atom. Note the electron "Cloud" of possible positions for the orbiting electrons. (Uncertainty Principle).

So you can see that the closer our observation of the "stuff" that we and our world are made of, the more we move into a box or room, the walls being made from more and more bizarre questions. Most of those questions with answers we don't like, answers that imply that our world is more bizarre than we thought, and even an illusion. Thus the Threshold Guardians of disbelief kicks in, the modern, scientific human mind desperate to find logic and empirically proven answers, pushing forth the limits of trying to prove logic and disprove the opposite. So deeper into the dead end they go, cutting and drilling into the rock wall of the confined universe of unanswerable questions—blind to the dead end they reached, they wander forth instead of retreating and getting a fresh new perspective. They stare blindly at the details instead of incorporating it with the bigger picture. But some were not so content with it, and retreated, looking for a fresh start.

"Particles" of the aging Standard Model of Quantum Physics all interact with each other by forces known as electromagnetism, the strong force and the weak force—the three forces of the quantum world.

But the large world of planets and galaxies work with a force we know as gravity, and this was the problem. Mathematically, these two different worlds didn't "add up." So, a theory called Super-symmetrical String theory was developed that could try and unite these two worlds by explaining the different particles (of which too many were discovered with atom smashers that were good for anyone anyway) and their properties as well as the four major forces of the universe.

Basically, Super String Theory, or M-Theory (as it is called now after five different points of view on Super String theory were unified by Edward Witten) states that particles are actually "strings" or "branes" of a certain finite length (Planck length) that create the properties of a particle as it vibrates on certain wavelengths in ten- or eleven-dimensional space, of which six dimensions are curled up or hidden, while the other four dimensions are experienced as the combination of space-time (three spatial with one time). In other words, there are no different particles, only frequencies that give rise to, dare I say, the "illusion" of particles. In his book *Parallel Worlds*, Michio Kaku, a leading theoretical physicist, puts it quite elegantly. He compares it to sound or music, where a string or "brane" is a violin string, the notes played by the strings are subatomic particles, melodies are chemical compounds (atoms and molecules, thus us lot) and the universe is a symphony. Beautifully explained I think.

Thus, you and I and Joe Ordinary, the cat, the tree and the universe, are mere infinite combinations of vibration. We are the melodies and songs of the symphony of life.

Now that sounds nice (pardon the pun), doesn't it?

Yet again you may remark, "okay we are vibrations, so what?"

Stick with me a little while longer, you'll see.

Focusing

Now that we have the basics of particles and strings in our vibrating little heads, we can move freely into the next part, which will hopefully astound you.

In the early nineteen eighties, Alain Aspect, a French physicist, and his team conducted an astounding experiment. They found that when two electrons were separated from the "mother" atom, no matter what distance they were from each other, they kept the same wave property — if the one's spin was changed, the other's would change at the exact same time. Somehow they "communicated" with each other faster than the speed of light. This of course broke the laws of Einstein's special relativity theory, and everyone shook their heads in disbelief.

But looking at the Uncertainty Principle of Heisenberg, which roughly states that an electron's position and speed can't be accurately measured, as well as the phenomenon of non locality, quantum entanglement or "spooky action at a distance" as Einstein called it, it becomes clear that something connects particles (or more correctly waves, as stated earlier). How else could two "separate" things each know what the other is doing, no matter what the distance, and better yet, unrelated to time?

Enter the David Bohm Factor. David Bohm was a contemporary of Einstein, and a physicist with a different view on things. Bohm, observing all the above, believed that separateness did not exist. According to Bohm, physical things, made from "separate particles," were only an illusion. Everything was part of an invisible wholeness, which looked separate from different points of view. He compared it to a whirlpool in a river that seemed to be a separate entity, but was essentially part of the river. It only seemed to manifest as a separate thing. Thus, the two "communicating" particles are not communicating. They are connected in a yet unobservable quantum state. They are the same thing from two different points of view. Bohm called this the "implicate" and "explicate" order of things, which meant that the universe was enfolded and unfolded at certain "points," and kept on doing this on a continuum. Matter, or the stuff we see and experience, is then the unfolded part, and the rest, the unobservable or enfolded part. It's almost like a space or room filled with water vapor, "invisible" to the eye, with certain areas of the room a bit colder than the rest. These colder areas condense the water vapor into droplets, which are visible. As the droplets fall, they reach an even colder area and turn into snowflakes. Then, encountering a warmer area, turn from snowflake into water droplet, and then back into vapor again. The whole vapor-space, droplet and snowflake phenomenon is one "entity" — phases of water — which only gives the illusion of different properties by means of temperature changes. Crude example, but it makes it more understandable for me.

Recapping on the phenomenon in physics called the "Observer Effect" — where changes happen in an event being observed, like the pathway of an electron being changed as it is observed or changing things as we observe them — fits with the ideas of David Bohm. In effect, the observed and the observer are the same thing, just different points of view and manifestations of the same thing. The "room" with its different temperature areas I mentioned above can be likened to consciousness, and the vapor and its changing phases to the enfolded universe unfolding as it comes into contact with different "areas" of consciousness. In essence, the "room" and "vapor" are interdependent on each other to give rise to the vapor-droplet-snowflake phenomenon. Just so, consciousness and infinite vibratory quantum states are interdependent on each other, where consciousness will change possibility (invisible or enfolded quantum states) into "reality," thus the unfolded and visible world we experience.

What this boils down to is that everything is connected. You, me, Joe Ordinary, the cat and the Universe are all one thing, just different areas of vibration in it. The enfolded part of the universe is then the world of all possibility, and the unfolded part, the world we experience everyday, the world of one fulfilled possibility due to consciousness (through the Observer Effect).

We can even take it a step further. The abovementioned correlates with a hologram. A hologram is a specialized picture, made by photographing something like a tree by using linear or laser light reflected on special holographic paper. When the holographic paper is viewed after development, we can only see vibratory patterns, but when shining the laser through it again, we can see the tree as a three-dimensional picture. Better still, if you cut the holographic picture in smaller and smaller parts, each piece of the original picture will retain the whole three-dimensional tree in a smaller format. Every little part of a holographic photo contains the whole image of the tree. Hence the name "holo," meaning whole. This same principle applies to our cells and bodies, where each cell's DNA, no matter what kind of cell it is, contains all the information of the body. The same can be seen throughout the universe, where everything is reflected in everything. Our cardiovascular and neurological systems resemble the shape of trees and river deltas. The atoms resemble the movement of planets around the sun, and they in turn resemble the movement of solar systems around the center of the galaxy. This can also clearly be seen in chaos theory by using fractal pictograms. As you choose an area of a fractal pictogram and magnify it continuously, you will soon reach within the magnified pictogram a pictogram that resembles the whole original pictogram you started with. Our universe is like a giant hologram that continuously "moves" or changes from "within" to "without." But looking at the Observer Effect again, it appears that it is our observation or consciousness that moves it or makes it change.

At the same time that David Bohm worked on the holographic "un-separate" nature of the universe, neurophysiologist Karl Pribram started to think of the brain in the same way. On problems with the "location" of memory, as well as its vastness in such a small space, Pribram started to think of the brain functioning holographically. A hologram can store enormous amounts of data in the same space, depending on the point of view of the laser and, as mentioned before, contains the whole picture in every part of itself. This also correlates with the brain, as it has always been a mystery how such a small piece of fatty organic tissue can store such vast amounts of information. Come to think of it, if we are made from the same stuff as the universe, which is holographic vibration with the illusion of being separate or partial, then our brains must be the same. We, and everything "around" us, are all "different" manifestations due to different vibratory states in the whole.

Thus we can conclude that the universe is Possibility unfolding from "within" and as a result manifesting different vibratory states experienced by Itself as you, me, Joe Ordinary, the cat, the tree, the galaxies and everything else we experience due to consciousness.

As I've mentioned earlier, we are all melodies, part of the symphony of life. And to augment the fact that we (our bodies) are mere patterns of vibration, consider the atoms you are made of. At your present state, you are composed of different atoms than you were a few months ago. As your older cells die, they are replaced by newer ones, composed of the food you eat, composed of the atoms of the universe. You are then just a concentration of the in and out flux of energy in the form of atoms, this "concentration" arranged in the form of an atomic vibratory entity you know as Yourself.

Starting to See

Now you might wonder how this might help you, how this might help the Hero tell a better story. If you think carefully about the abovementioned, you will realize the implications it holds. In his book *The Holographic Universe*, Michael Talbot explores the possibility of these implications, and reveals that this model can explain everything from unanswered questions in science to "taboo" topics like telekinesis, miracles and psychic phenomena. If this weird holographic theory of the universe is correct, then it implies that our so-called universe and we ourselves are a mere illusion. Only our consciousness, which is inseparable from that of the entire humanity, living creatures as well as earth itself, has the possibility of being "real" by creating this holographic universe through and around ourselves by means of the Observer Effect. It seems, studying the paranormal (BS man aside), that certain individuals unconsciously know this to be the "ultimate truth," and can by mere thought change the holographic illusion around themselves. This could explain telekinesis (moving an object with your mind, because you know it to be a mere illusion). It reminds me of the film *The Matrix*, where Neo bends the spoon after the child prodigy tells him, "there is no spoon." It can also explain telepathy (as consciousness is not separate), spiritual healing ("there is no disease") and other paranormal phenomena.

If the Hero, thus you, can properly understand and use the holographic theory as well as M-theory, you can illuminate the road on which you travel in the dark forest of your story.

See and Understand

Ooh, that Threshold Guardian wants you badly. How in the name of Pete can everything around you, including yourself, be an illusion? It feels so bloody real for goodness sake!

Have you ever dreamed? Ever had a nightmare so real that you woke up screaming, your heart pounding in your chest? It felt so real when you were immersed in that dream world that your body physically reacted to it, hence the pounding of the heart, your arms shaking. According to western thinking, the dream world isn't real. It's a mere (yet not understood) state of the "brain" when you "sleep." The brain has, according to western science a few consciousness states—awake, hypnotic trance states, light sleep to deep sleep and meditative states—all with their own unique brain wave patterns. There we go again—brain <u>wave</u> pattern. The EEG or electroencephalogram is a wave pattern picked up by electrodes when in contact with the electromagnetic activity of the brain. It clearly mirrors the wave properties of the brain again. But back to the dream state. Westerners are of the few who believe the dream state to be an illusion. Most ancient civilizations and indigenous groups believed the opposite to be true. It can be seen in Tibetan and Zen Buddhism, Hinduism, Jainism, Gnosticism, Kabbalism and of course in Aboriginal, Dogon and Native American thought. But we westerners think that we are always right, and all those others are wrong. After all, Western Civilization has been around for hundreds of years, (whereas the others have been around a few thousand years), and we are so perfect with our pollution, wars and global devastation. But all of a sudden, our own empirical mouthpiece, science, is starting to challenge western thought with M-Theory and the Holographic theory. There is also a lot of controversial thought on the nature of brain, mind, consciousness and "reality" by new and of course laughed-at thinkers.

Looking at a lot of research done in the last few years, it would seem that the brain is more than just the thinking tool in our heads, as believed by most present-day scientists. Dr. Rick Strassman, author of *DMT: The Spirit Molecule,* has done extensive research on Dimethyltryptamine (DMT), a molecule similar in structure to our neurotransmitter serotonin, with strong hallucinogenic properties. DMT is produced by the body (most probably by the pineal gland, as postulated by Dr. Strassman) and has no other yet known function in the body, apart from being a natural occurring psychedelic substance in the body. It was also noted that DMT concentrations were higher in those with Near Death Experiences and in certain forms of meditation, as well as in some cases of schizophrenia, this being one of the main reasons for the research. Voluntary subjects were given higher than "normal" occurring doses of intravenous DMT and experienced profound "hallucinogenic" experiences, some even life changing. In his recent book *Supernatural*, author and researcher Graham Hancock, in response to South African archaeologist David Lewis-Williams's work, has linked hallucinogenic experiences with the sudden emergence of rock painting approximately forty thousand years ago. Hancock takes it further, postulating with rock solid research, that hallucinogenic experiences can also be linked to the start of shamanism and early religious thought. There are very strong correlations between hallucinogenic patterns, visions with various hallucinogens and cultural backgrounds. Rock paintings in upper Paleolithic Europe, as well as those found in South Africa, share major characteristics. All paintings seem to be ordinary hunting scenes etc. But with a closer look, you will find a common theme of humanoid figures with shared human-animal characteristics. Take a look at the world's mythologies, and soon you will notice the golden thread of therianthropes (human-animal hybrids) running through all of them. A further shared characteristic is that of humanoid figures "suspended" in midair with lines entering or crossing their bodies, formerly thought to represent wounded men, but some thinkers' opinions have changed (which will arise in just a while). There are also patterns of waves, circles and dots accompanying most rock art. Now if one takes a closer look at hallucinogenic experiences, most subjects will start their hallucinogenic journey with waves and dots flickering in front of their eyes (known as entoptic phenomena).

Usually with low doses, the world would seem to become morphed, with some subjects seeing people who look like animal hybrids, or feeling like some kind of animal themselves. I remember an incident as a medical student when someone in our dormitory used a hallucinogenic substance. He kept on staring at himself in the mirror, touching something next to his head. When asked what he was touching, he reported touching his horns as he was slowly changing into a bull.

Subjects will also report seeing beings like elves or aliens that will arise from these humanoid figures, which will approach them and implant things into their heads or bodies with needles or spearlike objects (remember the changed opinion of the wounded man pictures?), through which new thoughts will be sent or programmed. Some will say that they then feel at one with the universe, and that there are many more dimensions than we think. This also correlates a lot with psychosis experienced by schizophrenics and those with bipolar disorders. Schizophrenic patients with various backgrounds will report hearing voices instructing them to do things, or will say that a god or the government have planted something in their brains and are communicating with them. They will also report losing their boundaries with the world around them, feeling interconnected to everything, with their thoughts not being private. They see meaningful coincidences in almost everything, and even sometimes hear or see (in rare cases) how angelic and demonic figures will fight for their souls.

Dreams are equally weird. Things rapidly transform from one to another. We dream about our family homes' transforming into dark and nightmarish places. We dream about snakes and spiders, public bathrooms and sometimes even global catastrophes. We wake up in a sweat and then brush it off with a smile—it's not real. But why does it feel so real? Why have I woken up after dreaming to have fallen with my body still aching a few seconds after waking up? Ever had sleep paralysis, where you are awake, but can't move your body or open your eyes, and then become aware of a malign presence in the room with you? You fight the paralysis until you wake up almost screaming. Sleep paralysis (hypnopompia or hypnogogia) is experienced by approximately thirty percent of the western population, and references to it can be found from India to China, Russia to North America. It has even inspired some artists like Henry Fuseli and Ernest Hemmingway. It is a state of consciousness between the fully awake and fully asleep states, which can give the poor victim from mild to vastly distressing "hallucinations." And as soon as the poor victim wakes up, the hallucination is gone. But for the schizophrenic, this dream state never ends. It is there when awake, causing severe emotional distress and social decline. Can you imagine waking up, but the nightmare not ending, following you around like a bad habit?

What if hallucinations were waking dreams? What if schizophrenics couldn't distinguish between the dream state reality and the awakened state reality, as some current minds in psychology and psychiatry are starting to think? What if the majority of us had a safeguard that kept our dream state and awakened state separate, distinguishing "us" from certain individuals like for instance schizophrenics? The cause for schizophrenia is unknown and merely speculative, and there is a growing support to groups feeling that mental illness is only society's way of separating themselves from ones who act outside expected social boundaries. One of these thinkers was a psychiatrist named John Weir Perry, who approached schizophrenia in an "unorthodox" way, his thoughts based on that of the Swiss psychologist Carl Jung. Contrary to Freud, Jung believed schizophrenia not to be the "incurable disease due to chemical imbalance" as Freud thought, but "when the dream becomes real." Jung saw the acute schizophrenic episode as the subconscious mind revealing itself through archetypal imagery to the fully awakened state of a person, showing the need for the "affected" person to confront his/her subconscious "demons," so to speak. Contrary to "orthodox" psychiatric management, where the psychosis is suppressed with anti-psychotic drugs for the remainder of a person's life (naturally supported by pharmaceutical giants profiting from this lifelong "disease"), John Weir Perry followed Jung's advice. He created a safe and comfortable environment in San Francisco, where these young individuals could face their "inner apocalypse" without suppression or confined and locked rooms. Help was given to these individuals in the form of support in a friendly environment, without suppressive drugs, and the results were remarkable. After about forty days, the "psychosis" would end, and with a further integration period in a safe halfway house, these "scizo's" returned to society happier and more functional than they were before the breakdown! Perry's "patients" also had near zero relapses. We can see this in non-western societies as well, where "scizo's" are seen as special, being supported through their period of "rebirth" to become the shaman or holy man of their people. Again in western society, we can see the Threshold Guardians at work in the shape of "conventional" psychiatry and pharmaceutical corporations, clinging to archaic ideas or even profiting from them, while destroying young people's lives and that of their families. If we look at Perry's success, the "conventional" method of treating schizophrenics, could be "one of the biggest human rights violations in the history of mankind," as Michael O'Callaghan puts it. This, simply because modern science refuses to let go of their reductionist approach to anything vaguely "paranormal."

Looking at the abovementioned, could it then be that hallucination (or waking dreams) and "normal" dreams are an unknown consciousness state where the mind dwells in the enfolded world where all realities (all quantum states) are possible? This would suggest that being awake and being asleep are equally real, where one state of consciousness only seems a bit more linear or organized, and the other more radial or "irrational." This suggestion can be found in all different schools of thought, as mentioned earlier, except in our new and improved western "supermarket" folk. What if we supermarket folk were wrong? What if different states of consciousness were like radio stations, all with different frequency or wave ranges? After all, we have thus far started touching on the idea, with solid arguments, that our universe is a complex vibrating hologram. Thus, the "awakened," "asleep" and "in-between" states all have their own frequency ranges, almost like radio stations.

Now take the brain (which is also a holographic wave form). The only way the brain "knows" what is "out there" is by interpreting electrochemical impulses or information from the five senses (eyes, ears etc.). For example, photon waves from the sun will strike all the details of an apple. Some of these photon waves will interact with the apple's waves and be absorbed, but the others will be reflected into the eye waveform of a human being. These reflected waves will then interact with the eye waveform (retina) to create a message waveform, what we know as an electrochemical stimuli, that miraculously moves to the visual cortex of the brain waveform, where the message will be decoded — a tone of red with green spots, semi-ball like object with little stem. The brain will scramble through the archives of holographic memory, and the interpretation of "apple" will be presented to the "higher functioning part" of the human's brain. It is like your PC decoding html or "internet code."

It would seem to be, BS man aside, that our brains have built-in limited frequency reception ranges, and that certain factors like DMT, meditation and rhythmic dancing (in the case of some tribes in Africa) can broaden it. DMT, like our brain, is a waveform that can reprogram the brain's limited wave function reception ranges to come in closer contact with the enfolded universe, where all quantum states are possible, almost like a software plug-in program that updates your brain's reception ranges. In other words, there is more around us than we can perceive due to our limited reception range, with DMT and other factors helping us perceive it clearer.

Let me put it like this. Say for instance that our normal day-to-day existence ranges from frequency level D to P, and our brains are thus tuned to only receive and perceive from D to P, but that other realities exist from ranges A to C and Q to Z. Then, if a substance (frequency pattern) called DMT could adapt and change this range from D to P, to range B to W, then we would be able to experience more frequencies, thus these other realities. Now the problem is, we are not used to these frequencies. As we have seen, our brain knows how to interpret all those millions of frequency patterns between D to P and turn the apple frequency into a picture of an apple in our heads. But now come these other unknown frequency patterns, some of them probably not even complete (like television interference patterns), and our brain gets stuck and doesn't know how to interpret them. It will start scrambling through the subconscious archetypal archives in search of some picture that will closely resemble the new and unknown pattern. It is this that could explain why shamanistic dream states and modern-day visions or hallucinations share the same properties. As noted in Hancock's book "Supernatural," dream states will start with patterns, like waves and dots, and then take the dreamer further into a surreal world with brighter colors, therianthropes or human-animal beings and even into contact with dead relatives. He also notes how, as humans evolve, so do their visions.

It would seem, yet again BS man aside, that hallucinations are not something abnormal. They are the mere tuning in to different dimensions or realities and their wave or vibratory properties, and as we evolve and our archives get fuller, we connect these unknown frequency patterns to clearer and clearer pictures. This could give us a clearer understanding on hallucinogenic "illnesses" like schizophrenia, and also why folklore elves are turning into modern-day aliens.

I will leave this topic here, lightly touching on it only to make you more aware of our vibratory nature and to make you question more and more things. Let us now return to "reality," and try little by little to make it less rigid.

Deconstructing Illusion

Quiet yourself again, and let this idea start to manifest itself clearly.

Your body and your mind, the chair or bed that you're on, the room you find yourself in, your family members, animal companions, your community members (even those who annoy you tirelessly), friends and foes, our lovely planet earth and the whole universe—are One. We are one "thing" with different vibratory patterns here, there and everywhere. Only here, there and everywhere, as well as time, is an illusion. We experience space-time and "reality" only because of the superpositioning of projected waveform from its "entry point" at super string or "brane" level. It is like watching a 3-D movie, where more than one projector's projection will intersect (**superimpose**), with the combined intersection, giving the illusion of 3-D. In the above example, the light of the projector resembles the "energy" coming from the enfolded dimension. The lens resembles the "point of entry" as string or brane, the film and its projected light beam the different vibrations from subatomic particles to organisms (us) and galaxies, and the intersecting projections the illusion of the universe.

Let's take a closer and simplified look at...

Time as Illusion

If one compares the human race's history of approximately 100,000 years, of which only the last 4,000 years are "adequately" recorded, to that of the earth's 4.5 billion years, then our existence here is almost negligible. Better put, if earth's time so far were a twenty-four–hour day, our existence would be less than a second. For earth and our universe, our time here is nothing, while for us, it feels very significant. It's like the holiday whizzing by, but a working day dragging by.

Does time really slow down when we work and speed up when we enjoy ourselves, or is it our perception of the illusion of time changing? The Relativity Theory of Einstein showed how time is not a fundamental universal constant, but changes with regards to individuals' perception of it, especially when they moved at different speeds! In plainer terms, do people in the east really experience New Year first? What happened on earth before we were here for all those billions of years? Why were those billions of years there anyway if we are so special? On earth, we have a 24-hour day in a roughly 365-day year because of our planet turning at a certain speed and orbiting the sun at another. If we lived on Mars, our day would be less than 24 hours long, and a year 686 days.

See what I mean? It is only points of view that differ, not "time" itself. And just as time is an illusion, so is space or place.

Space as Illusion

Keeping to the Greenwich, if one sends a letter from London to Johannesburg by plane, it will take an approximate eleven hours of flight over a distance of roughly six thousand miles to reach its destination. If one e-mails it, it's there instantaneously. You will probably argue and say, the one is "real" and the other is "virtual." Hmm, remember our universe's vibratory nature. Sending information via airplane instead of e-mail is just the detour or "primitive" version of doing so. Both letters have the same meaning. They both contain the same message or wave pattern. E-mail just uses the non-local properties of the universe, and the message will resonate non-locally at the illusory "other end." Just as this message is information in waveform, so is our DNA. At present, we only know how to use the "local" ways of "transporting" our complex waveforms, thus the detour.

But there is progress. These days, with video conferencing, your smile is seen instantaneously over thousands of miles. If we had a holographic camera on the one side, and a holographic projector on the other, a complete three-dimensional "you" would be in that room, interacting with everyone there. Yet again you will argue and say the holographic picture is not real.

Now consider this. You are talking to a friend, face-to-face. You "see" him or her because photonic vibration reflects of his or her fermionic vibratory state, and enter your fermionic state via your "eyes," and your "brain" translates that vibratory pattern into a three-dimensional, recognizable friend. Now, if your friend was 500 meters away, he or she would seem "small" or "far away," and you would need to shout at each other, or use a mobile phone. But if you remember the holographic picture, cutting it into smaller and smaller pieces would yield the whole picture, only "smaller." See the resemblance? The so-called "distance" between you and your friend is like cutting the holographic universe into smaller holographic bits, and you both appear smaller to each other.

If you could place a massive magnifying glass and sound amplifier between the two of you, things would appear the same as face-to-face. If your friend was thousands of miles away, using a holographic camera and projector, it would also act as a "magnifier," and it would seem as if your friend was in the room with you. Both of you interacting with each other like normal. The only difference would be not being able to touch each other. But what if both of you acquired more atoms and became as big as earth? As both of you grew larger in proportion to your "center" points, you would also expand toward one another. At some stage in this expansion you would be as close to each other as before. Immediately you would be able to reach out your arms and touch each other.

Elaborating on the idea of the illusion, some theoretical physicists are sheepishly smiling at each other over a drink when they discuss the idea that our whole universe is just organized information, that is, like a massive and extremely complex program, not unlike a computer program. That we ourselves and everything we experience is information (like bits) expressed in waveform, and that it is possible that all this information can be stored like a computer program. Instead of on a CD or DVD, it would be possible for this information to be stored on a black hole's event horizon (event horizon being the surface area of a black hole, which is the last thing one would experience before being drawn into a black hole for eternity). Interesting idea, isn't it?

Can you see? Space and time, or space-time as it is called by special relativity, is an illusion, and we are mere points of view in it, interacting with it, oblivious of the fact that it is only an illusion. We only use this illusion to help us "order" our daily existence, and we are so used to "knowing" that it is "real" that we struggle to cope with the mere idea of the world around us being an illusion.

Now, I've always believed an idea should have more than one point of view. So far the idea of us and our universe being a holographic complex of vibration, emanating from a yet undiscovered dimension through our collective consciousness, is interesting. But it is also distressing and emotionally uncomfortable, always calling for the false comfort of the Threshold Guardian. So far we have various scientific points of view, but let's balance scientific thinking with some golden oldies.

Reality Check

Tantra

You may have heard of a term called Tantric sex, or maybe even have read the hype about it. But Tantric sex as the west knows it is only an obscure and adapted and sometimes vulgar version of a very small part of Tantra to fit the limited mind-set of typical western thinking, which these days has a mere "Money, Sex, Booze and Rock & Roll" mentality. Instead, Tantra is an ancient and mysterious body of knowledge, of which the origin is speculative. It was incorporated into Hindu, Buddhist and Jain religions thousands of years ago, and has had its fair share of different formatting by these belief systems. But before these religions, it was an ancient and impartial science, rich in metaphors and other archetypal elements.

Tantra comes from the Sanskrit root *tan* meaning "expand." It impels its student to become more aware or conscious and to change their actions into active participation and creation of evolution and our so-called reality through various systematic rituals and practices. Furthermore, if closely studied, it will reveal uncanny similarities to the science of today, and it is on these similarities I want to focus.

If we look at cosmogenesis in Tantra, we find parallels to our current scientific explanation, which is quite remarkable.

Roughly, according to Tantra, the universe began as a single point of unmanifestation called Prakriti, consisting of indeterminate elements before manifestation. These elements are Sattva (Essence, or intelligence), Rajas (energy) and Tamas (matter). These three elements or "gunas" as they are known, existed in perfect unmanifested unison—Prakriti. Cosmogenesis begins as this equilibrium is disturbed by Purusha (Universe of consciousness), and an expansion and evolution take place with these three elements starting with ether, changing into subtle matter (charged with vibration), then into progressive stages of this subtle matter's becoming denser and denser matter or particles, interacting with each other, and giving rise from subtle to strong forces. This dense matter and forces will then interact with each other to form the world as we know it.

Now, let's have a look at the Big Bang theory, or cosmogenesis a la modern:

Modern cosmologists believe that the universe started as a state of perfect symmetry, the Planck era of the universe, with all the forces we know today unified into a single force of super symmetry. Symmetry was broken by something "mysterious" (maybe a slight quantum fluctuation), and as the equilibrium was broken, this single force became unstable, expanded faster than the speed of light, and as it cooled, gave rise to the four forces we know today, as well as denser matter. Free quarks, leptons and gluons, settled into more complex atoms as the universe cooled over billions of years, giving rise to the universe as we know it today.

The Tantra version is more than three thousand years old, and if compared with today's version it is nothing less that mind-boggling.

Tantra also describes time as a continuum, with a moment in time being the transition of matter from one point to another. The rest of time is latent, and the whole universe revolves around that singular and relative moment. Further, space or location and time are also described as relative to consciousness, and are only "real" in finite terms. A very special importance was also given to sound and vibration-like qualities of the universe and its attributes. Sound and vibration in the universe can also be subdivided into audible vibration, which is sound; supersonic sound, which might or might not be audible; and then transcendental vibration or more subtle and spiritual sound. This concept formed the basis of mantras and chanting, the rhythmic vibrations in ritual that awaken the spiritual energy within. It can be seen in the religions (Hinduism and Buddhism) that incorporated Tantra into their belief systems, believing the universe to have been created by a spoken Word. It is written in the Rig Veda, "In the beginning, there was Brahman, with whom was the Word. And the word is Brahman." These same words are reflected in the Christian version of John 1:1, "In the beginning there was the Word, and the word was with God, and the word was God." A remarkable similarity don't you think?

Lastly, the concept on One—the universal energy known as Prana, which connects everything and which is responsible for the manifestation of all things as we know it. This concept is described well in *The Tantric Way* by Ajit Mookerjee and Madhu Khana, a remarkable book on Tantra: *Prana, or the energy of One is the ultimate reality. Behind the world as we know it, matter and thought, there is the eternal One without a second. All things, physical and biological are finite versions of the One.*

Yet again, compared to Einstein's Theory of Relativity, where space and time are relative to the viewer, Super String Theory, where atoms are mere vibratory manifestation, and especially the holographic nature of the universe and mind, we see a remarkable similarity.

Now how did the writer/s of Tantra know this? Better yet, who or what was the initial mind behind the concepts found in Tantra?

Kabbalah

The same can be said of Kabbalah—a new word spoken by many celebrities, which probably makes many of us cringe and believe it to be some cheap fashionable kick. In fact, Kabbalah is an ancient esoteric teaching of speculative origin (not unlike Tantra), believed by some to be as old as humanity itself, and safeguarded by a single few in Judaism for the last 5,000 years. It is closely linked to Gnosticism, Rosicrucianism and Anthroposophy and gave birth to Christianity and other western religions (the old testament of the Bible and parts of the Holy Qur'an translated from the Kabbalistic Torah), as well as mystery traditions like Astrology. Unfortunately, a lot of these mystery traditions have been morphed by "fakers" and ridiculed by "modern" western thinking, especially by the science community. It is also described as the "devil's" work by some Christians and other modern religious groups, inherited from middle-age Catholicism fear of losing power to "gnosis."

But Kabbalah is a very powerful way of learning about one's consciousness and spiritual growth, as taught in its many books like the Sefer Yetzirah (Book of Formation), the Torah (translated into the biblical old testament) and the Zohar (book of splendor, a commentary on the Torah), which is considered by many Kabbalists as the most influential. Kabbalists also believe that the writings in these books are not meant to be translated literally, but to be seen in context of metaphoric and archetypal instruction. It is a code of life.

Now, as with Tantra, Kabbalah has very striking similarities to our modern, scientific view of the universe.

According to Kabbalah, before time began, the universe was bathed in a universal light of no-thingness called Ain Sof Or, Ain Sof being "the One without end" — thus God or Godhead. Then, as God or the Universal mind wanted to "behold itself," the light contracted into a single point, creating a void of potential, and then rapidly expanded, giving rise to three primal Words of God — A, M and Sh. A universe of universes (olamot) was created, of which five survived — the universes of Adam Kadmon, Atzilut, Beriyah, Yetzirah and Asiyah, each of these expressed as the Ten Holy Sefirot (tree of life). The Ten Sefirot, or tree of life, is the collection of the ten dimensions of these universes — Kether, Binah, Hokmah, Geburah, Chessed, Tiferet, Hod, Netzach Yesod and Malkut. There is also a hidden eleventh sefirah called Da'at (knowledge). Through this came the separation of light and darkness and the notion of the universe or Godhead to give and receive simultaneously (light and dark, give and receive, positive and negative, yin and yang — the opposite poles of a fluctuation or vibration).

The Kabbalah goes on to explain the eternal truth of God and the universe(s) — that there is no time, as everything is a simultaneous event in space-time-consciousness. Also, that the sefirot (ten to eleven dimensions) in the olamot (five universes) are "currents in the river of light and channels through which creation-revelation transpires" as explained by Tau Malachi in his book *Gnosis of the Cosmic Christ*. There is a constant flux of light from "God's world" into ours and back, like God breathing in and out, manifesting our world with each exhale and un-manifesting with each inhalation.

Now if we closely study the wordplay between Kabbalah, Tantra and modern scientific thought, we will clearly see the remarkable correlations. As you will remember, in Tantric cosmogenesis, the universe came from an unmanifested state called Prakriti (breath or life sustaining energy), called into action by Purusha (Universal consciousness), which gave rise to three elements called gunas, which in turn gave rise to denser and denser matter. These three gunas correlate with the three primal words of God, A, M and Sh, as well as the triumvirate group of free primal matter, forces and their interaction that shaped just after the initial "Big Bang."

Looking at modern cosmology and physics, we will see the parallels to the Big Bang theory, but more strikingly, we will see the coincidences with String or M-Theory. Remember in M-Theory how matter is manifested by vibration of strings in a ten- to eleven-dimensional space. Look at the "words" of God (being vibration) and tree of life, with its ten sefirot, the eleventh, Da'at, hidden. Again, remarkable similarities. There is also the correlation to the holographic model, where the ninety-nine percent world (God's world) and the one percent world (our "reality"), according to modern Kabbalists, is represented by the enfolded and unfolded universes in holographic theory, the breaths of God being the constant flux of light between the seen and unseen world or enfolding-unfolding process. Also, there is the illusion of space and time, whereas in Kabbalah, everything is a simultaneous event in space-time-consciousness.

Jean Erasmus

TANTRA	KABBALAH	MODERN PHYSICS
Prakriti (State of Unmanifestation)	Ain Sof Or (Light wihout end)	Planck Era of Super Symmetry (All forces in Unison)
Changed by Purusha (Universal Consciousness)	Changed by God (The need to create: Give & Receive)	Symmetry broken by 'mysterious' quantum fluctuation (Big Bang)
Sattva Rajas Tamas (Essence) (Energy) (Matter)	A M Sh The three Primal Words of God	Energy/ Matter Forces Primal Matter interaction (EMF) Bosons (SNF) Fermions
The concept of Sound or Vibration giving rise to:	The concept and importance of the spoken Word in Kabbalah (word=sound=vibration)	(WNF) (Gravity)
Universe of Illusion (Maya)	Shaping the 5 universes: Adam Kadmon Atzilut Beriyah Yetzirah Asiyah With 10/11 Olamot (dimensions) (Tree of Life)	Concept of Vibration in M-Theory 10/11 Dimensional Universe needed for M-Theory concept EMF - Electro-magnetic force SNF - Strong Nuclear Force WNF - Weak Nuclear Force

Comparison Chart - Tantra/Kabbalah/Modern Physics.

So modern science (relativity, quantum physics, M-Theory and modern cosmology) correlates with Tantra (ancient eastern thought) and Kabbalah (ancient western thought) on the following points—cosmogenesis (with striking similarities of the three gunas, three primal words of God and free quarks, leptons and gluons) and the importance of vibration, space-time and our universe to be an illusion and the existence of multiple dimensions and universes.

By now, one must ask why these themes, both modern and old are connected, and to such an accurate degree.

We have to look deeper, past the gates of the Threshold Guardian called Dogma, and follow the trail of bread crumbs.

Understanding

On one hand, we have our modern view on the world around us, and how we fit into it, and have concluded that it is vastly stranger than fiction. On the other, we see how it is mysteriously and beautifully echoed from the past in the form of vastly ancient scriptures from both the west and the east. It somehow feels that we have had this knowledge all along since ancient times, somehow lost it and now are rediscovering it by means of modern science.

Is it mere coincidence that two vastly ancient bodies of knowledge from different parts of the world can correlate in such detail to one another, and then also to today's ideas?

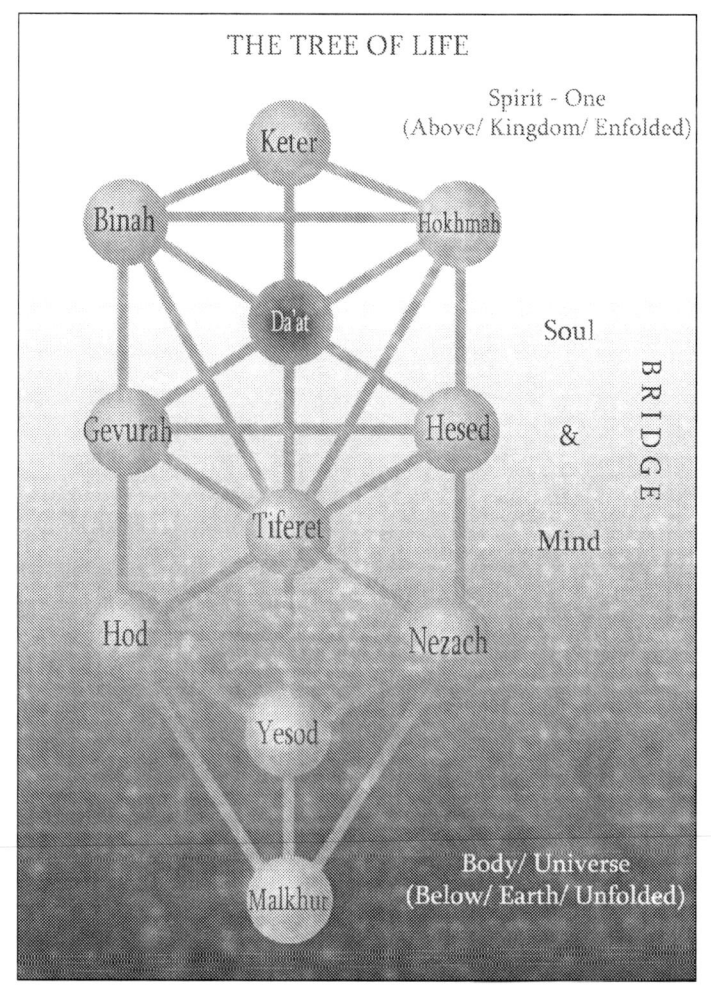

THE TREE OF LIFE

Spirit - One
(Above/ Kingdom/ Enfolded)

Keter

Binah   Hokhmah

Da'at   Soul

Gevurah   Hesed   &   BRIDGE

Tiferet   Mind

Hod   Nezach

Yesod

Body/ Universe
(Below/ Earth/ Unfolded)

Malkhut

The Kabbalist Tree of Life depicting the Olamot of the five universes. It can be seen as a map of the path between the unfolded and enfolded universes, thus, from outer to inner space.

Or shall we pass the Threshold Guardian of coincidence, and accept the calling of the Herald called Synchronicity?

For those unfamiliar with the term, synchronicity was named by Carl Jung, the Swiss psychoanalyst mentioned in the first chapter. If random events, or "coincidences" become meaningful to individuals, it is called synchronicity. I'm sure all of us have experienced very meaningful "coincidences" in our lives, and if you want to be awestruck by historical coincidences, read Martin Plimmer and Brian King's *Beyond Coincidence.* But unfortunately, synchronicity has been ridiculed yet again by the Threshold Guardian in the scientific community, coining it nonsense as it is not scientifically proven. It thus makes us believe the BS man again and dispel meaningful occurrences in our lives. As I've mentioned earlier, unexplainable hocus-pocus has always been explained later — flat earths became round, little balls became vibratory strings and mad people became geniuses, saints and prophets.

In "controversial" works by Graham Hancock, Robert Bauval and others, it is postulated that our generation is the remnant of an ancient and forgotten civilization that collapsed, were scattered by and survived a global catastrophe, and have since then re-evolved through the stages of Egypt, Maya, Inca, Greece, Rome and China, all the way to our modern way of life. They also postulate that these ancient ones tried to leave clues to their existence, as well as ways to avoid the next catastrophe. Their arguments are very solid, linking the ancient ruins like the Sphinx and Egyptian pyramids to the ruins in South America and the far east with erosion patterns and building style (megalithic and very purposeful) as well as very significant "coincidences" in their religions and connections to a remarkable knowledge of astronomy and astrology. Their work is definitely worth considering in using as one of your tools on your journey.

So, looking at all the abovementioned, it seems to be that we have known certain things all along, lost it long ago, struggled through the years trying to find the ancient knowledge kept from us to leave us powerless, and then ironically found it in the mouth of one of the biggest Threshold Guardians — science.

Also, taking all of this in account, we can distill it into an understandable unison.

It seems clear that modern science, Tantra and Kabbalah (and many more falling beyond the scope of this book) synchronize to give us the following:

The universe(s) manifested from a single point of unison, a point of infinite energy that was in total equilibrium.

That something (God, The Universal Mind or a Quantum Fluctuation) caused a moment of "imbalance" or asymmetry that made this point of unison expand rapidly, giving rise to light elements that gradually became denser and denser, forming us and the world as we know it today.

That reality consists mostly of an unseen part or dimension(s), and unfolds or manifests into the seen by means of consciousness as vibration, and that everything is connected, forming each other's infinitely large and small worlds simultaneously — as above, so below; as without, so within. It can thus be simplified into the unseen or enfolded "dimension" likened to: Above/Inner/Kingdom of Heaven; and the unfolded dimension(s) likened to: Below/Outer/Body-Earth (universe).

Space and time or space-time are all relative and dependent on the observer and his circumstances — an illusion so to speak.

That vibration is the key — The Words or Names of God in Kabbalah, the detailed focus on sound and vibration in Tantra, and wave or vibratory properties in String Theory that give rise to all the different "particles" we experience as matter.

By this we realize that our ordinary little lives are much more than that. We are tiny little whirlpools in the ocean of existence who have not made the choice to join in the current of "real life" yet due to the Threshold Guardians. The Threshold Guardians who keep us thinking that we are safe in our little boxes with the pictures of life. We are those lost children on the island or in the labyrinth I spoke of earlier, oblivious of what we are and how deeply we are connected to one another and the One. But the oblivion is breaking. We are slowly but surely waking up to the truth that lies dormant in all of us.

We have to climb out of our little restricting boxes and know what we are — We are all One, resonating together in an ocean of vibration. We are the songs in the symphony of life.

And life — what is it then being a mere illusion? What is the purpose of it?

If one looks closely at Kabbalah and Tantra, the "forefathers" of so many schools of thought, coinciding with each other and with modern science, the answer can be found. Life is the story. Life is the adventurous game where we find ourselves to learn how to evolve from mere actors playing out the part to the writer-director of our stories. Life is the holographic vibratory illusion we find ourselves in and part of, and by guiding our consciousness, we can use the Observer Effect and the Uncertainty Principle to change an unfavorable quantum state or reality into a more appropriate one.

Applying the Tools to Our Lives

But how could this be? Better yet, how can we use it in our daily lives? In order to do this, we have to recognize it in and around us first.

Let's have a look at vibration. What is vibration exactly? Simply put, vibration is fluctuation between two or more states. We see, feel, hear, taste and touch vibration everyday without even knowing it. It could be simple, like a swing swinging from left to right (fluctuation between left and right with an upward-downward combination) or a ball hopping up and down till it comes to a standstill. Or it could be more complex like the sounds we hear, colors we see and emotions we feel.

Sound is fluctuations in air density. If you say "ahh," your vocal chords vibrate at a certain frequency. This in turn makes the air in your throat and all around you resonate with the same frequency. This resonance will enter someone's ear, and his eardrum will start to resonate with the same frequency pattern. This vibratory pattern is then converted into a chemo-electrical vibratory pattern by the nerves connected to your eardrum, and travel to the audio part of your brain, where the pattern is analyzed and recognized as "ahh." Everything has a different sound because of tiny fluctuation differences in the vibratory pattern. Music, for instance, is a very complex melange of sound frequencies and patterns, which if utilized correctly, will cause something that makes us cry with melancholy or jump with joy and even augments the healing process. Furthermore, some sounds will fall above or below our range of hearing because our eardrums can't resonate at that particular frequency. This is called Ultrasound (higher than audible range), and Infrasound (lower than audible range).

The same applies to light. White light, (photons, which are part of the electromagnetic spectrum of frequencies) is the super combination of all colors of light. Different colored light is merely photons vibrating at different frequencies. Shades of red light vibrate at low frequencies, and as the photons vibrate at higher and higher levels, will change in color till they become blue and then violet. Or shall I say, our minds interpret these frequencies as color? These photons, vibrating at their respectable frequencies, will fall onto an apple. Some of these photons will be absorbed, reflected and deflected, and the ones reaching our eyes, will have a certain frequency pattern converted by the eyes and interpreted by the brain as—red, semi-round ball-like object you came to know as "apple." As with sound, some of these electromagnetic frequencies fall beyond our scope. Infrared to radio waves vibrate at lower frequencies than visible red, and ultraviolet to gamma rays, higher than visible violet.

The same applies to touch, taste and smell, and as previously mentioned, the perception of other realities.

You can experience this vibration all inside and around you. Look at the trees swaying in the wind, fluctuating to and fro. The ocean's waves and tides, the day-night cycle, the weather patterns, hormonal cycles, financial patterns, mood swings and arguments—all vibration in vibration in vibration. It is the yin-yang, male-female and light-darkness phenomenon.

We can also see how our universe creates vibratory "pictures." It was discovered by researchers as early as the eighteen hundreds that sound could translate into complex geometric shapes. Hans Jenny, a Swiss physician and scientist, started the study of wave phenomena called Cymatics, where he photographed the complex geometric shapes created by sound in liquids and semi-solids. Even earlier, Pythagoras discovered and explained the remarkable relationship between mathematics, geometry and music with his circular lambdoma, deciphering music and breaking it down into harmonics or the study of intervals of tones. The mandalas used with chanting in eastern religions are the geometric representations of the sound created, also correlating with the chakras or energy centers of the body. Looking elsewhere in our "reality," we can see these geometric shapes of vibratory creation—from the golden-mean phi-ratio geometric shape of seashells to sunflowers and complex fractal images of fern leaves, mountain ranges, snowflakes, cardiovascular systems of animals and flow systems of plants. Look at most animals, and you will see resemblances that only differ in certain ways for functional and environmental adaptation. Most of us have a head, harnessing the brain, with eyes, nose, mouth and ears. We have necks, torsos, abdomens and extremities with the same organs doing the same stuff, again with minor changes to adapt. A human, as well as most other animals, will be "built" in the shape of the sacred geometric pentagram, if arms and legs are stretched out, and it is interesting to note that our DNA differs only approximately one and a half percent from that of the chimpanzee. Another example is that of a dolphin's flipper. If one looks at the skeleton, one will notice the striking similarity to the human hand with the forearm (radius and ulna) and upper arm shorter to be more practical in water. The same applies to a cat or dog's hind leg. Most people think that their knees are bent backwards. In fact that "knee" is their ankle, with the foot bones elongated (walking only on the toes to give them more agility), and the upper and lower leg shortened.

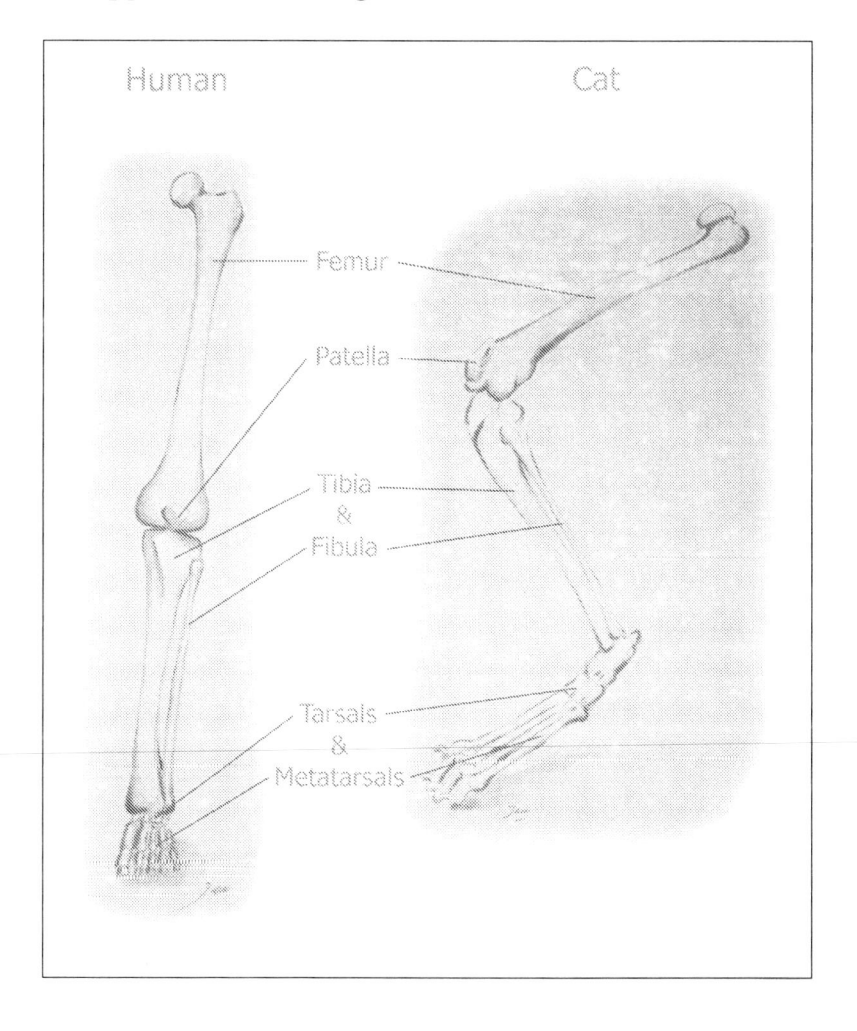

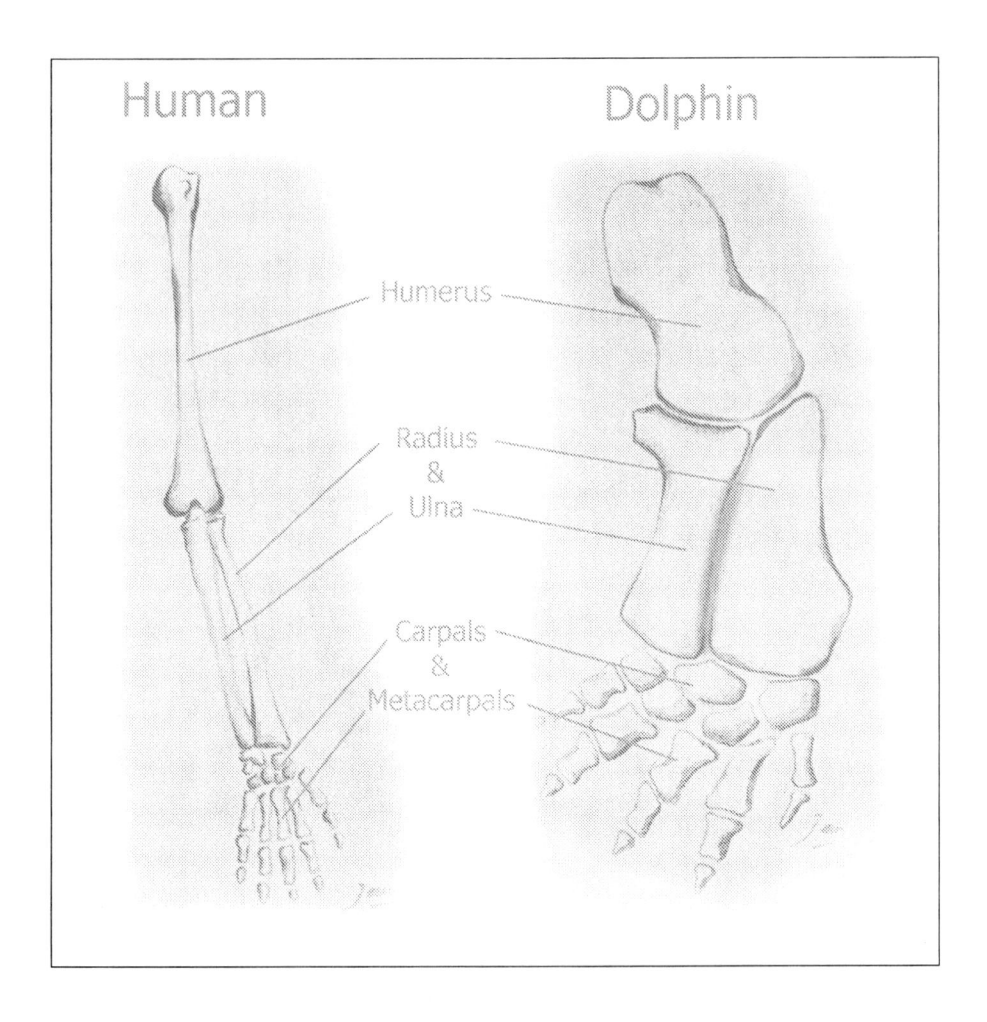

![Human and Dolphin forelimb skeletal comparison showing Humerus, Radius & Ulna, Carpals & Metacarpals]

If we look at embryonic development, we will notice that most embryos will look exactly the same up to the point of differentiation and adaptation. This is controlled by DNA, the molecule-complex all living creatures possess. DNA can be seen as the sheet music or recipe for how that particular organism's song will be played. It is the profoundly mysterious organic software that controls all life on earth.

The similarity goes even further. If we look at our cardiovascular and neurological systems, we will see that they share a structural similarity to that of trees and other plants, and that they in turn share structural similarities to rivers and their deltas and even lightning patterns.

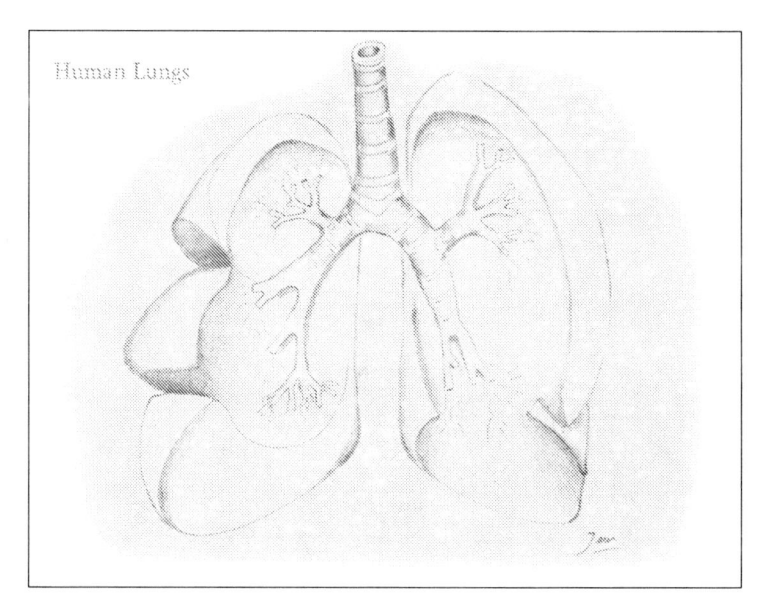

Lungs

Tree

River Delta

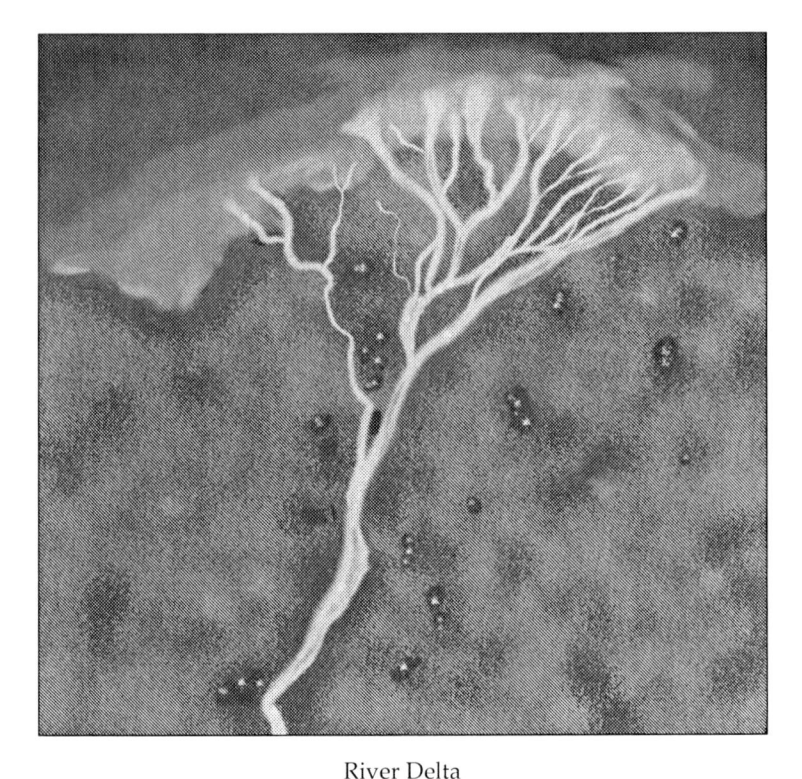

Comparisons showing how nature uses the same template

As we can see, these are more examples to show us that we are vibratory patterns in millions of other vibratory patterns all continuously interacting with each other.

But if everything is vibration, and all vibrations act and react with one another (the so-called Butterfly Effect), then we can see that vibration is not always in harmony, and it is here where the problem (and solution) lies.

It would seem that before our creation, there were no fluctuations or vibrations, but only a steady state. Since the initial "disturbance," our world of infinite interacting fluctuations and vibration was caused, and I think it is in our power to harmonize these vibrations. Do you remember the Observer Effect? Our consciousness changes our surrounding environment, and the effect can be very subtle to moderate and then severe.

Let's start with the basics—moderate to severe.

If you wanted to take a break now, and have a glass of water to drink, then you would simply get up, walk to the kitchen and pour yourself a glass of water.

What happens in this new "out of the box" way of looking at things, is the following:

Your complex body-vibration is slightly dehydrated, thus lacking a vibratory pattern known as water. Your body will then vibrate at a certain frequency, interpreted by the brain as "thirst" by resonating at the same vibration via the nerve-synapse vibratory pattern. A new vibration is created by this "thirst" vibration due to action-reaction or Butterfly Effect—the "desire" for water. The brain will vibrate at this desire for water vibration, and soon the body will resonate at the same frequency. The body, a complex vibratory pattern on its own accord (excuse the pun), starts changing its vibratory pattern ever so slightly by utilizing other vibrations called sugar molecules to make the muscle vibrations vibrate to such an extent to move the entire body to a "space" called the kitchen. Here a lot of exchanges in frequency patterns will arise, from the glass being placed, to the water being poured and then eventually drunk and assimilated into the vibratory pattern called your body.

This simple (yet complex) thing you made happen was done with a whim of thinking, thinking itself being vibration. This could be applied from picking up a pencil (defying the gravity of an object with the vibratory pattern called hand) and drawing plans for a major building to later constructing this building. Thousands of other vibratory life forms (humans) will move around in this building, taking it for granted by thinking it to be "just there" by chance. But it's not there by chance. It is there by thought.

Are you getting my drift? Mere thoughts make things happen, from the minuscule to the insanely profound. And it is in everyone's power to do so. We are all one and the same, vibrating at different patterns and thought vibrations, guided by Consciousness, to change all the vibration around "itself."

The reason why some are "clever" or successful is because they unknowingly use this principle. They use their thoughts productively. They look past the Threshold Guardian of Can't, and just realize their thoughts. They turn their thought patterns into "reality" patterns, thus waves of probability into fermions via the Observer Effect.

Now, for the subtle. At the Princeton Engineering Anomalies Research Lab, founded by Robert Jahn, it was shown that conscious focus could change physical instances (telekinesis as an example). Although to a minor degree, it was statistically proven. It was also found that some individuals could do this more profoundly than others, and interviews with these ones revealed that they saw themselves less separate from the event they had changed than the others not having such a great effect.

This could be linked to the paranormal findings I touched on after discussing the holographic nature of the universe, and is covered extensively in Michael Talbot's book *The Holographic Universe*, ranging from telekinesis to spiritual healing. It is easy to turn to the BS man again and say it is nonsense. But with careful consideration, one can start to put two and two together. We can't see infrared or ultraviolet light. We can't hear radio waves or dog whistles. But that doesn't mean they don't exist now, does it? Our senses are our sensors of this reality, and our brain the filter and interpreter. You would be amazed at how much your brain filters out.

Can you feel the chair, bed or beach under your bum? Can you feel your clothes surrounding your body, or the light breeze tucking at it? I'm sure you became aware of it just now. Remember the topic of dreams and hallucinations? It would seem that our brain-waveform is a complex vibratory "machine" created to receive and process information, not unlike a radio-computer chip combination. We will explore this metaphor in chapters to come, where it would seem that our brains are not the originator of thought, but merely the processor of it after receiving it from a "higher" or inner source (the higher self, inner self, mind or spirit). But later on this.

The Obstacles Ahead

Problems in our bodies, our lives and the world arise due to disharmonic vibration. Vibration has the power to damage or destroy when disharmonic, or heal and build when harmonic. An example can be found in the earth, which used to vibrate at a soft hum of 7.8 Hz, but has increased to a range of about 9.0 Hz, and is still steadily rising. This steady climb in vibration (with other co-factors), will sometimes be replaced by a very slow, high amplitude wave called an earthquake, which will destroy our cities. I heard someone once remarking that it is not earthquakes that kill people, but falling buildings. The reason for the buildings to crumble and fall is due to their disharmonic nature in comparison with the earth's. They are simply "out of tune" with the earth's wave field at that particular moment, the building's harmonics and that of the earth not being synchronous or in "harmony."

We can also see this in resonance between glasses. If we have two identical crystal glasses, both having the same frequency pattern, and make the one "sing" by slowly stroking the rim in a rhythmic and circular motion, the other will "sing" as well. It's because of their identical resonance pattern. If we could mimic this pattern with a sound generator, but the amplitude or volume was too high, the glass would resonate at that frequency and then break because it couldn't contain the amplitude. We all know this phenomenon as the humorous event when an opera singer shatters a glass with her voice. In this, we can also see the destructive power of sound and vibration when incorrectly used.

Everything in life has its own unique resonance pattern, and so different tones together will cause what is known in music as an interval or harmony, better known as chords. If two people sing together, using the correct notes, they will create a soothing song. If not, it will be a cacophony that will irritate the hell out of anyone. The soothing or irritating effect is due to our vibratory patterns' natural reaction to other vibratory patterns. A lot of research has been done on the effect of sound and music on things, ranging from people's moods to plant growth to patterns in water and ice. Masaru Emoto, a Japanese researcher, has done research in the field of sound effects on water. He demonstrated how pure water would have harmonic crystal formation when iced and polluted water not, but better yet he showed that this property could be changed with consciousness as well. Pure water's harmonic crystallization would change to disharmonic when in the presence of disharmonic music, but most strikingly in the presence of harmful thoughts (thought is electromagnetic vibration — remember the EEG as an example). The opposite also happened, as polluted water's crystal properties improved after Buddhist monks chanted in its presence with good intent. This again sounds like hocus-pocus, but if closely studied will reveal the "because" behind the "why."

Let's take a glass of water. The water will vibrate at a ground state of being water (which is two hydrogen atoms fused with one oxygen atom at a certain temperature vibration, as temperature is an effect of increased or lowered thermal vibration). The water vibration is contained by a glass with its own ground state vibration. It is important to note that both glass and water are excellent conductors of sound. Now if we play a disharmonic sound or music in the presence of the glass of water, which is disharmonic sound waves or sonic vibration, it will touch the glass and water, and the disharmonic sonic properties will start changing the ground state vibration of the glass and the water. In plain terms, the glass and especially the water will "record" this disharmonic property. When the water is iced during this contact, the effects will be seen in the malformed ice crystals. Now if you find it difficult to believe that water can record music, let's have a look at how music is recorded on tape (the analogue method).

A woman sings, her vocal chords vibrating at certain resonances that will change the vibration in the air. This vibration is carried through the air toward the microphone. The microphone (an electrically charged micro plate) will vibrate at the same frequency pattern as the woman's voice, changing the sonic vibration into an electric vibration, carried to the recording device. This electric vibration (mirroring the sonic vibration of the woman's voice) will then be "written" on a tape, which consists of metal "particles" arranged in a uniform manner. As the electric waveform strikes these uniform metal particles, it will rearrange their pattern into a mirror image of the electrical waveform, which is a mirror image of the sonic vibration. Thus, the woman's voice is "recorded" on the tape. If you want to play it back, the rearranged metal particles will be "transcribed" back into an electrical waveform by the tape deck "heads." This electric waveform will then be turned into a sonic vibration again by the speaker.

Metal is used because it is relatively stable and reliable to keep the mirror image of the recording for a while. But everything that comes into contact with each other will change each other's waveforms. From sound and metal particles on celluloid to light and electrically charged sensors in your favorite digital camera. From wind blowing through the leaves of a tree to your thoughts and emotions being "captured" by the walls of your house—hence the bad vibes some sensitive people can pick up when purchasing a home. Ironically, a proverb in Luke 19:28-40 states, "… the stones will cry out." Thus, it makes sense that water can "record" sound and thought. It is a natural phenomenon nobody thinks about—everything has a vibratory effect on everything else, which changes vibratory states and in plain terms is called "record." As our bodies are sixty-seven percent water, we can just imagine the impact of daily disharmonic sounds on our well-being.

The same can apply to anything in our lives from health to wealth. When we feel happy, it is a sign of harmonic vibration, and when we don't, the opposite. When looking at relationships, for instance, we can sometimes feel those bad vibes, can't we? Looking at the world of today, it is clear that we, with ourselves and each other, all living creatures and the earth, are not in harmony with each other, and this is what we must address. We need to learn how to create that harmony. In the next section, we will see how.

Approaching the Point of No Return

In the next part of act 2, we will explore what has been discovered so far, and how you can apply it to your life. It does, however, contain elements that are controversial and hotly debated in the science community, as they can't be proven (yet). Science limits itself to the "I will believe it when I see it" philosophy, and the problem with that is clearly noted in the following scenario.

Say for instance you were an ingenious software programmer in the far future and decided one day to write a game. In this game will be an incredibly realistic world, inhabited by software "people" programs that are highly intelligent and self-aware. You also write this program so that it is impossible for these sentient "people" programs to access your world outside their own computer-generated world—an enclosed universe so to speak. These sentient program people will start to ask questions, as all intelligent life forms do. Questions like, "who are we, where did we came from, who made us, is there life after death?" But because it is an enclosed system, they will never be able to know the answers. They will divide into two groups—those who "blindly" believe that there must be something outside their realm, and others who adhere to "seeing is believing." The first group will believe in your existence as their creator (even if they don't have a clue to who or what you are), while the others won't because they need proof in a world that cannot give them any. The fact that your existence as their creator can't be proven in their limited little world does not mean that you don't exist. It just can't be proven from their point of view.

The Sleeper Must Awaken

This is exactly the problem with science. We live in a universe with limitations or boundaries where reason, logic and mathematics bounce back from the walls. How can you prove something that exists outside the framework of your universe? Better still, how can you believe something exists or doesn't exist if you don't even know what it is and what it appears like? For that matter, we can't even prove the existence of ourselves. How do you prove that you really exist? By saying, "Easy, here I am" does not cut it. Remember the dream I mentioned earlier in the book? Some of our dreams are so realistic, and we dream of things equally realistic, but that does not make them real, or does it? Which life is real, this "awake" one or the one where you go to when asleep? Or are both of these worlds real? Looking at the runner-up to these words, it seems that our world is a holographic projection from another vast and unseen world anyway, manifesting us in the form of vibratory patterns if looking at our world through the eyes of quantum physics, String Theory, Kabbalah and Tantra.

Fortunately it would seem by following the bread-crumb trail of the ancient ones that we do have access to our "Programmer's" world (unlike our computer program friends), and it is this access and potentially firm link that we will focus on and apply to daily life.

Now, before you continue, here are the tools to light your path gained from the previous section's discovery:

- Life is not what it seems. It is much more.
- Our world or universe seems to be a moving, holographic projection from a vast and unseen reality and so are we — all seamlessly connected.
- We are manifested in this world through vibratory patterns by consciousness.
- As everything we know is vibration, then in vibration must lie the key.

- Vibration can be harmonic (balanced) or disharmonic (unbalanced), and can clearly be seen and felt from relationships to world matters.
- Creating vibratory harmony is then the key; harmony not simply taken in its metaphorical context, but being used with the same principles as with sound and music.
- Guiding this vibratory harmony by the correct application of consciousness is the lock into which the key fits.

If we look at the abovementioned, one can't help but to think that Shakespeare was right when he said, "all the world's a stage." It feels like this vibratory manifestation or hologram we live in was created purposefully to act like a stage—the stage where we have to tell our stories using the secrets of harmony as the pen. Let's see how.

Our Allies

Your Best Friend

Continuing your journey, meet your first and best friend—You. Face it; you are the one that you will have to live with everyday for the rest of your life, waking up with You every morning—the foul taste in the mouth, the dreary look in the mirror and all the heartaches you will have to endure through years and years. Yes, you are stuck with You for a lifetime (literally). Why not just become best friends from the start? Anyway, if you and You become best friends, you can mean so much to each other in body, mind and spirit. You could be your best friend for life, and will never let you down, ever faithful and always there to listen and to give a helping hand. You are so much more than you can ever imagine, so let me introduce you to You…

You are the center point of your universe. Yes, your world revolves around you, just as others' revolve around them, and all these parallel universes superimpose with each other to form this illusory story around us we accept as real. You are where the Unseen World flows through. The One consciousness flows through every cell, every atom and every string or brane you are made of. You are the portal to the other side. A journey into you (and everything around you for that matter), will reach the world of light, where everything you see, hear and feel in this illusory world, sprouts from. From this world of light, where we are all undoubtedly connected, will flow the energy, changed by your will and thoughts, into the world that is manifested around you. The Uncertainty Principle, which makes it possible to have any quantum reality and future, is changed into "reality" by the Observer Effect, utilized by us in the shape of thought and choice. Think about it. Your thoughts in the shape of millions of choices per day will create your destiny. You are with that particular partner because you chose him or her. You chose him or her because you chose to love him or her. We met them because of millions of choices before meeting them, placing us on a "collision course" he or she devised by his or her choices as well. You were in that car accident because you made a decision to climb into your car at that precise moment that would unfold into events synchronizing with others' choices to be in the collision as well. You might ask, "what about those who didn't have a choice?" Ever had a "gut feel" that you ignored, just like I did before my car accident? Don't we sometimes ignore danger signs hidden from plain view, but subtly known? And as we will explore in Confessions of Spirit later in this Act, it would seem that we even make choices before entering this world. Life and choices are not just limited to this small holographic world of ours.

Each "individual" is a portal through which the Source (enfolded universe of the One) flows, our thoughts creating our reality through the Observer Effect, and where these "realities" intersect or synchronize, creating the world we know. We are all like crystals bridging the gap between the Light World and our Dark World, and because of our unique vibratory pattern (represented by our DNA), the light or energy flowing through us will have a different color, sound and feel - quite remarkable.

Looking at what has been discovered so far on this journey, it is silly to part or divide something in our holistic universe, but to make it practical, let's give ourselves (our being) three practical "parts," or better put, phases—the everyday terms of body, mind and spirit. They are seamlessly connected and shape a complex continuum from this world to the other. Unfortunately the western world mostly stares blindly, and only lives and acts in the physical plane, debating about the nature of the mind (as it is not empirically possible to prove the existence of a mind), never mind the spirit.

As mentioned earlier, it would seem that this illusory world is there to learn from, to learn how to tell your story the way it should be by listening to that "voice" within that guides you into making the right choices, or as modern day Kabbalists put it, play the game of life. You need your holistic existence in order to do so, that is, your spirit, mind and body, and they should be in harmony. But before you can do this, you need to know a bit more about this trinity. As you are the portal between the world of possibilities and the world where possibility becomes "reality," you are in fact the one co-creating your world with all the other holistic beings around you, also being portals to the other side. This is why you need to know more about yourself. And if you have doubts about us (thus you) creating the world around you, just remember that everything in civilization that you see, taste, smell and use started as an idea in someone's head, which became reality — from a simple match to a skyscraper. Now, let's start with the body-mind-spirit unit.

In a nutshell, your Spirit can be seen as the part of you that is eternal, seamlessly connected to everything and everyone. It is where all the "ideas" emanate from. Spirit is the "entry point" from the spaceless-timeless-boundless Knowing, where eternal memory lies (the legendary Akasha). This "entry point" of Spirit lies in each brane of each subatomic particle that you and everything in this universe are made from. Spirit and thus the One consciousness can then be seen in everything. This point of view can be augmented by David Bohm's observations with electron plasmas (gas filled with high concentrations of electrons), where the electrons didn't act individually anymore, but as an interconnected whole. It was almost as if they were "alive," as Bohm remarked. Thus we can see that Spirit resides in everything, and not just in egocentric human beings.

Your Body is the dense vibratory pattern that unfolded from the "World of Light" through the phases of brane, subatomic particle, atom, molecule, DNA, cell, organ, system and organism (you). It is the vehicle that will be used to experience in this plane.

Your Mind can be seen as the bridge between Spirit and Body.

Let me use a crude but effective metaphor.

Your body is like a PC. The casing is your physical dimensions—skeleton, muscles etc. The other hardware is your organs—the microphone represents your ears, the web-cam your eyes, speaker your mouth and vocal chords and most importantly, the CPU (microchip) and hard drive and other memory devices your physical brain. Your body is the hardware that will enable you to function in this world. Your mind is represented by the software, most importantly the operating system (like Windows, Mac Os or Linux), forming the interface between the hardware and the user of the PC.

Thus the User is your spirit, which is the true you, and must coexist with mind and body, cooperating in harmony. This "PC unit," thus the body-mind-spirit union, is also linked to the "internet," where all users (spirits) are connected via one giant information-laden web (a level of the enfolded universe). Ironically, looking back at "fiction" reflecting "fact" in the archetypal nature of the story, we are subconsciously recreating this truth in the way we deal with day-to-day information—millions of PCs connected to each other via the internet. We see yet again the "as above, so below; as within, so without" phenomenon.

From this you realize that the spirit is the "boss." Not the mind, and certainly not the body. We know how irritated we can get if the hardware and software start doing things on their own accord. This applies to life as well. Unfortunately, most of us let our bodies and minds run the show and are not even aware of our spirit, completely shut to it. This is where the trouble starts. Our tri-nature gets out of balance and can affect the way they reverberate with each other on a two-way street basis. But before we go into the health and well-being aspect, let's have a closer look at each of the three. I will start with Spirit, as this is where everything you know starts.

The Sleeper Must Awaken

2 Dimensional Entry Point Diagram

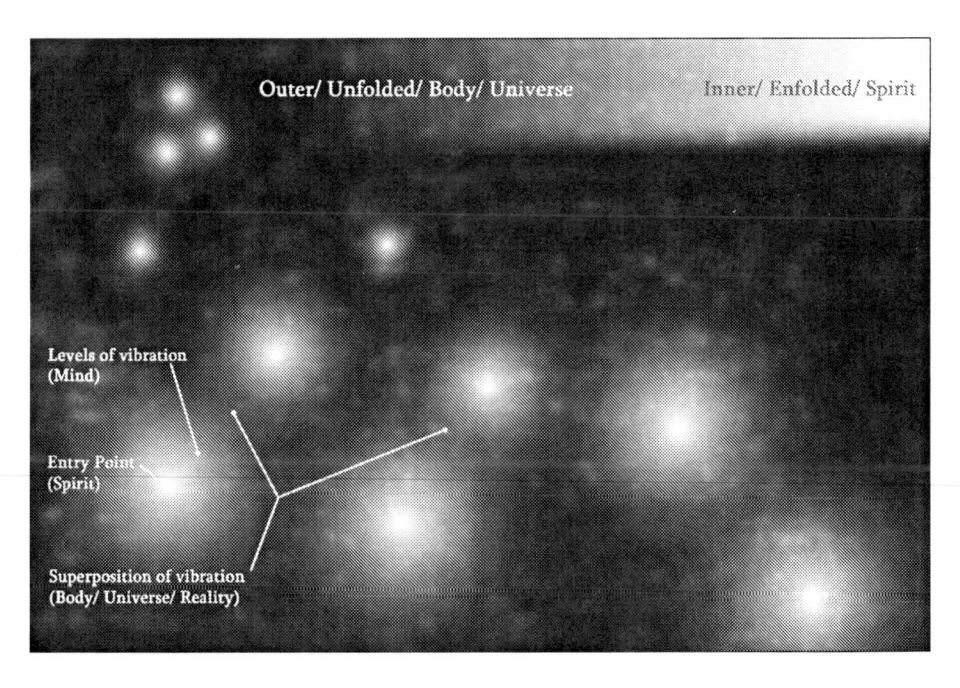

Outer/ Unfolded/ Below/ Earth (and our universe)

Superposition of vibration is our illusion of Reality (Body)

Levels of vibration: atoms - galaxy (Mind)

String/Brane or Entry Point (Spirit)

The 'Veil'

Inner/ Enfolded/ Above/ Kingdom of Heaven (The One)

3 Dimensional Entry Point Diagram

Outer/ Unfolded/ Body/ Universe

Inner/ Enfolded/ Spirit

Levels of vibration (Mind)

Entry Point (Spirit)

Superposition of vibration (Body/ Universe/ Reality)

93

Confessions of Spirit Existence

Now what is the spirit exactly? Difficult to say, as we can't even scientifically prove its existence. But on the basis of other investigations, we can get an idea of what it is and how it works. This is by the study of Near Death Experience (NDE), Out of Body Experience (OBE), hypnotherapeutic case studies of past lives and controlled experimentation on hallucinogenic substances.

We have all heard of Near Death Experiences, and some of you might even have had one, as approximately eight million Americans have experienced one (according to the Gallup poll). NDE is a controversial topic in the science community (how else—it can't be empirically proven), but research done by Raymond Moody, Elizabeth Kubler-Ross, Kenneth Ring (cofounder of International Association of Near Death Studies or IANDS) and many more have shown that this is a phenomenon that needs to be reckoned with. Studies have shown that NDE has nothing in common with race, gender, social background or belief systems—NDE can happen to anyone.

NDE has particular trademarks. People feel that they leave their bodies, are aware of this world and another, travel to the other world through a "tunnel," feel peace and calm and meet beings of light in this other world who manifest themselves as spiritual beings either known or unknown to the person in NDE, as well as relatives who have passed away. Here they usually have a Life Review, where they themselves are the "judge," seeing the seeds they have sown and the harvest they have reaped while supported by the beings of light, offering comfort in difficult reviews. They then return to this life, having a remarkable change in attitude toward life, spirituality, ecological sensitivity and sense of oneness with the universe. Another trademark seen while in the NDE state is that the person experiencing it can manifest him- or herself as they see fit. Some will be auras of energy, while others will transform themselves into the body they have known from that particular life, only fit and healthy. They are boundless, and it seems that their thoughts and focus are free to manifest their desires. Their life reviews are also intensely detailed, running by like a self-immersed movie, simultaneously super fast and slow, and they also have access to a vast and incalculable knowledge (the legendary Akasha?) of things that are mainly difficult to recall once back in their lives as they are so difficult to contain.

The same can be seen with past life regression, where some also see the phase in-between two lives (coinciding with that of NDE) and of course Out Of Body Experience (OBE). Most OBE experiencers "fall back" into their own selves out of fear, but there are some who travel further and "astral" project themselves to distant locations. Some have even crossed the barrier between this world and the other.

A good example is a well-known genius of his time called Emanuel Swedenborg (1668–1772), a Swedish scientist, philosopher and later in life mystic, who could go into deep trance-like states and project himself into the realm of the afterlife. His early life was spent in science, politics and astronomy. He could speak a dozen languages and even designed prototypes of an airplane and submarine. But on developing his OBE and remote-viewing skills, he became very spiritual after "being shown" the other world—the "world of God" where everything emanated from. Here, he also saw the spirits from earth having their life reviews, appearing to be waves of light and energy. Swedenborg believed the other world, or the world of light, to be the origin of our world, where energy flowed down from the divine world as thought form, becoming slower and denser, and giving rise to an almost "frozen" existence as we know it now. It's almost as if there is a constant wave-like flow from the divine, echoed from the non-divine, and where these waveforms intersect gives rise to our illusion of a world.

From these sightings and experiences, Swedenborg wrote numerous volumes of work, where he broke away from the usual restrictive church doctrine and claimed that our conception of God, Jesus Christ and Holy Spirit is inaccurate (our current Christian views on the Trinity are based on the first council of Nicaea in 325 CE, at which the nature of God and Jesus were decided) and said that the Father-Son-Holy Spirit aspects were not separate, but parts or phases of one God. This in itself is one of the main causes for Islam to be opposed to Christianity, as Islam believes that God is not three separate beings, but only one God. He also stated that what he saw was as real as anything we believe (words he spoke on his deathbed), and that one day, we will also see.

If one thinks that this was a man who devoted his life to science, politics, astronomy, invention, economy and color theory and postulated workings of neuroscience (which were accurate), spoke more than five languages and also acted as psychic and mystic, it is difficult to just disregard him as "insane" as some would. Instead, I would rather take a closer look at his experiences, see how they coincide with the findings in OBE, psychotropic drug research and regression to past lives and use them by balancing out all the elements to distill them into something useful.

By the abovementioned, it seems clear that yet again, OBE, NDE, Tantra, Kabbalah, entheogenic experiences and modern physics coincide on a number of matters - this world (dense, sluggish and dark) and that world (light and peaceful), vibration and energy and the illusion of space and time.

Yet again, the spirit or soul can't be empirically proven. But with all these "coincidences" storming in, I would say that it is pretty stubborn not to simply say, "where there's smoke, there must be a fire." Yes, it can't be proven, but it's simply daft not to believe that there must be something outside this dense and fragile world of ours. So, either one believes, or not. In the end, the choice is yours.

Mind the Mind

Yet again a controversial little thing which can't be touched, can't be proven, hotly debated on what it is exactly, how one can divide it or separate it from emotions and make scientists fall into different groups opposing each other on the subject.

The mind and its nature have had a long history of thought, debated since the days of Plato and Aristotle. There is a substantial view that the mind is not physical, but an entity separate from the body, and a functional or more scientific approach that the mind is a mere product of the brain, where the brain becomes aware of its own workings and existence termed mind or thought. The mind is like a cloud; it can't be pinned down, can't be categorized or put into a specific box by science—it just is. To believe it to be a mere product of chemical reactions in the brain is fair enough if you look at life in general through "seeing-is-believing" glasses. But one must remember that the brain, like everything else, is a complex wave pattern. Chemicals and their reactions are also complex wave patterns. It then boils down to whether one believes that the mind—a lighter less dense waveform—is produced by the denser wave pattern called the brain, or that the mind is created by the interference pattern caused by the rendezvous between the spirit reflected from the denser brain waveform, like light reflects from an apple, revealing the apple to the observer. It doesn't matter how one looks at it, the mind is a bridge, and a bridge usually has two-way traffic. I believe that the mind is the interference pattern between spirit and brain (which is part of the dense body) that forms the bridge between this dense and "physical" world and the light and "ethereal" world, the body being the portal. In the words of Christ—"your bodies are the temples of God." And this brings us to…

The Body Re-viewed

To most of us, our bodies are just a collection of meat, bone and some weird disgusting organs drifting about in it. In actual fact, the human body (and any other body for that matter, ranging from plant to animal) is an amazing feat. If one studies the anatomy and physiology of a body in a purely scientific way, it is still a thing to marvel at—sheer genius. From the skeleton, made and maintained by bone cells (osteoclasts and osteoblasts), using calcium as a building block, to the microscopic actin and myosin proteins in muscle connecting and disconnecting to make muscle contract, to the way the liver will use worn-out blood cells in the production of bile (to, in their turn, help with digestion).

Our bodies are not just functional in the sense of day to day life, but also aesthetically pleasing creations when well maintained. We use our bodies to move about in this world, work and play, break world records and make love. We take them for granted, abuse them daily with unhealthy foods and habits and in the end when they start to malfunction, we anguish.

Our bodies consist of various systems that work together when all is well. We have a nervous system consisting of the complex brain and millions of nerve pathways and neurotransmitter chemicals, which in unison with the hormonal or endocrine system, form the communications department. We have a cardiovascular system consisting of the heart, veins and arteries, which is the transport system, transporting all the oxygen, carbon dioxide, food and waste molecules. We have the musculoskeletal system for strength and movement, the renal system for cleansing and the hematological system for oxygenation and defense. Every day, while we worry about our next dental appointment or broken nail, our bodies work silently and efficiently, hardly ever complaining about the various abuses they suffer under our modern way of life—stress, smoking, drinking, fast-foods and various other nasty habits.

But the body is much more than just this complex collection of systems. When looking at it from all perspectives—western and eastern, modern and ancient, scientific and metaphysic—the body forms the first step on the ascension to our spirits and the "unseen" world. According to ancient Tantric texts that are used in Yoga, our bodies consist of three "parts" or "layers"—the physical body, the astral body and the causal body—each seamlessly integrated, the physical body being the densest of the three and perishable, with the causal body being the less dense, eternal and in contact with the divine. These bodies are also connected to each other via 72,000 Nadis (the root *nad* meaning vibration in Sanskrit), through which universal energy flows, and where they strongly intersect will form the seven chakras or "spiritual" foci of the body. The seven chakras are specific areas in our bodies, from root to tip so to speak, and form the strong connection points or portals of the body–mind–spirit relationship. They are metaphorically associated with flowers that need to unfold as they are awakened.

The Base Chakra (Muladhara) is at the base of the spine, associated with the pelvic organs (excluding the sexual organs) and adrenal glands, and forms the basis of survival, the primal focus. Its color is red, with associated musical tone in the frequency range of C (thus around 256Hz), and it is said to be in this chakra where the mysterious kundalini energy resides, waiting for awakening. Disharmony in this chakra will give rise to physical problems like constipation and hemorrhoids as well as fatigue and lethargy.

The Sexual or Sacral Chakra (Swadhisthana) is in the area of the gonads (just above the testes in males and just below the ovaries in women), linked with the gonads. Its function is that of pleasure, sexuality and creativity, and it is linked to the color orange and associated with the musical tone D (292.6 Hz). Disharmony in this chakra will give rise to abnormalities in the sexual organs of both men and women, as well as abnormalities in libido, inhibition and lack of creativity.

The Solar Plexus Chakra (Manipura) is in the area of our solar nervous plexus, an area with a concentrated nerve center just above and deep to the navel. This area also houses the pancreas and adrenals and is linked to the maintenance of the physical organs, as well as giving logic, drive and ambition. Its main color is yellow with associated musical tone in the range of E flat (315.1Hz), and disharmony in this area will cause physical problems of the associated organs, as well as a lack in drive, ambition and logic.

The Heart Chakra (Anahata) is in the area of our cardiac nervous plexus (in the heart region, hence the name). Its physical connection is that of its surrounding organs and thymus gland, and it is associated with love and kindness. Its main color is in the green range, with associated musical tone F (336.1 Hz), and disharmony in this chakra will give rise to abnormalities in the surrounding organs, as well as anger, insomnia and lethargy.

The Throat Chakra (Vishuddha) is in the laryngeal plexus area, situated at the juncture of the medulla oblongata and the spinal chord (just behind the throat). With a basic color of blue and musical tone G (388.4 Hz) it is associated with the thyroid, communication, willpower and expression. Disharmony will be associated with the area that it presents, as can be seen from previous chakras.

The Brow Chakra (Ajna) is situated deep to and between the eyes, associated with the pineal gland, basic color of purple to indigo, musical tone A (436.9 Hz), and has the function of intuition and extrasensory perception. Interesting to note again how this area, coinciding with the pineal, is postulated to be the producer of the natural hallucinogen DMT, which causes OBE and NDE under controlled circumstances.

The Crown Chakra (Sahasrara) is situated just above the head. This is meant to be the area where the kundalini energy, which resides in the base chakra, traveling up the other chakras after being awakened, will end and connect to the divine. It is to be the portal to the spiritual world, and is associated with the colors white, gold and silver and musical tone of B (485.5 Hz). One can imagine what happens when this chakra is disharmonic.

It is interesting to see how these areas, detailed in their description by the ancient Tantric texts, coincide with very particular areas in the body (described by western science) as seen in the above notes, especially the brow chakra and the pineal gland. It is also interesting to mention that each chakra has its own vibratory value or musical tone, starting with low vibration (or bass tone) in the base chakra, becoming more treble (or higher) as one goes up the chakra ladder. It is also interesting to note that the colors associated with these chakras start with lower vibratory light, as red has a very low vibratory value, while orange, yellow etc. have progressing higher vibratory values. These colors and tones also coincide with the values of the Pythagorean lambdoma. The lowest of the chakras are also associated with the four basic elements: base with earth, sacral or sexual with water, solar plexus with fire, and heart with air.

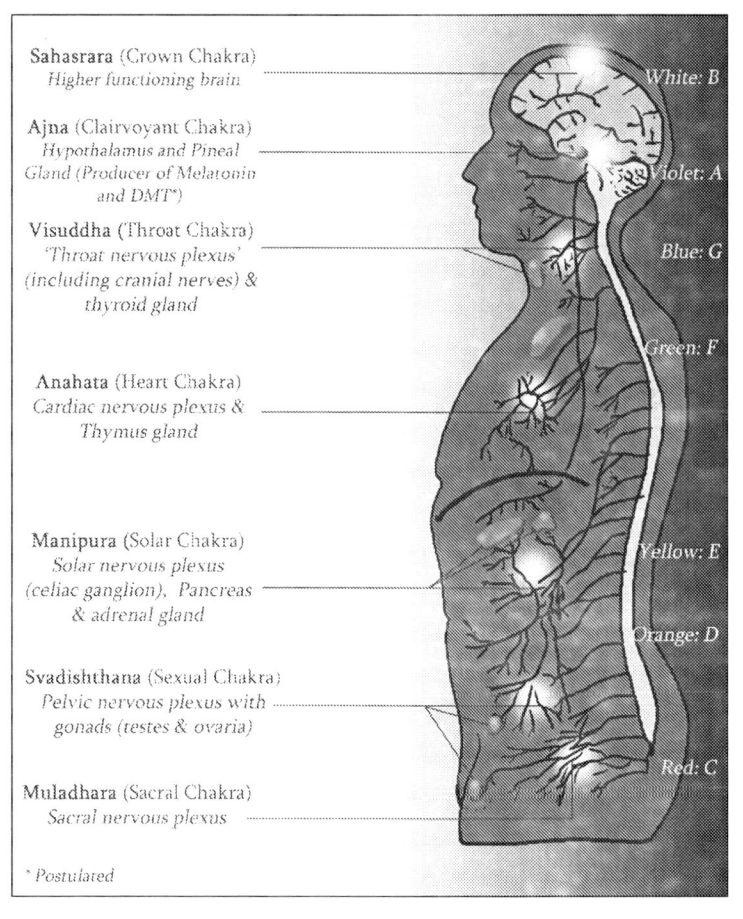

Sahasrara (Crown Chakra)
Higher functioning brain

White: B

Ajna (Clairvoyant Chakra)
Hypothalamus and Pineal Gland (Producer of Melatonin and DMT*)

Violet: A

Visuddha (Throat Chakra)
'Throat nervous plexus' (including cranial nerves) & thyroid gland

Blue: G

Green: F

Anahata (Heart Chakra)
Cardiac nervous plexus & Thymus gland

Manipura (Solar Chakra)
Solar nervous plexus (celiac ganglion), Pancreas & adrenal gland

Yellow: E

Orange: D

Svadishthana (Sexual Chakra)
Pelvic nervous plexus with gonads (testes & ovaria)

Red: C

Muladhara (Sacral Chakra)
Sacral nervous plexus

* Postulated

A schematic representation of Chakras in the body

The higher chakras are associated with the lighter elements, ether and radium. The crown chakra has no element. Another interesting thing to note is that the colors of the chakras represent those of a rainbow, which is white light split into different colors or vibratory light values by a denser body than air. Thus, white light is a product of all different colored light that unites. As the crown chakra is white, it would seem that it represents the unison of all the chakras, especially viewed from above — God's view so to speak. Or can we think of it as the Light entering our bodies through the crown chakra, and then split into the "rainbow" as it encounters the denser areas of the body?

   These chakras, with the three different aspects of the physical body, produce the energy field seen around the body, known as the aura. Some mystics and spiritual healers can actually see auras and the areas that show disharmony reflected in them. It is by using this that they can perform their healing techniques by correcting the imbalances. Auras have also been shown with a more conventional method known as Kirlian photography, but even you might be able to see it. Ask a friend or family member to stand in front of an even-colored white wall. Stand a few feet away from him or her, and let your eyes drift from the top of the head to focus somewhere between the head and the wall. After a while, you might be able to see a faint glow around them. This would be the first and densest layer of the person's aura. If you are more connected, you might even see more of the layers, which would have a certain color.

   Of course western science will sneer, how else, yet again. For it is a typical mistake to part anything in the body — the brain is the brain, the heart is the heart etc. Surely it must be nonsense that emotions and disease can be created or controlled with so-called energy foci. In a very basic and western way of thinking, a disease such as pancreatitis (inflammation of the pancreas), which is mainly caused by gallstones or alcohol abuse, looks very benign in the beginning (apart from severe pain). But soon, if not well looked after, it can cause the whole body to fall down in an endless spiral of organ failure. This one small piece of tissue (about the size of a quarter of your hand) can cause the whole body to die, because everything in the body is seamlessly connected. Even in plain basic western medicine, failure to realize the interconnectedness of everything in our bodies, as well as our bodies to the environment, will lead to failure in correct diagnosis and treatment. The brain is not separate from the nerves, as the heart is not separate from the arteries and veins, but forms a continuum of functionality. These systems are not separated from one another either. They are connected via electrochemical receptors, the one not changing without the other's knowledge nor reaction. The body was "separated" into smaller and smaller parts in early (and even primitive) days of medicine to make it easier for the student to understand and learn. Unfortunately, the problem of seeing in "separate mode" arose from this way of teaching, a problem that has been passed down generation after generation, causing modern medicine and the like to partition things even smaller and smaller, even in their specialties. The bottom line is we are holistic beings, part of a holistic universe, all seamlessly connected, and failure to realize this will lead to blindness to the truth. And as the saying goes, "In the land of the blind, one eye is king." The body then (again BS man aside) would also seem to be much more interesting than we imagined.

Now What?

Now what indeed. Now we can take all this information and try to use it as the tool on our further quest in order to tell our stories. As mentioned earlier, your universe surrounding you sprouts from you. You are the portal through which the Enfolded dimension or the world of light unfolds and manifests the world as you see it, intersecting with all the others around you. Where these parallel realities of ours coalesce and synchronize is where the events of life happen.

Our thoughts and focus, intersected with each other's, create the world. In a sense, the change starts within you. It starts with all of us. Everything, it would seem, arises from the spirit or soul (connected to the Godhead or the One), but in order for it to do its thing accurately, we need to ready and maintain the vehicle and the bridge. We need to maintain the lens through which the spirit looks at the Ordinary World and will eventually shine its light. Let's start with the vehicle, or body.

Body

Maintenance: An Introduction

The body acts like a vibratory lens through which the spirit's light will shine and create your reality. Therefore, the lens needs to be clean for the light and energy to pass. All in all, balance is essential. Many a person will go on a rampage to eat and drink as healthy as they can by chomping greens only, or using only the best mineral water from a certain area or following some diet that does more damage than good. In the end, one needs to balance a healthy lifestyle with pleasure. If you burn yourself out with health tyranny, you will become unhappy anyway, which in turn will harm your health. I would suggest a diet and life plan that suits you best. Although we are all more than ninety-nine percent the same (DNA wise), we do, however, differ in small variations, which are enough to make us all utilize and react to certain products differently. Some of us have faster metabolisms than others, some of us have certain food sensitivities and some of us will feel energetic with some foods while others may feel lethargic on the same foods. We all need to find our own golden pathways.

But a word of caution: Human well-being has in the last decade or so been used and turned into a billion dollar industry, preying on the need for well-being as well as the ignorance of yearning for it. One diet revolution is replaced by the next, and the absolute need to look good has been brainwashed into us so that we can let go of our hard-earned cash. The motif behind everything in a capitalist society is that of making more money. Now, there is nothing wrong with money nor having a lot. How you earned it and how wisely it is used do matter, however. So please don't fall prey to moneymaking schemes. There are a lot of good people out there who want to help others be well, but the majority lack the morals—they're out to make money. Avoid them.

Base line is: back to the basics. How would we have lived in a less artificial world?

Below are a few guidelines that are meant to break through all the technobabble and rosy colored lenses. They are very basic, and could prove firm ground to build on. But remember, they are guidelines, not rules.

Maintenance: Energy in = Energy out

What you don't use after intake will be stored for later famine-stricken days as, yes you know the word - fat. Fat is the way of the body to just store access energy. Obesity has become an enormous health problem for the west as the percentage of obese individuals has dramatically risen in the past thirty years. As we all know from the media hype, obesity is extremely bad for our well-being, and a lot of us struggle with the weight-diet tango. While many obese people will deny their intake of high amounts of calorie loaded food (I had many in general practice denying their binges), the fact remains that if I stuff anyone in a padded room with only water for a few weeks, they will lose enormous amounts of weight. With no energy intake, the body will start to use its own resources—the stored fat. The problem doesn't lie in that some can eat all they like and stay thin, while others eat like mice and become fat. When you eat loads (especially calorie-loaded and high glycemic-indexed food) and you don't use that energy, you will become fat. It's a matter of balance. Now it is true that some have slower metabolisms than others (especially with some rare diseases and genetic disorders), but that just means that such a person can eat less for the same energy value. He or she preserves and utilizes energy more efficiently. The real problem lies deeper and has a combination of causes.

It seems with recent studies that obesity has dramatically risen in the last thirty years in especially the United States and United Kingdom. The rise has been connected to the intake of higher calorie dense foods, especially in fast-foods and "ready meals" as well as more food produced than is necessary. In the United States, more food is produced than is consumed. Certain foods have also been advertised as being "good" for you in the past, before all the hype went bust. In the eighties and nineties, American fast-food franchises sprawled over the world as if they were colonizing the world in stealth mode as they became household names. The habit got stuck, and on a lazy night, it's easy to go and grab a burger or a pizza made from cheap and cheerful ingredients. Mood disorders are also associated with obesity, where the lack of pleasure or "the void" must be filled with something pleasurable, and food comes easy. These factors are all associated with the Energy-in mode. On Energy-out mode, we have other problems. We are much less active than we used to be in the past. Everything became so much easier. Public transport is now much closer to home. Cars and fuel became more affordable post-World War Two, and by the nineteen eighties, almost every family owned a car or two, driving everywhere. Now we are stuck with the car habit, no matter what the fuel price. There is now Playstation for the kids, so no more running around and climbing trees. You can also do almost anything online, from organizing your holiday to ordering some more food. It would seem that the Energy-in as well as the Energy-out has a problem. A double whammy so to speak. Millions are spent on diets per year, while the fat sticks around like a bad habit. Fads come and fads go, making millionaires out of some. But it still boils down to one thing — Energy in = Energy out. One has to adhere to this rule no matter what. If you pick up weight, you are not necessarily eating too much, but you are getting in more energy than is used. You either have to become more active or eat less calorie dense foods or both, again not necessarily less food per se. It's advisable to get yourself a program that works for you. That which works for one doesn't necessarily work for another. The same applies for when you lose weight. An unknown cause for weight loss should not seem like a blessing in disguise—it could mean that you have a serious condition underlying. We are unique in some ways. You are what you eat. Thus try to eat as healthy as you can, following sound advice from dedicated professionals, not media hypes who want to make quick bucks from people struggling with weight due to ignorance of the elusive food industry, a sound knowledge of the physics of their bodies and some emotional problems that they try and solve with binges. Get to the root of the problem. Maybe your habit lies much, much deeper. Maybe even in past life memories. BS man aside, look at the work of Sylvia Browne, who has regressed many people with disastrously bad habits - where they found their problem in a past life and dealt with it. Thus the problem can be a simple one, like eating too much or too little ("monkey see, monkey do" in the family), or be deeply rooted in a previous life memory. Find it and deal with it.

A small tale from my side to maybe help you with difficult habits—I love, no, I adore Italian and French food, especially thin-based pizza and croissants in the morning for breakfast. But in the last few years, my stomach has been giving me the hump, and got worse and worse. Details are not necessary, but the IBS-like symptoms became unbearable. So, I realized that something I ate was causing it, and by a process of elimination, I discovered the problem—I had a serious wheat or gluten sensitivity. So that meant all my favorite food was making me ill, and more so everyday. I tried to eat less of it, but the symptoms became so bad that I made the choice to cut it completely. It's terrible to stop eating the most lovable food, and as I love good food and preparing it, it struck me harder than I imagined. I then realized how much I couldn't eat anymore due to wheat and gluten content—bread, pastry, pizza, pasta, biscuits, wavers, most confectionery chocolate, stock cubes, beer, sauces—the list is almost endless. It makes it particularly bad if I want to go to a restaurant with my wife, who is then restricted as well if I can't eat anything on the menu, not to mention everyone digging into my favorite but forbidden foods when we do find an appropriate restaurant. I have to say, it's not easy. Sometimes the craving drives me insane. But my gut does not like wheat, and I have to respect that. My gut, and the rest of my body, give me a lot that I could be eternally grateful for, and thus I compromise. It's like all good relationships, I suppose, and unfortunately you can't chicken out and divorce your body. You have to adapt or die.

Maintenance: You Are What You Eat

An old saying, but very true. If you think of it, you put some stuff into your mouth, swallow it and then your body will break it down and incorporate it into itself (yourself). Thus, if you eat crap, you absorb that crap into your system, where it will travel to every one of your cells and stay for quite some time (as we don't drink enough filtered water and don't exercise enough to boost our circulation). Problem is, we don't know half of the crap we ingest everyday. That supermarket food looks good, but that's because of all the "behind the scenes" stuff you don't know about. Pesticides, genetic modification (GM), color enhancing, hormonal boosting, antibiotics, water injection, preservatives, flavor enhancing, partially hydrogenated oils — and so it goes. Very bad for you. All those chemicals are absorbed by your system, and there it will do its damage year after year. And GM foods cannot be good for you. With genetic modification (GM) the DNA has been tampered with, and thus the basic vibratory code of the plant or animal. We are only just beginning to grasp the fact that the "machine" can be altered a bit, but that doesn't mean that we know about the long-term harm it can cause, especially with the narrow-minded view of science and the money-hungry wolves sitting behind the motive. If we look back at scientific and medical history, we will see countless cases of tampering that years later resulted in serious damage. And then all of a sudden the lawsuits come. It's like the bone meal fed to cattle. How can you feed a species its dead brethren's bones? It's like eating the powdered local graveyard for goodness sake! And then, CJD or "mad cow disease" struck. The protein (prion) responsible spread from one to the other via the nervous tissue in tainted animal tissue used in feeds. Herbivores need to eat grass as nature intended, not their dead brothers and sisters. It also reminds me that we supermarket folk, especially the children of the supermarket folk, don't appreciate meat anymore. Those chops are laid neatly in cute little packs, only to be half consumed and then pushed away by a spoiled little brat and thrown away. We forget that animals (who we have learned so far are not so far removed from ourselves as we would think) have endured suffering and then death to make us not live, but enjoy. We don't need meat. We can do well without it. We are omnivores by nature, meaning we can live from plant as well as animal material, but close examination of our intestine reveals that we are more adapted to plant consumption than meat. We should then act as such. I am not preaching vegetarianism or veganism, but after visiting a modern abattoir, I realized again the cruel nature of humans. It struck me deep to see the whole mechanized and cold environment in which the slaughter of animals took place — the long queue of nervous animals, the zap to the brain, the pickup and slaughter by machines, and then the electrical beams tendering the meat artificially as the fear makes the muscle (and thus the meat) go tense and less enjoyable to us supermarket folk. It is done by such a cold and machine-like disregard for the suffering of the poor creatures, which have no choice in the matter. And meat consumption goes beyond that. For the same amount of soil used to feed forty people with maize or soya, you will only be able to raise one or two cows, not to mention their water consumption. Thousands of acres of forest are destroyed per week to make grazing for more cattle than is necessary, to make hamburger patties for a species who don't need it for survival, but because it's so nice to eat. We are destroying the world's lung so that we can eat a nice little hamburger, or have a barbecue or cookout. I realized that I could give up meat altogether. How could I eat Daisy that followed me around on the farm as a child? Yes, I remember this cow on the farm that used to be happy to see me and follow me around wherever I walked. She used to enjoy being stroked on the head. How could we eat veal (the flesh of a baby cow) or lamb (the flesh of a baby sheep)? How could we get it over our hearts to stuff these beings in a truck with no place to sit or lie down, standing for hours in their own excrement while the truck swings to and fro? If you can get it over your heart, then at least be thankful to that animal that gave its life in a holocaust kind of way, so that you can enjoy its flesh. The same goes for plants. Cleve Backster did research on plants with polygraph machines (the machines used in lie detectors to show fluctuation in emotional response) that showed how plants responded in a similar way to humans and animals when threatened. Even with a mere thought of threat, the polygraphs showed signs of distress. It would seem that even plants feel "fear and happiness," and we should keep this in mind when we kill them to eat. We do, however need to eat and live, and luckily, plants want us to eat their fruit. It helps them spread their seeds to further their species' survival. But remember to be thankful to all animals and plants that had to die so that you can live or enjoy.

Simple guidelines then:

First of all, make your own food, and stay away from ready-made meals and other processed food. They are loaded with harmful ingredients like partially hydrogenated vegetable oil, preservatives, color enhancers and all other so-called "E" numbers. Processed and bleached wheat, found in almost any processed food, is the thing to avoid. It is a "quick calorie" thickener, and its high glycemic index causes quick surges in your insulin levels, causing hypoglycemia is some people, but mostly hunger, which leads to eating more in a day than is needed. Hence, the weight problem. Overall, a low glycemic index diet and life plan are a good idea. *The GI diet* by Rick Gallop is a tremendously helpful book in this regard.

Another problem with wheat is its storage (as with maize and other products, like peanuts). Compressed in bales, it lies waiting to be processed while the center of the bale is dark and humid. This is good news for aflatoxin-producing fungi, but bad news for humans, as aflatoxins can cause liver cancer. It's better to eat as little wheat products as possible, and if done, preferably stone-ground organic whole-wheat. Best is to use organic whole-wheat that hasn't been stored in bales for long periods of time.

Try to eat as much fresh produce as you can, particularly organic produce, as they exclude the use of chemicals and genetic modification. Organic produce is a bit more expensive, but if health is important to you, especially your children's health, you will "invest" in it. I'm also sure that a lot of you have unhealthy habits costing you a fortune that could be dropped. The money saved on the bad habit can then be used to buy decent food.

Try to eat more fruit, vegetables and whole grains that suit you, rather than too much meat. If you can, cut out meat altogether (replacing your protein intake with nuts, dairy products and plants like soya). Use trial and error to find the fruit and vegetables that will suit you best. If you can't do without meat, try to eat the meat of animals that are smaller in stature than you are. Their muscle fiber is finer and easier to digest, and thus the use of energy on your behalf is less. Smaller animals also have a less strenuous impact on the earth's resources. Also try and obtain meat from humane facilities that go out of their way in the benefiting of animal and environmental welfare—in the end its good for you, your family and the whole planet in general.

Try to use more steaming and cooking with water (filtered) in preparation rather than frying in saturated fats—it's healthier.

Try to lower your refined complex sugar intake. It is bad for your teeth and lingers in the gut a bit longer, which could cause bacterial balance disturbances. Less complex sugars are better (like fructose from fruit). If at all possible, avoid it all together.

Chocolate and coffee have their advantages as well as disadvantages. Caffeine in teas and coffees is a culprit when it comes to insulin surges and interference with the normal ATP cycle in muscles, so use it in moderation, and try to use it in a pure form without too much sugar and additives. It tastes better anyway without all that added crap. And please look for Fair Trade logos. Companies in the developed countries make millions from coffee and chocolate, while the women and children working in the developing worlds to bring you that nice cup live in poverty. Fair trade at least tries to make it better for them.

Same applies to alcoholic beverages. Enjoy their taste, not their inhibition-numbing effects. Use it in moderation, and if you cannot stop drinking, no matter what the occasion, avoid alcohol, full stop. Alcohol is also a cause for struggling to shed weight. If you have problems with weight, cut alcohol out.

Try and avoid sitting in front of the television while you eat. It's much better to have an hour of the enjoyment of food with family and friends around a dinner table. Not only is it a way of bonding with your family, it will also provide a relaxed and cared-for atmosphere, which in turn stimulates your parasympathetic system, which in turn will help you absorb and utilize your food better. That is to say if there are no family arguments. I suppose then it's better to sit and eat alone, but hopefully the family matter will be resolved.

If you find it tough to be vegan (the complete exclusion of animal products, for those who don't know the term), remember that a lot of animal products can be obtained in a symbiotic way, symbiosis meaning a relationship where both parties and organisms benefit from exchange. Milk, which is used to make all kinds of dairy products, can be obtained in this manner. We benefit from the product, while the animals benefit from shelter, food and health. This is to say if obtained in an organic and humane establishment. Look into this, and make your life easier if you are having a tough time. On the other hand, if you are a "religious" vegan to the extent of becoming fundamental, remember that the food chain is natural. Nature intended for there to be a complex chain, going from simple bacteria and plants fed on by herbivores (plant eaters) fed on by carnivores (meat eaters) and omnivores (plant and meat eaters). One species will die in order to feed another. Plants are not less of a species than animals (remember the polygraph testing effects of stress on plants), so why shouldn't we fight for plant rights as well? Plants die for animals to live, and some animals die so that other animals can live. It's nature's way of balancing the species, and this we must respect. Going against this simple fact is going against nature. We are omnivore in nature, being able to eat plant and animal material, but we are also supposed to be the intellectually most advanced species on earth. Therefore we must know that we are not like other carnivores and omnivores that automatically fall into a category, blindly consuming as nature intended. We can think and adapt in order to make life better for all species, including ourselves and the earth, keeping the balance between need and pleasure.

Thus, be grateful for your food — plants and animals had to die so that you can live.

Don't waste food by making too much. There are people dying of hunger everyday.

All in all, let's go back to basics and keep a balance between enjoyment and need.

On a last and very important note, don't smoke. I know it's a great feeling, believe me, I have smoked in the past. There are few things as nice as lighting up on a crisp winter's morning with a steaming coffee in hand, taking that first drag. Ah, so satisfying. But it is death in small packets. It has so many toxins; it will take a page to list them all. Smoking is very bad for your health. You know it by now. To stop smoking is hard if you believe it's hard. I've stopped for more than nine years. Yes, I do miss it, but I know what's good for me and for people around me. I decided to stop because of various reasons. My grandfather died of emphysema, which is a nasty smoker's disease. He literally died for years. Smoking is also very expensive, and I felt to invest money in lung cancer or emphysema is pretty stupid. My wife complained of me stinking and tasting like an ashtray, and people around me were always bothered by the passive smoke. Passive smoking is not just a pain for everyone around you, it's also bad for their health. So I quit for good. But everyone moans and says it's so difficult. It's difficult if you believe it is. Why can some quit and others not? We are essentially all the same. The difference is in what you decide. First step is to decide to stop, and not to try and stop. There's an enormous difference between those two decisions. Second step is to smoke one less every day till that last one, which you don't smoke. You break it, throw it in a dustbin and walk away with a smile (crying) on your face. But in the end, it is very rewarding. Remember, you are in control of your body, not that little white cancer stick, and finding something healthy to replace the habit of lighting up is a good idea. Eat an apple or play with a coin or anything you fancy if you feel the urge. Eventually that neuro association of lighting up when you're idle will gently fade away. Very few things are achieved immediately in this world. So ease your way out of a bad habit into a good one. If you need help with quitting, remember they are Helping You quit, not quitting for you. In the end it is you who decides to quit, and not to try and quit.

Maintenance: Crystal Clear Water

Our bodies resonate with approximately sixty-seven to sixty-nine percent water. We find it in the four to five liters of our blood, cells and organs. Our water is saline (salty), housing various salts and minerals vital to our functionality. If we are essentially water beings, then water is very important to us. We can do without food for a while, but the lack of water will soon end in disaster. It is then essential to take enough water during the day, and this water must be of high quality. Your tap water might look clean and healthy, but in fact is full of harmful ratios of chemicals used in the cleansing process. It needs to be filtered well. Mineral water is not necessarily always healthy either, as many mineral water companies are not well monitored. Some sources could be unknowingly polluted in small quantities or be from an area close to granite, which could house quantities of radon. Furthermore, mineral water is mostly shipped in plastic containers, which are high in metal contents. Also, as seen with Dr. Emoto's research and cymatics, water reacts to and retains vibratory energy from sound to thought (which are all vibration as seen so far). Thus, not only water per se is important, but in what form it will be taken. Trusted mineral water companies could be one, but expensive option, or you could invest in a good filtration system. It needs to be cleansed via filtration, kept in glass containers and also "reprogrammed" to break its retention patterns from previous sources. Can you imagine all the memory in our recycled water, coming from everyone in your city? Hoo!

Thus, you can play harmonious music to your water, or simply put your hands around the glass and think wholesome thoughts while focusing on the water. It sounds silly, I know. But so did it when Pasteur told surgeons about germs. Try and see if it works. Try and test everything, and keep what suits you.

The amount of water needed to take is always recommended as "so and so" liters per day. We are not all the same size, and we all process our water differently. You can monitor your hydration status (fancy term for if you drink enough or not) by checking your urine output amount and color. It sounds a bit grim (there is a Buddhist saying—pay attention to the bodily processes), but if you go to the loo regularly (in a balanced way) and the color is not too dark and not too light (yet again, balanced), not smelling too strong, then you're on the right track. All liquids add to your daily fluid intake, but crystal clear water is the best. It works better in getting rid of waste products and toxins in the body. Think of it this way, would you wash your clothes with soap and water, or with soap and coffee?

Maintenance: Exercise

As I've mentioned before, we are not all exactly the same. We are songs in the symphony of life, and seamlessly interconnected, but our notes are written a bit differently, and thus we should take care how we are played. If you were not built for running, then don't. It's bad for your joints. There are many more ways of getting into shape than running. There's swimming, in-line skating, cycling, gym, yoga, tai chi, brisk walking — the list is almost endless and there for you to choose from. Assess your build and see which exercise is best suited for you, and also which one is most enjoyable. Exercise should be fun, not a tyranny. If it's not enjoyable, it overrules the health benefits. An exercise I would recommend is Yoga (if you are suited — extreme high blood pressure, obesity and vascular abnormalities in the brain could cause harm during Yoga). Yoga is more than just exercise. It is a lifestyle, and keeps your body as well as your mind fit. See if you are equipped to do it, and for heaven's sake, it is not from the devil. It is from the east, rooted in the body-mind-spirit tradition. It has been practiced for thousands of years with one thing in mind — to focus and attune the body and mind to the spirit and reach enlightenment. Not everything outside "normal" dogma is from the devil.

And yet again, keep balance. Don't overexercise yourself into a skeleton that urinates myoglobin (muscle breakdown products) nor slob in a sofa, bitching and moaning about your ass. Keep the balance, exercise moderately, and enjoy it.

Maintenance: Supplements

Try to get in all your vitamins and minerals through a natural process by eating the right foods. If it's not possible, then use a trusted and self-researched brand, preferably natural. Also beware of supplement bandwagon campaigns. Every so often comes another bandwagon fad that propagates everlasting health, beauty or intelligence. The new one is the Omega 3 fad. Yes, Omega 3 is good for you, but don't let them insult your intelligence by fooling you into buying the whole ocean's Omega 3 contents. Use everything in moderation, short and sweet.

Health as Wealth

The body's health is not a black-and-white issue. As the body is seamlessly connected to mind and spirit, I will start with the mind-body relationship in health matters. As we can see, the basics of the body's health lie in the abovementioned brief topics, but are also deeply connected to the mind, and I will give a brief overview on the mind's influence on the body and its health and then gradually move over to health matters in general and then on pure mind and then spirit matters. Here we go.

The Mind-Body Tango

You are watching a horror movie, knowing that it's only a movie while you chomp your popcorn, but as soon as the werewolf approaches, you start to sweat with your heart pounding in your ears. I remember when I was watching Jurassic Park, the woman next to me squealing with every scary scene until near the end, when the velociraptor almost grabbed the heroine from behind, she jumped up and left with "screw this, I had enough" trailing behind her.

We know that what happens on the screen isn't real, but our bodies react to it nonetheless. The scary movie makes us activate our sympathetic nervous system or "fight or flight" system. Our fictional scary mind-set makes us release adrenaline, which stimulates the heart to beat faster and stronger, blood vessels to our brain and muscles to dilate but also enhance the vessel muscle tone to provide more oxygen flow to the stuff in our bodies that will make us fight or flee. The same applies to a sexual fantasy. Just by imagining, we can change our bodies to respond as if ready for love play. I even have a "party trick" where I can lower my blood pressure from 130/90 mmHg to 110/70mmHg within five to ten minutes if I concentrate on it. You probably thought I was going to say I have a party trick that involves sexual fantasy—hah! You can change the way your body functions by your thoughts. Research in a relatively new field called pscychoneuroimmunology has shown that the mind-body relationship is very strong indeed.

In his book *The Sickening Mind*, Paul Martin explores this profound connection, ranging from the mind-body connection in death prolonging, to how personality types are more prone to certain diseases, to mind-over-matter scenarios where cancers went into remission with positive visualization (where one creates mental images of white cells proliferating and beating cancer cells). With my own experiences in the medical world, the patients coming in with a lighthearted and positive attitude made startlingly fast and complication-free recoveries, while the pessimists got complication after complication. Both my wife and I have talked about this numerous times, and after years' experience, we could quite accurately predict which patients would do well and which wouldn't. Both my wife and I have seen our fair share of miracles as well, where patients healed with all odds against them. In Michael Talbot's *Holographic Universe*, the mind-over-matter scenarios were also explored, ranging from faith healing to walking over red hot coals without harm.

It would seem that there are some individuals who know the "truth"—that our world (as well as our bodies) are vibratory projections from within (from the enfolded world or higher realm of God or the One), and that through focus and correct intent, this illusion of a world and its contents can be changed. Miracles have not ceased to exist after Christ. Only our belief in the truth has, obscured by power-seeking Shape Shifters and Threshold Guardians. The truth is, however bizarre it may sound, that body, mind and spirit are seamlessly connected, and that this unit is, and should be, connected to the higher realm of the One. Knowing this, especially on our starting level of mind-body connection, can set us free to start our exploration of ourselves and our path.

Thus, on the mind-body connection, you are what you think, and you think what you are. Today's thoughts are tomorrow's reality, especially in your body and health. It only seems to take such a long time to become ill or heal from a disease because of our limited perception of the illusion of time and also because of how slow energy moves in this dense world of "matter" or semi-frozen vibration. It takes a lot of focus and belief to move something in this dark world, so be patient and exercise your focus. Every second is a small step closer to your goal.

Body, Mind and Health

As said, the mind has more power over the body than imagined, which is shown more and more in the field of psychoneuroimmunology. Patients are shown to have postponed their death until the very last moment of opening their Christmas presents. Type A personalities (ruthlessly ambitious and perfectionist) are shown to have a connection to heart and peptic ulcer disease, while Type C personalities (pleasant, submissive and painfully law-abiding) are prone to certain types of cancer. It was shown that Natural Killer-T cells (the cancer fighters), are prone to diminish in quantity with prolonged periods of background stress and feelings of being trapped in a situation. Equally, research has shown that the reverse is possible. Cancers thought incurable by the oncologist have gone into remission with focused positive visualization or a mere blind faith in a drug that later proved to be useless, as in a famous case in Russia. Diagnosed with terminal lymphoma (a particular cancer of white blood cells concentrated in the lymph glands), the patient begged his oncologist to give him the new, thought-to-be revolutionary chemotherapy drug at that stage, as he believed it would cure him. He improved remarkably, going into remission, while the others on the trial hardly showed results. After the drug was shown to be useless, the poor man's lymphoma returned with a vengeance, and his oncologist decided to try something unorthodox since he improved so miraculously on it while the others didn't. The oncologist convinced him that there was a newer, yet untested version on the market, and that he would give him some if he consented. The poor man did, and the oncologist gave him sterile water injections, which miraculously put him back into remission for a few months. Unfortunately, the man found out that there were no newer versions on the market, his lymphoma recurred soon after the news, and he died. There is another case, where a boy diagnosed with a malignant brain tumor was not responding well to his chemotherapy. But then the boy started playing Star Wars games at night, where he imagined his white blood cells to be the star fighters and the tumor the death star. He went into remission remarkably fast, and only a calcified lesion was seen on his brain scans.

But it goes further. The mind or combined effort of minds can "fix" the bodies of others as well. The occurrence of healing and remission has been shown to be higher in those who are prayed for than in those who are not, in studies where the patient wasn't even aware of the prayers. It also showed that the particular religion didn't matter, as long as there were good intentions behind the prayers. Even in my family have I seen a miracle or two, where terminal malignant melanomas miraculously disappeared after prayers, as well as a family member's leg being healed by a faith healer after western doctors threw in the towel after months of struggle. Being a western-trained doctor myself, I found it hard to believe, but true.

The mind-thought unit is an incredibly powerful phenomenon. It can create and heal as well as destroy on a worldwide scale. Unfortunately, it is mostly used for the latter, as it is possessed by cosmic ignorant fools using their powerful gifts only for self gain. Even on smaller scale, hating someone or secretly wishing harm upon someone has the power to destroy. Remember the polygraph tests of plants? Thus, know the power you possess, and use it wisely. Use it for creation, healing and harmony. Never abuse it, for you shall reap what you sow.

But yet again, there must be balance. As we are in our utmost infancy realizing this mind-body truth, there are some who want to fly before they can crawl. I've seen some patients who refused orthodox western medical input on the basis of faith only, which ended in disaster or death. It reminds me of a scenario where I once as a kid had to write an exam that I didn't study for very well, and being scared to fail it, asked my mother to ask God to help me. She smiled and said, "God helps those who help themselves." I was furious with her, and naturally failed my exam. In later years I realized the absolute truth of those words. Balance is essential, and in the beginning we need all the help we can get, no matter what the circumstances, but we also need to pull our weight and do and think the best we can while we evolve into beings of pure thought. Without the combination of engine, metal shell, wheels, superior engineering, driver, support team and crowd, there will be no formula one racing, but only a bunch of people with unused intellects standing between piles of unused metal, scratching their heads. So, when you become ill, use all the resources you can find - western as well as complementary medicine. The human is a holistic being, the body-mind-spirit union being seamless, and we must remember this with our healing techniques. Your body is also integrated into your environment—the air that you breathe, with all its loaded chemicals and so forth, will circulate through every cell in your body. The local water and produce from all over the world and their chemicals, will circulate through every cell as well. Thus you need to first try and avoid the most harmful areas and produce, but because it's not always possible, keep your body-mind-spirit unit strong with good habits and positive thoughts.

With western medicine, we work on the "hardware" of a human only, and it mostly does the trick. But sometimes the "software" and "operating system" gives trouble as well, and the one can affect the other just the same. This is why we must approach ourselves (and patients if we are physicians) on a holistic level, using alternative therapies such as acupuncture (absolutely great for musculoskeletal pain), Reiki, sound and color therapy to name but a few. With my research into this book, I had to cross the Threshold of skepticism of alternative therapies because of my prejudiced training in an orthodox western medical school. On my journey into the alternative therapy world, I was stunned at how scientific some of these worked, especially acupuncture. It also reflected the holographic and vibratory nature of things perfectly. I believe that one day, when we fully connect to Spirit, we might be able to heal ourselves or not even become ill in the first place. But on our journey to that time, let us approach our illnesses on a holistic basis.

Now let's explore the…

Mind

A strong bridge connects worlds. A weak one will wither and break, and the two worlds will lose contact, the segregation causing the worlds to drift apart. It is this bridge, our minds, which have been weakened over millennia by the skilled manipulators, the puppet masters of which I will speak later. The bridge between this world and the world of the One is weak and creaky, and only now and then will a messenger run across and tell us about the paradise on the other side. Because of our ignorance, arrogance and bitterness being stuck in this dense world, we simply ridicule or kill the messenger. We must realize that our minds are the key that will unlock the door to the other side. It is the bridge that we have to reinforce, and sometimes even rebuild, to reach paradise.

But our minds are like a wild horse, which acts on fear and impulse. It has been programmed with so much fear over the millennia that it can't function properly anymore. It has also been programmed lately to think that it, the so called Ego, is in charge. A software operating system can do a few things automatically to help the user with day-to-day activities. But it cannot think for itself, nor be in charge. It will run amok. The mind is the same. It is a bridge that needs to be cared for, reinforced and made beautiful. It is that horse that needs to be tamed and taught not to fear, but to know that it is loved and cared for, while Spirit gently blows its breath of "Thy Will" into this world.

Repairing the Bridge

A bridge basically consists of two anchoring points, one on each side of the divide, two parallel and horizontal beams with a platform connecting the two anchoring points and sometimes pillars or an arch. Bridges come in all shapes and sizes, but the basics always stay the same, and the function of the bridge is always the same — to connect divided worlds.

Our minds are very similar. One anchoring point is in this dense world most of our consciousness lies in, and the other in the world of the One. The anchoring point in this world is our body-brain-chakra complex, and the anchoring point in the other, Spirit. The two beams and platform connecting the two worlds are the "body" of mind and can be likened to the tree of life in Kabbalah, each sefirah being a pillar supporting the transition from this world to the other, and the two beams being the two points of resonance in our world's wave function — yin and yang or male and female in the tree of life.

At present, most of our bridges are tacky and stringy, wildly swinging in the air currents of the divide. We have to reinforce it by starting with our anchoring point in this world, namely the brain-body-chakra complex. We have already spoken about how to reinforce and care for the body. With the brain it is simple. Brain is wholly incorporated into the body by neuro-endo-vascular systems, and thus caring for the body, one cares for the brain as well. A healthy body leads to a healthy brain. But furthermore it needs to be trained. The brain is like a muscle, and if neglected, will wither and atrophy. One must train it with knowledge, explore the creative receptors of the mind union, and burn them full blast as much as one can. The more you use your brain, the stronger and faster it becomes. But unfortunately there is a flip side to the coin. The brain doesn't care what you do with it. It obeys your will perfectly (if looked after). So if you repeat bad habits and nasty thoughts, you will enforce the wrong neuro-pathways. For example, change two of your kitchen cupboard's contents with one another and see how long it takes you to remember the simple move. It took me more than two weeks! Same goes for smoking, drinking and all other habits you have. The more you do it, the more your brain will submit to and enforce this pathway, and the more difficult it gets to break free from it. Thus, be careful what you do with your brain.

It is a powerful tool, ready to carry you to the sublime or the opposite, depending on your will. Fill it with books, fictional as well as nonfictional. Fill it with movies and music of all genres; don't be so picky. How can you know you like or dislike something if you haven't even tried to explore and understand another world? Try some science fiction or jazz, for example, if you never have. It won't hurt you to try and understand why so many others adore it. Explore the world of art in history and form. Look at architecture (a perfect blend between art and math, aesthetics and functionality). Explore the beauty of Victorian, Georgian and Art Deco in your town or city. Stroll down the aisles of modernism and postmodernism and the philosophies behind them. If you can afford it, try to travel to a foreign destination on your own steam (if it's a safe country). Get there by plane or boat, and struggle alone around the foreign language signs; eat their food and live their culture. You will soon realize that they are as human as you are with dads playing football with their kids, teasing them till they throw tantrums. It might just heal you from your silly xenophobia. Try learning more languages, pronunciation and all. Teach yourself how to fix your own PC or water pipes, and not just run to the nearest Yellow Pages. Try everything, and then see what you like best and why.

Now before we come to the mind-spirit complex, we have to know something very important.

The Difference between Religion and Spirituality

This is important, as most of us are to a lesser or greater extent trapped by ignorant dogma about what is right and what is wrong in the eyes of God. Whether you are Christian, Muslim, Jewish, Buddhist, Hindu or atheist, you have a certain belief system that you absorbed and transformed over your growing years. Some of us get force-fed strict religious dogma, filling us with so much fear that we dare not break away from it. Others refuse to swallow the force-fed dogma and overcompensate by becoming completely atheist, believing that there is no deity.

Yes, you can argue all you like, but it is your belief system not to believe. You choose to believe that this "God" they shoved down your throat does not exist. And religious dogma always teaches you that the other religious dogmas are wrong. So if you grew up as a Muslim, then the others are kafir. If you grew up Christian or Jewish, then those others are heathens. They will all "go to hell."

Looking at these particular three religions, which seem to always be locked into hatred and wars with each other, it is interesting to note, yet again, that they share the same root. They are all Abrahamic religions, meaning that they worship the God of Abraham. They just do it in different ways. Islam even acknowledges Christ as being one of the greatest prophets that ever lived, but not that he is God. The Jewish faith believes that the Messiah is yet to come, and one branch of the Christians believes that Christ is God, and another believes that he is man, for how can a god be born from a human woman? If we look at a coin, how many sides does it have — one, two or three? Which side is the right side — heads, tails or the rim? Which one is wrong? The truth is, it is one coin with three sides. Each side is as important as the other, because if one of the sides were missing, we would have no coin. Abrahamic religions are just three points of view of the same thing — the belief in the God of Abraham. If one fails to see this, then one sees the world from only one point of view, and this is severely limiting. And if one looks at Buddhism or Hinduism, one will soon realize that there are strong similarities. In Hinduism, there is Brahman, the one true God. Funny enough, it looks like wordplay of Abraham, doesn't it? Coincidence? But many will argue and say, Hindus have other gods as well, the sub- or demigods. If one looks at Abrahamic religions, don't they have archangels and demons? Are they not in a higher realm than us mere mortals? In pure Buddhism, there is no belief in gods, as they are seen as the illusion of the One truth — to break free from the wheel of karma (suffering) and ascend to enlightenment. There is only striving to become like the Buddha himself. Buddha is not worshipped by the pure form Buddhists, but only used as a divine teacher figure to which one strives by walking the divine path. One can easily fit God into the equation of Buddhism, as Buddhism discriminates against no gods, as long as the worship of these gods does not cause suffering. What's more is that there are a lot of similarities between the teachings of Buddha and Christ. There are also similarities between Christ and important figures most of us haven't even heard of. Viracocha, Kukulkan and Quetzalcoatl, three South American deities of the Incas, Mayans and Aztecs respectively, share similarities with Christ. These deities were described as in the beginning being the creator of the heavens and earth, then to walk the earth as a man described as a bearded Caucasian and disguised as a peasant. They (he) traveled from village to village teaching the people how to live good lives, performed miracles (healing the sick and raising the dead) and eventually left, promising to return. The eastern figure Krishna also shares similarities. There are numerous versions of stories of Krishna in Hinduism, Jainism and Buddhism, but a general characteristic of him is that he is God incarnated in physical form, here to help humanity. In the Baha'i faith, Krishna is believed to be one of the many physical manifestations or prophets of God, who periodically comes down from the heavens to assist humanity in its growth in the likes of Abraham, Moses, Jesus, Muhammad and Bab. The most striking similarity is between the Dionysus/Osiris figure of ancient Egypt and Jesus Christ. Both were prophesied virgin births born in the time of the winter solstice, visited by three wise old men (Mentors), performed miracles, had twelve disciples (correlating to the twelve months of the year), used the bread and wine metaphor for body and blood, were killed because of their teachings or way of life (Osiris was placed in a wooden coffin inside a pillar, and Christ was nailed to a wooden cross). Both descended into the underworld or hell, and both were resurrected, taking their place in heaven, where they will "judge" humanity on their return. It is also interesting to note that Christ spent a lot of his youth in Egypt (of which the details strangely elude) and that according to the *Aquarian Gospel Of Jesus, the Christ*, a book transcribed from *The Book of God's Remembrance* by Levi. H Dowling published in 1908, Jesus received his spiritual initiation in Egypt. Another interesting thing to note is that modern independent Egyptologists (like the engineer Moustafa Gadalla) are shedding light on the typical dogmatic thoughts of western Egyptology (which still regards ancient Egyptians as a primitive and confused polytheistic society). Refreshed thoughts on ancient Egypt show that they had a monotheistic religion, with the incorrectly interpreted neteru as gods, being correctly interpreted as the <u>aspects</u> of the one God. These aspects were metaphorically represented by animal-like qualities, just as we will say "as strong as a bull," for example.

If two people see an event that later they tell their children, the versions will be different. Each of us tells our stories in different ways. The children hearing these stories will tell it to their children in different ways as well, spreading the legend in their own sweet ways. Then, two or three families will decide to part, some of them looking for greener pastures, taking with them the different versions of the legend, which will keep on evolving into different versions.

Take a look at our modern history (the last two thousand of the past hundred thousand human years). Christ came for all humanity. He favored none, and peacefully opposed only those who manipulated the meek by using their indoctrinated fear of God. With his sad departure, being skillfully killed by those same Puppet Masters he opposed, the puppets started to dance (with the puppeteers skillfully pulling those strings). The crumbling Roman Empire changed Christ into a franchise, using his popularity, and turned it into one of the most successful empires ever. Still the Vatican is one of the richest and most powerful elements in the world, while other Roman Catholic children, especially those in developing countries, are completely poverty stricken. The stories of Christ changed over the years. Some believed him to be God, some the son of God, and some the greatest prophet that ever lived. The Christian faith is split into so many different sects it's unimaginable. Roman Catholic, Greek Orthodox, Lutheran, Dutch Reformed, Reformed, Apostolic, New Apostolic, Christian Revival, Rhema, and so it goes. All different variations of the same thing, namely the life and works of Jesus Christ. Who is right and who is wrong? In my humble opinion, you can worship in any way you like, as long as you don't hurt others and yourself, and don't obscure the pure truth. So far, none of the above have not hurt others or not obscured the truth, from early days of Catholic inquisition (ranging from Europe to Central and South America and Africa), destroying not only individual people's lives (especially women's), but also wiping out entire civilizations (the Taino people by Christopher Columbus and his men, and the Aztecs by Cortez's), to the modern-day Evangelists. This affects the modern Muslim world as well, where dark political agendas will abuse the fear of God (Allah) to create Islamic fundamentalists who will do their dirty work for them, promised the holy land. The greed overtakes them, and they abuse the teachings of the Teacher and the fear of God to prey on innocent souls.

And if it comes to understanding the nature of God, then the whole cookie crumbles. We can't even prove His existence. We never see Him, hear Him nor feel Him. Isn't it maybe because we don't have a clue what to look for? If I were to tell a color-blind child to go and pick me blue flowers in the forest, he would simply return saying there are none, or if he fears me, come back with any flower, regardless of the color. God, Allah, Brahman, the One, Ain-Sof or the Source is something far beyond the reach of our physical bodies or brains, and as we struggle to try and comprehend it, we make up our stories along the way.

Can you see? We, regardless of where we were born and grew up, were taught a particular version of something greater than ourselves called God, Brahman or Allah. We were also taught that to reach heaven and escape the fires of hell, we had to only believe in this particular god and that all other versions were wrong. As a child, you believe what you are told. How else? Your parents and those scary church folk can't be wrong. It is yet again the fear of going to hell that drives our beliefs. And it is this fear that is abused by those in power.

Religion is the worship of the metaphor for the One we don't fully comprehend, and not the One "Himself." With our indoctrinated "limited" mind-set, we see the One—the limitless and most profound Source of eternal Light, Possibility and Energy—as a limited single personified deity that glares "down" at us, waiting for us to make a mistake so that he can throw us into the fires of hell. This limited view of God (Allah, Yahweh, Brahman, Ain Sof), in my opinion, is a slap in the face of "God." In the "words" spoken to Moses, "I am that I am," God reveals what "He" is—I AM. To help us understand this, close your eyes for a moment, and try to imagine that YOU ARE—Do it now.

"God" IS—full stop. "He" is EVERYTHING. He is brane, atom, molecule, DNA, cell, organ, organism, Earth, solar system, galaxy and universe. He is time and space. He is you. His very "breath" dwells in everything, exhaled from the Source of Him/Her.

Religions then, are merely the shattered pieces of the original window of God. They are the puzzle pieces that each of us holds dearer than life, believing them to be the only truth, and thus trapping us in a domain of limited thought, fear and hatred. But we need to let go of this fear. Our puzzle pieces need to fit back together again, to reform the window of God so that His light can shine through it again, casting light onto this dark world of ours.

This is where "spirituality" comes in. I believe that the only way to the truth and to the One is through one's Inner Self, which is connected to the global consciousness of not just humanity, but to the whole Kingdom of God. The Kingdom of God is simultaneously within and without. It is within all of us, and if permitted, projected through us to the outer world we believe to be real. God or the One is an eternal light or "breath" of vapor and sound, and we and our world the crystallized version of the One. We are the cast net in the ocean of experience that will soon be retracted. This ocean of experience is what the Kabbalah calls the "game of life." It is the story world we are starting to remember, the fairy-tale land in which we are desperately trying to tell our stories right so that when the net retracts, we will be able to go home satisfied and content, returning home with the elixir. But how do we do this? How do we learn how to tell our stories right? The answer is—by connecting to Spirit, which is seamlessly connected to the One or the Source, so that the light can shine through into this dark world, eagerly awaiting the light it was created to receive.

Spirit

The Glass Elevator

Moving to Spirit through the brain/body-mind-spirit connection is like ascending on a glass elevator away from earth. First, you see your house, then your town, your state or province, your country and then the earth, solar system, galaxy and universe. You realize that being in your house the whole time, you can't see what happens in the world "out there." You are confined to the four walls around you, where you are only preoccupied with yourself and your own thoughts. As you move higher and higher, you realize that there are millions of others "down there" struggling with the same chores as you do. You realize that we all live on the same planet—a living sapphire in a black void. We are all trying to find the forgotten truth that haunts us in our dreams night after night, trying to wake us up from the real nightmare called reality. But how does one do this? Not easily, as it is difficult to break free from years of programmed belief. Believe me, it is even difficult for me now. Some days in writing this book, the Threshold Guardian of modern reductionist thought will try and ridicule these "new" found ideas from the corner of my mind. But the dogmatic side of modern civilization just can't win the argument anymore. There are just too many fingers pointing toward the glow on the horizon promising the new break of dawn. Thus, we choose to believe and start by walking into the glass lift, the body-brain-chakra complex.

When it comes to your body-brain-chakra relationship, it gets a bit trickier. Most people will submit to the BS man and just say bull to the chakra idea. But remember all the abovementioned arguments. Remember that we are all one in our own special ways. We can focus on this by meditating. Meditating comes in different shapes and sizes. Most people will think it to be nonsense or something of the devil. But meditating is calling that glass lift and getting in, ready for the ascension to a higher view of oneself as well as the whole universe. It is learning how to tame that wild horse of a mind we have. A simple way is to find a quiet spot somewhere, anywhere quiet, and to just focus on your surroundings, taking in every detail. Look, listen and feel carefully. If you are in a garden, look at the flowers swaying in the wind. Listen to the bird song and feel that light breeze on your skin. Try to feel your connectedness to your surroundings, feel that you are a vibratory field within this vibratory field around you. Feel that this vibratory complex of you and your surroundings are seamlessly connected to the whole vibration of humanity and the universe. It will take some time, but it will come. Then, after exploring this outer interconnectedness, start focusing within. Realize that this reality around you is a mere projection from the world within through yourself and that we all contribute to it. We are all collaboratively painting a massive painting. But because of our selfishness and egotism, we fight each other more for a particular piece of cloth than concentrating on the painting. Focus on your own collaboration rather than competing with the others. There's ample space for all of us to paint our pictures and write our stories. You have to align your outer self with your inner self, or put in another way—find harmonic resonance between your body, mind and spirit. What will help in achieving this is by balancing your chakras with sound and color, as each chakra has its own color and tone if you remember. Remember that we are only vibration in a vibratory universe, and that our chakras are concentrated points of this vibratory energy. If they go out of harmony with each other in sound and color vibration, we will be a false chord, so to speak. This we can correct, and we will be a more harmonious chord in the song of life. There are chakra chants available from Jonathan Goldman's (specializing in sound therapy) website healingsounds.com. With colors, you can get yourself colored paper charts, and focus on them and the particular chakra it coincides with. Explore the different ways of meditation and stick to the one that suits you. In the end, with meditation, you will strengthen that bridge we call Mind and the glass elevator will reach higher and higher into Spirit, revealing more and more the nature of the One.

Remember Slumberland

Last but not least, try to remember and jot down your dreams. Remember the part on the DMT molecule and hallucinations, how these "hallucinations" gave insight into many people's lives. Our brains are the receivers of vital information from the enfolded world of light and infinite possibility. We can say that dreams are sleeping hallucinations, and hallucinations are waking dreams. They are they way to expand our wavelength pick up or "tuning in" to higher (and sometimes lower) realities. It is in this zone that space and time are more relative, or shall I say irrelevant, than in this illusory world. It is here that the messages from Spirit come to you in weird and wonderful flavors, the reason being that you are not familiar with this vibratory pattern. It is like a language you only partly know, filling in the gaps with more familiar pictures and sounds from your memory banks. It is like the wave function of a red cricket ball coming to you when you've never seen one. You can see that it is round and red, but the only round and red thing you can come up with in your memory bank to interpret this wave code is an apple.

I must agree and say that most of our dreams are silly, or even "garbage," depicting the daily routine etc. But I think that the dream state has levels. If you don't go "deep" enough, you will swim in a messy ocean of thought waves, created by you that day, week or month. But, as you go "deeper," you pass this phase, and enter the quiet zone where your Inner Self awaits you with archetypal messages.

I had a few dreams where "messages came to me." I once dreamt that I was looking at a world map. There was a cup of black coffee on the right-hand side of the map, which tipped over, the coffee turning into blood, spreading all the way from the Middle East over Europe with its "fingers" to North America, one of the fingers touching the New York area. Two days later 9/11 was on the news. I also somehow knew that things would escalate, but brushed it off as coincidence. A few years later, I wanted to take my wife to the Maldives. One evening, I dreamt that we were standing on a beach at the Maldives. In the dream, my wife was about to walk into the crystal blue waters when we felt a tremor, and then the water became bubbly and muddy. When I woke up, I thought of putting the Maldives trip on hold. A few days later, there was a huge underwater earthquake, and the tidal wave hit the east. Another coincidence? I had some other dreams that came true as well. I also knew just before my car accident that I was in the wrong lane, and before every illness, I dream of swimming in murky waters or of an alien chasing me in a dark building. One of the most bizarre things that happened was the morning when my mother told me about a dream she had that matched mine of the same night to a tee. It was of giant phantom faces, one woman and two men drifting outside our house, smiling benevolently.

Most of us have the "odd" dream now and then, and these metaphorical messages must not be brushed off. I am surprised to hear how many people, especially living near coastal areas, have escalating dreams of tidal waves (we will explore this in the third act). I believe that dreams come from our higher selves or our Spirit as clues to the game, but because the vibratory pattern is unusual it is sometimes interpreted by our brains in some bizarre way. We must learn how to decipher them and learn from them.

There is also the element of psychedelic experiences from substances like psilocybin (found in "magic mushrooms") and ayahuasca (found in brews of the native South American). Firstly, these substances are not the drugs that are taken for euphoric sensations like cocaine (crystalline tropane alkaloids) or heroin (synthetic opiates like diamorphine), which are highly addictive and thus profitable. Psychedelic substances are tryptamine-based molecules (like DMT and serotonin, manufactured in the human and other mammalian brains), which, in the correct doses, could change the way you perceive things via "hallucinations." These "trips" are not just the mundane feelings of euphoria you get from addictive substances, but a breakthrough in consciousnesses, as so many once users of it reported. It is a substance that is reapproached (after once used) with a sense of dread, as Terence McKenna put it, for the experience could be unsettling in the sense of losing oneself in the universe of possibility. Many a "tripper" has not tried it again because of this feeling of anticipation. This is one of the reasons why it is not a profitable "drug," other than the ease of acquirement in nature. It is also interesting to note that open-minded scientists are seriously considering promoting psychedelics as therapeutic substances. Recent studies have shown how these psychedelics can give people profound life-changing experiences, which create a long-lasting insightful and positive outlook on life for several months with only one session. Researchers have warned that these experiences are not always pleasant (as mentioned earlier), but usually involve the "tripper" taking a subconscious tour inside his or her dark subconscious mind as well.

Psychedelics can be used to connect to "the other side" quicker. It is like an express train compared to other methods (meditation, tantra, yoga, dance rituals etc.), but if one is not ready for that "speed," it could be an unpleasant experience. One needs to prepare and be ready (by using the non-express methods first). These sacred plants should be approached with care and respect, and not used for recreational purposes (especially mixed with sedatives like alcohol). "Bad trips" usually result due to this, as the "spirit world" will reprimand the abuser. In the end, the "dream world" can be reached with psychoactive substances, but the problem lies in not being able to wake up from the dream, as the half-life of the specific substance (especially psilocybin) can reach hours and keep you in the dream state "against your will" so to speak. If the experience is an unpleasant one, you will be trapped in it for a while. Thus, it is safer to reach the dream state by sleeping. You can always wake up from a nightmare. In order to recall your dreams better, it is advisable to get more quality sleep, thus longer hours, pitch dark and quiet room and eating melatonin-rich foods.

Some of us, however, don't even need psychedelics, as more and more of us are born with the ability to ease through the barrier spontaneously. There are children and adults born in the period from the sixties up to the present who are naturally opposed to dogmatic male-dominated oppression, most with the ability to "see" and "know" things others "cannot." Maybe you are one without even knowing it, hence the search for the Great Unknown.

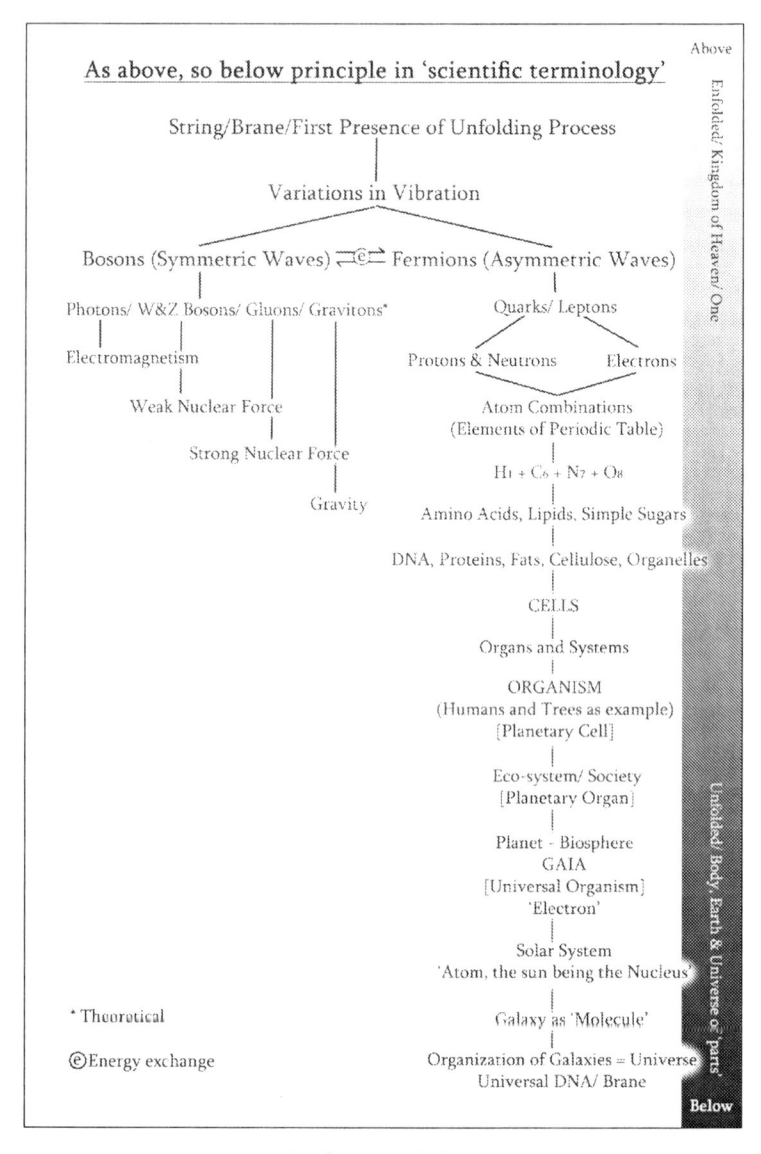

As above, so below principle in 'scientific terminology'

Above — Enfolded/ Kingdom of Heaven/ One

String/Brane/First Presence of Unfolding Process
|
Variations in Vibration
/ \
Bosons (Symmetric Waves) ⇌ⓔ⇌ Fermions (Asymmetric Waves)

Photons/ W&Z Bosons/ Gluons/ Gravitons*
|
Electromagnetism
|
Weak Nuclear Force
|
Strong Nuclear Force
|
Gravity

Quarks/ Leptons
/ \
Protons & Neutrons   Electrons
|
Atom Combinations
(Elements of Periodic Table)
|
$H_1 + C_6 + N_7 + O_8$
|
Amino Acids, Lipids, Simple Sugars
|
DNA, Proteins, Fats, Cellulose, Organelles
|
CELLS
|
Organs and Systems
|
ORGANISM
(Humans and Trees as example)
[Planetary Cell]
|
Eco-system/ Society
[Planetary Organ]
|
Planet - Biosphere
GAIA
[Universal Organism]
'Electron'
|
Solar System
'Atom, the sun being the Nucleus'
|
Galaxy as 'Molecule'
|
Organization of Galaxies = Universe
Universal DNA/ Brane

Below — Unfolded/ Body, Earth & Universe or 'parts'

* Theoretical
ⓔ Energy exchange

A Above, so Below

All in all, we all range from eggs to caterpillars to cocoons to butterflies. None of us is good or bad, but merely in a stage of spiritual development. Unfortunately, most of us are stuck in the caterpillar phase, where we consume and pollute brainlessly. We need to move into the cocoon phase, withdrawing into ourselves occasionally, to find our Inner Self. Only then can we emerge as the butterflies intended. We need to realize this as soon as we can, and travel our journey into self-realization by starting with what we know, namely Body, and work our way up to the butterfly stage via Mind into Spirit.

Conclusion

We can summarize everything so far in the following:

We and our world are a vibratory holographic projection or crystallized manifestation of the One.

It seems from various ancient scriptures, which coincide with each other, as well as modern physics that the One was in a state of no-thingness or complete balance where nothing happened. Then the One went into a state of imbalance (quantum fluctuation) and gave rise to a world of illusory parts, of which all have two distinct points of fluctuation called a wave function. It goes by different names—light and dark, male and female, summer and winter, yin and yang, positive and negative charge, proton and electron, north and south poles, good and evil—and it is this potential difference between these poles that gives rise to wave function, energy and possibility. Consciousness in the One binds these endless strands of possibility into a magic carpet we call our reality.

The reason for this reality is the One casting Him/Herself into the denser world of "darkness" like a net into the ocean in order to "catch" the fish of knowledge of Itself. The One wants to experience Him/Her self through every living and "non-living" thing in existence, and we are a "part" of the One, bringing home these experiences for another cosmic adventure to follow.

We are all living our own stories in this wonderland of God, and one day will return to tell them around the dining table of the One. God, or the One, "wants" us to succeed. As we are vibration, we follow the law of harmonics, and things will "manifest" according to our thoughts. Thoughts are vibration, and the Universe will "answer" with harmonic resonance, whether the thoughts are "good" or "bad."

This is why we must learn to tell our stories well, and we can do this by first realizing this truth, by looking after our bodies (temples of God), building and reinforcing our minds (bridges) and ascending into ourselves and our spirit, which is seamlessly connected to the One.

Our (humanity's) task here is to follow all the clues in all the stories around the world. Follow the white rabbit or the bread crumbs in the forest, and remember the paradise from which we cast ourselves. Our task is to remember the tower of Babel, when we shattered the window of God into different puzzle pieces, and to realize that we must unite these pieces and ourselves into the original window of God, so that His/Her light can shine through to illuminate us and our world. Then will we be able to rebuild ourselves and our world until the time when we will go home for another adventure.

Again, there is no way of proving this at present. It is simply a matter of belief. It was especially difficult for me being raised in a country of racial and cultural divide with the Protestant church's fingers in every place one looked. A Protestant church of God who refused African people entry because they were different. But somehow my connection with Spirit kept going. I remember as a child, getting up in the still dark early hours of the morning with everybody still asleep, going outside in the garden, marveling at the stillness and freshness of things. I just felt peace around me and was afraid of nothing. It was this memory that kept me from submitting to the fear and hatred that are so drilled into us from childhood. I decided to adopt an attitude of "skeptic open-mindedness," and to look for a truth where harm would diminish until everyone was content and kind. Following my bread crumb path through the forest, I found my own thoughts reflected back at me by ancient as well as modern teachings. I realized that I wasn't alone in this quest for the truth, and I believe that more and more are awakening to it. Yes, it cannot be proven, just as super symmetrical string theory can't be proven yet. But there are so many "coincidences" connecting to shape such a wonderful and peaceful belief system, that it becomes difficult not to believe. If one can't prove something's existence, then it is arguably possible to say that it exists till otherwise proven. Yes, it seems strange, but so does love play when you grow from childhood into adulthood. What is important, though, is that in believing this, we will be able to live and let live and collaborate instead of compete. We will build instead of destroy. So the choice is yours and yours alone to answer this call, and cross the threshold of belief into a world of wonder. But after crossing this threshold, you must confront the biggest Villains and Shape Shifters.

Let's explore in more practical ways the real Villains and Shape Shifters of our story as humanity, and how we can defeat them, so that we can move into Act three of our adventure and reach the conclusion of our story.

Obstacles

Enter your most profound Obstacle/Villain — You. Huh? But aren't You supposed to be the best ally in the world? How can You be the most profound enemy? Simply because You are, just like the rest of the universe, a wave equation vibrating between two points of fluctuation — good and bad. It is called free will by some. Just as You can be your best friend, You van be your worst enemy. You can make yourself drink till you get liver cirrhosis and die an ugly death. You can take yourself into the depths of darkness where you abuse others — not being grateful of others serving you, being mean to others, humiliating others, hating others to such an extent that you physically abuse them and eventually kill them. Yes, You are a wave equation swinging between good and evil as intended from the start. It's there to bring balance. But at present, looking at the world, there is no balance. It seems that darkness, or in the case of the Tree of Life, the Severity, is ruling our world and that we are falling prey to it. We are lost. We are those cancer cells that went rogue, because we are no longer connected to the One. We serve ourselves only by taking what we want, no matter what the cost. We take from each other, we take from nations and we take from the earth. Take and consume, stuffing ourselves like black holes sucking up all the light. And as we do this, we multiply and spread all around like malignant cancer cells, consuming further while we grow. Consume and grow until eventually, we kill our mother — Earth. And we will die with her. Yes, we will destroy ourselves long before there is spaceflight advanced enough to carry the human cancer to another world. And we will deserve that death, because while some of us destroyed actively, most others have passively watched them do it while burying their heads in consumerism sands. We are all guilty.

And You fit right into that equation. It is because you have free will to decide to be your best friend or your worst enemy. If you are your best friend, you will wake up to the truth of Oneness. You will know that you are seamlessly connected to everything and that there is a higher purpose for you. You will look after your body and mind, and will desperately try and connect to Spirit and the One. By doing so, you will teach others this, who will then follow the path, and so the destruction will diminish, and the process of rebuilding start.

Let us have a look at obstacles leading to the darker You.

Ego

Ego means different things to different people. Let's say that your ego is your PRO (public relations officer). It is the persona you created through life to help you cope in this world. Unfortunately, most of us think that we and our Egos are one and the same. This is not true. Ego is like a software program, which can be reprogrammed. Numerous people start out as "nice" people, and as soon as they move into a world of fame or power, they become monsters. The opposite is also true. Some people start out monsters, and then after some life-changing event like a near death experience will change into angels.

Most of us will see ourselves somewhere on a hierarchical ladder with those who are higher up and those who are lower down. This is a point of view that has damaged many lives, and still continues to do so. Nobody is either lower or higher than you. Famous people are only famous. Fame is merely to be known by many as one's face is splashed all over the world by film and television. The famous are merely "well advertised." But higher or better than you, no. They are human just like you. When contracting a bug, they will become ill and might even die. They need to eat like you do, go to the bathroom, wash themselves and yes, they also look like crap in the mornings with smelly breaths that needs a toothbrush. They grow old (and by George do some of them know that), they have fears and they also lose family members through death, experiencing the same heartaches as you do. And no matter how much money they have, most of them are completely unhappy. Why do you think they behave so badly? Drinking, abusing drugs, getting caught up in sex scandals and going through marriage after marriage. They have their own problems and own stresses. Work is getting scarcer with all those fame seekers in overdrive; thus competition has to become second nature to them, or else they feel they won't survive. Every time they want to go for a quiet walk, the paparazzi swamp them so that you, mister or miss obsessive, can have a nude picture of your demigod. And the reason for that obsession is because of the belief that they are "up there." Fans project their fantasies upon these normal people, and believe steadfastly in this fantasy without flaws. Some go overboard and become celebrity stalkers to the extent of being criminally insane. Others will make a job out of the famous by writing nasty remarks—putting them on pedestals only to knock them down again—because they feel "lower" than these demigods, the jealousy in them making them write ugly things about other human beings. All this because they see these normal human beings as "above themselves." Their Egos are programmed to "be less."

The same goes to you rich, famous and powerful ones "up there." Those people serving you day in and day out—cleaning your house, looking after your kids (which are mostly spoilt rotten), wiping your doggie's poopoo, doing your makeup, doing your manicures, bringing your café latte and making your special required diets — are not less than you are. They are not the scum of the earth that needs to be treated as such. They are human, just like you. They love and feel and get heartbroken, just like you. They have families like you, and have Christmas dinners like you, but maybe less extravagant.

In the hospital setups where I have worked, especially in the United Kingdom, the feel of hierarchy is super tangible. You have the managers "up there" who will bark orders at medical and surgical consultants of twice their age as if they were their lapdogs. But then, these same consultants will treat the "junior" doctors and nurses like scum, not to mention the cold and heartless approach most of them have with their patients. These junior doctors and nurses will treat the cleaning and catering staff like scum, and so it goes. So many times have I seen the hurt on those "simple" little faces when someone "up there" treated them like crap. If you would only stop and think for a while how important everyone in this whole team is, you would be amazed. If you would only talk to some of those "lower" ones, would you find the warm hearts they have and even sometimes be surprised by their profound hidden talents. There were many "lower" people I talked to with these hidden talents — writing, singing, painting and songwriting — and on my encouraging them to not place themselves on this hierarchical ladder, but to take that talent and run with it, they reached personal heights. Yes o rich and famous ones, there are those "below" you who may not have your money and two hundred pairs of shoes, but they are quantum physicists who understand things you cannot even start to fathom; they are doctors who have the knowledge to save your life when in danger; they are policemen and soldiers who keep you safe in your bed at night and they are your cleaner who has to endure your bodily remains when cleaning your bath and toilet, enduring your spoilt tantrums because they need to pay their humble mortgages. Your Ego, rich and famous one, is merely programmed as, "I am holier than thou." Think back into the distant, gray past. You were once "down there" as well, and the faintest hiccup can pull you "down" amongst those whom you have treated so badly.

    No one is above or below another. We are all links in the chain of humanity. But then you might ask, "what about those terrorists?" Simple answer - Why do you think these terrorists hate the west so much? Isn't there maybe a hidden agenda that you don't know about? Don't you think that their fears are being abused by the cunning few, indoctrinating and brainwashing them into believing that what they are doing is right? Those "savages" in those "savage countries" have families and mourn them just like you do when they lose them. And those serial killers and pedophiles, have you ever stopped and thought about their childhoods? Yes, what they are doing is completely unacceptable, and nothing makes me angrier than a person willfully hurting others, especially the ones who can't defend themselves. But we must know that these individuals are lost. They have lost their connection with Spirit, their mind bridges completely destroyed. They are the example for the rest of us, showing us what happens if we lose our connection with the One. And believe me, they are sowing the seeds that will only grow into fruits of darkness. They will eat of that fruit and fall into utter despair. We are all creating our own life cycles, or karma as eastern philosophy puts it. What we sow, we shall reap, as Christ put it. And we have to know that these individuals are replacing our natural predators of so long ago. They are social predators, and we have to defend ourselves and our children against their onslaught by the measures known to us now, until the cosmic ignorance veil lifts, and they are completely gone. But also remember that something made them into predators. Behind every evil, you will find a tragic childhood, a tragic childhood that leads to delusions used to mask the pain by hurting others.

Ego is a tool, and not you. Ego is and can never be "the boss." There is no boss. There is only connection with the One, or not. The more you lose your connection with the One, the more you will fall into despair, and the more you will hurt yourself and others, which is known to us as committing evil. The more connected you become, the more you will understand and the more "good" you will do to others and the world. You will become a builder of yourself and society, and not a destroyer. Ego must be programmed to be user friendly and multi-interfaceable. Ego must be friendly and kind to others, no matter how hard it is. When another barks or sneers at you, it is because his or her Ego is not reprogrammed yet. This individual still lives in the delusional belief of "I am holier than thou." When a person keeps invading your personal space, suffocating you, it is because his or her Ego is programmed "lower" than yours and desperately needs your attention. No need to become angry at it. Resist the anger, because it's only a primitive reaction of the primate body you dwell in, and try to understand. Egos act like shields. They can be used to hide secrets of fearing failure. They are the sneering masks on a Venetian ball, hiding a crying face behind it.

It reminds me of a day when a nurse ran to me and said she couldn't handle this particular patient anymore. "She is absolutely impossible," she said, and wanted me to help. This lady was coming into hospital for an operation and needed all the prep before the said incident of the next day. I must agree, she was difficult. She was angry and interrogative, finding fault with everyone and everything we did. I asked to be alone with her while she kept on rampaging. I closed the door and waited for her to take a breath, feeling the anger boiling in me, but resisting it. When she took her first breath, I asked her what really bothered her. Almost immediately she broke down in tears. She was absolutely terrified of the operation and hid her fear behind a mask of nastiness. She was so afraid of getting caught for being afraid that she had to hide it behind her mask—an Ego programmed to fight to the death.

So you could become a light You, or a dark You, depending on what you do with your obstacles, Ego being the most important one. And saying this, Ego needn't be an obstacle. It must be used as a tool to interface with the world around you. It is your unique persona that makes you, well, you. But it must be the best "You" you can be, and not accepted as "I was born with anxiety" or "this anger runs in the family" or something like that. Break free from your darker self by reprogramming your ego and connecting to Spirit via your mind.

The Holy Grail Called Happiness

The reason why nobody can ever find "eternal happiness" is because of their lack of understanding of what happiness really is.

What is happiness? Think carefully. What is it? How do you define it?

If one clears the mind, and carefully thinks about it, happiness can be thought of as a positive emotion. Then what is an emotion? A "feeling" you might say. Then what is this "feeling," and with what does one "feel" this feeling? Hmm, bit of a dilemma, isn't it?

The key, yet again, lies in the universal truth of vibration. Emotion is the "sensing" of harmonic or disharmonic vibration. If it feels good, then it is a harmonic vibration, and if it feels bad, the opposite. Thus the good and bad "vibes" we often talk about. With some part of our being, we can sense the harmonic properties of the universe. If you think about it, that "feeling" is situated somewhere between your chest and your stomach, isn't it? When you fear, you feel an unpleasant shunt in the pit of your stomach, and when excited, a pleasant shunt in the same area—thus the solar chakra. When you feel love, you experience it as a "warmth" in your "heart," and when sad or "heartbroken," the opposite in the same area—thus your heart chakra. Interesting, isn't it? It would seem that one's chakras are sensitive to these vibratory harmonics, just as your eyes are sensitive to properties of photonic vibration (light), and your ears to auditory vibration (sound). Thus, if you feel "happiness," you sense vibratory harmony between yourself and the universe, ranging from your Inner Self to people and situations "surrounding" you. You are then resonating in a harmonic chord or unison with what you perceive "around" you. When you feel unhappy, sad or angry, it indicates that you are not in vibratory unison with the surroundings, and different harmonic intervals or "chords" will give rise to different negative emotions. Let's take an example—think about a period when you and your partner had an argument. Where, when and how did it start? How did it feel, and how was it resolved? It is often difficult to pinpoint the answers to these questions. But if vibratory harmonics can be applied, you will know that it started because of disharmonic or incompatible thought vibration. You and your partner, at that stage, had disharmonic thoughts, which "clashed" instead of uniting—a false chord so to speak. This disharmonic vibration will then be felt as anger, frustration and unhappiness, until resolved. The only way to deal with this, is by using your mind to change your vibratory resonance with everything around you. You cannot swim against the flow of the river–you will tire and "drown." In other words, you cannot physically change the world around you, as it is a mere illusory projection. One cannot change a shadow on the wall, only the thing that casts it. Thus, if you flow with the river, sensing the different currents, you can choose the right side-stream or current, and "move" into it. You then change the "projector" of the world around you, that projector being your thoughts. In due time, the larger universe will start resonating with your changed thought patterns—it is the law of harmonic resonance.

You might wonder how to do this. It is simply by silencing that burning desire to react to everything verbally and physically, in other words fighting and arguing. You have to distance yourself from your ego, know that it is only your personal interface or PRO with the world, and find that quiet spot within yourself. It is here that you will feel or sense the vibration. With practice, you will get it. Then, by thought alone, you can attune yourself to the flow, and change it with the action-reaction phenomenon. Your "surroundings" in the shape of the immediate world and people will then resonate with you, just like two singing glasses.

Now we must remember that the universe is in constant flux. It keeps changing due to its vibratory dynamics. Things will always fluctuate from one state to the other—yin and yang, good and bad etc. Therefore, eternal bliss cannot be found on this earth plane. It is not part of the earthly plane equation, and will never be found here—so don't pursue it. Eternal happiness is an illusion. One doesn't find eternal sunshine nor eternal summer. Happiness is part of the yin yang. It is the up in the happiness-unhappiness wave equation, just like day is to night and summer is to winter. Everything in our universe works on the principle of fluctuation. Electricity is constant fluctuation between positive and negative charges. Without those fluctuations, electricity wouldn't exist. Wind is the fluctuation between high and low air pressure, and without that we would have no wind to blow through the leaves of the trees, pushing clouds over the land to make it rain. Life is fluctuation. Male and female in unison gives birth to new life. The new life fluctuates from young to old, and from old to death only to be reborn when man and woman unite again. Just so, happiness must fluctuate with unhappiness in vibratory harmony.

Instead of hunting for eternal happiness, find content in the balance of even flux between happiness and unhappiness. As mentioned so many times before, balance and harmony are the key. Too much happiness can destroy just as much as too little happiness. Ask any person associated with or suffering from bipolar disorder (manic depression). Their "highs" can lead to bankruptcy in weeks as they become manic spenders or become promiscuous and cause themselves nasty illnesses and destroy their relationships. Just so their lows are the depths of hell, which equally destroy, and sometimes end up in suicide. Finding even flux between high and low, like the tides of a calm ocean will make us more content. But this fluctuation must be used as fuel. You will be surprised how many great works have been born from the depths of despair. Think about all the love songs. Think about thought-provoking films—most of them having a sad undertone. It is sadness and unhappiness that make actors or actresses do their best work. It is the portrayal of sadness that chokes the audience and breaks their hearts. Think of *Schindler's List*, *The English Patient*, *Empire of the Sun*, *Sophie's Choice* and *Bridges of Madison County*. The same with musicians, painters, writers and poets—heartachingly beautiful works have arisen from artists' sorrow. Use this unhappiness as fuel. Don't just sit there and feel sorry for yourself. There are lots of people out there with just as much, and maybe even more sorrow than you.

And the happiness point? A short burst of euphoria that ends in weeks of unhappiness, creating an obsession with euphoria. So many people are brainwashed into believing that a bigger house or the latest model of your favorite car or a yacht or a private jet will make you happy. This of course doesn't happen, and they search for it elsewhere — in the darker places of human existence where short-term pleasure turns into an eternity of despair. Forget about eternal euphoria. We are here to live our stories. You won't find a book or movie with eternal bliss from start to finish. It will bore the living hell out of anyone. We want suspense. We want to be thrilled. We want happiness and sadness, ups and downs. We want vibration, and not inertness. Our lives are reflected by stories, and our stories reflected by our lives. It's because we are living a story, and stories have ups and downs. It's life, and we have to live it and learn from it.

Things "out there" in the world will never make you eternally happy. They are only illusory projections. They can't love you or hug you. They can't hold you when you feel sad. They can't sit in the bath with you and chat away for hours about trivialities. They can't chuckle with laughter when they see the ocean for the first time, grow up and give you gray hair with their first dates being someone from hell.

Happiness, then, is the sensing of harmony, and only you can create it by "tuning" yourself to the world and others. By sensing the vibratory "value" of the universe around you, and your vibratory relation to it, you can "tune" yourself to it, just like a musician will tune his or her instrument before a performance. You then change the shadow caster, and not the shadow, the projector and not the projection. And life always goes out of tune, just like an instrument, and always needs tuning. It is the fluctuating nature of the universe.

Relationships

Ah yes. Probably the most important thing in our little existence that always gets overlooked. From your relationship with yourself, your spouse, children, family, friends and work colleagues to relationships between countries—a thing that can make or break. A bad relationship with yourself, and you sink into the depths of self-abuse hell. A bad relationship with spouse, children, family and friends, and you lose them, abandoned to be lonely and unhappy. A bad relationship between countries, and we have continuing wars and destruction. Yes, it seems to be the thing we are failing at most. Divorce rates are going up, children's drug abuse and suicide (especially in developing worlds) are on the rise, and wars are escalating into the obscene. All because of failed relationships.

Relationships are directly linked to our connection to the One. It is, per se, a relationship with the One. When you are connected to Spirit and the One, thus resonating with them, your understanding expands to such an extent that you will know that everything is connected, and that there is no need to compete anymore. We are the portals through which light can flow if we let it. If we do that, then we can glow together, illuminating the world, and bring balance. When we lose this connection, we fall into the primal "take no matter what" trap. We feel that everything is limited, that we are completely isolated and alone and have to fight to the death for our survival. This happens from the smallest scale, to the largest.

Relationship with You

You are just as important, and just as not important as everybody on this earth. You will love your child with all your heart; why is it then that you will hate yourself? What if you could stand aside from yourself, and take yourself back a few years when you were a child? Go and find a picture of the time when you were a child or baby. Look at that baby in the picture. Will you hate and abuse that little child you were (and still are deep inside)? Will you stuff the child full of unhealthy foods, make him or her binge drink and take cocaine till his or her nose bridges collapse? Or will you overfeed him or her, and then make the child vomit his or her food back into a toilet? If you won't do it to another child or person, then why do it to the child within? What makes that child who you are and were less important than your own child? We are all one spirit connected in the One, illusorily parted in the different bodies we posses that help us tell our archetypal stories on earth. You can't discriminate against yourself, for you will discriminate against another, and you can't discriminate against another, for you will discriminate against yourself. If you have two loving children, will you love the one and hate the other, barking at one and humiliating him or her? Will you, when that one brings you a little butterfly, just take and crush the butterfly and tell him or her to piss off? Of course not. Then why do you treat yourself with the same disrespect? You are no less important, and no more important than others. We are all equal with our own talents and quirks that contribute to humanity. The only difference is our stage of development in the chain of becoming spiritual butterflies — from the egg, to the caterpillar, to the larva, pupa and then ultimately the butterfly. Make friends with yourself, and keep the balance by vibrating in unison with others around you.

Before we go to relationships with spouse, children, family, friends and colleagues, let's take a look at...

Sex and Sexuality

Oh, that three letter word we gave to something we know so little about. As I see it, modern society is mainly divided into two groups where it comes to sexuality: group 1 — those who fear it due to generation after generation's religious condemning dogma, staying clear from it as far as possible or overcompensating by doing it in weird and wonderful ways, but feeling infinite guilt in the eyes of their forefather's god; and group 2 — those who completely rebel against the years of oppressing dogma, changing sex into an abomination called "fucking" (excuse my French). It is then a lot like with religion again — those who fanatically follow religious dogma due to fear of the same god, or those who completely rebel, becoming atheist. Now isn't that odd? Both groups are missing the point, as none of them are balanced, balance always being the key to vibratory harmony (no, not that kind of vibration some naughty girls might think!).

Sex, which I will call love play from now on, is like a state-of-the-art dream car that stands brilliantly clean and polished on a beautiful meadow. It gets discovered by a primitive primate species, knowing nothing about it, but using it nonetheless. Some will touch it carefully, feeling that it might be threatening. Some won't even get close, as their mothers warn them that it is a vehicle from darkness. Some will think this to be nonsense and start to play games on it. They will jump on it, slide over its bonnet, throw mud at it and write their names on it. Some will even tear pieces from it and hit each other with them. Then one day, some will realize that the door can be opened, and carefully go inside, sniffing the leather seats and tasting the steering wheel. After a while they will invite their buddies and have a ball inside it, rolling, screaming, and jumping in it, until one finds the key, pulling it from the ignition. He found something, and it's his alone. Another wants to take it from him, and the whole thing turns into a blood bath, completely ruining the beautiful machine.

Let's start from scratch. There's a beautiful, aesthetically pleasing, state-of-the-art car on a beautiful meadow. A beautiful woman and man walk toward it, open the doors and climb in. They sit for a while, marveling at its aesthetic design and technological wonder. They turn the key in the ignition, and the smooth engine comes to life. Carefully, the car is placed into first and then second gear, and the car slips gracefully into the sunset. (I apologize for using a crude metaphor such as a car for such a wondrous event, but the "physical act of love" is a vehicle that I will soon elaborate on).

Some of us eat fast-food on the go, quickly forcing the unhealthy beastie down while running for the next bus. Others will come home, lovingly prepare a wholesome meal, and sit down with a loved one, enjoying every mouthful.

Love play is something much more than we can ever imagine. Man and woman unite in a state of pure joy (when done as intended), and when the tide is right, a soul will cross the threshold from the enfolded universe or Kingdom of Heaven, infuse a single cell inside the woman's womb and then intelligently divide and differentiate to become a fetus and then a beautiful baby. The baby will be born, and when nurtured will grow into a lovely human being who could be the next World Teacher for all we know. If this soul is violently and vulgarly plucked from the heavens and stuffed into a fetus, intoxicated with cigarette smoke and bad diets, secretly hated and wished dead and when born treated like dirt, who can blame this child if it grows into a Hitler?

Love play is the opening of the gates to heaven, can't we see? It is probably one of the most important events in one's life — when taken to be born, or when preparing the flower bed for the one to come. And when not reaping a soul from heaven, use it as a vehicle to connect with each other and the One in a state of pure joy. This was the initial uncorrupted intention of Tantric love play, and not the stuff you read these days where it's all about getting laid better.

Tantric love play is about connecting to the One. It is about two devotees uniting to climb Jacob's ladder to the heavens and reach out to God or the Source. We have in our lives one of the most profound vehicles of connecting to our inner selves, with each other and with God, and all we can do is scratch it. We are the monkeys on that instrument, scratching and soiling it out of ignorance and primitiveness, or missing it completely because of our indoctrinated fear.

We discover this corrupted idea of love play when we reach our teens (these days even before that) by lustful magazines on the shelf with two big-breasted honeys mockingly licking each other. We feverishly scroll down the endless web pages looking for that better anal sex view, "choking the bishop" or "riding that dildo" till it hurts. We can't seem to fulfill that burning desire, and we keep looking for more distasteful pictures and events in nightclubs, onto the brink of becoming a sexual predator. We are bored with the gentle ones, looking for that beast or femme fatale, the excitement never eluding. And so the downward spiral into the depths of despair.

Wake up! It's an illusion. Pornography isn't real. It is a cheap, blown out of proportion imitation of the darker side of primate sexual rituals. Walk down the dark backstreets of porn land, and you will discover the real pain and suffering the women must endure to give you that fake orgasm. It is like eating a nice little piece of steak, not knowing the pain and suffering the animal had to endure at the abattoir so that you can stuff your face with it. Pornography is only a tool used for money and power. Why do you think it is always run by a male-dominated force? And why is it so successful? Because we are sex-crazed victims to our own primitive primate sex drive, trapped in this dark illusion created by the power seekers.

Casual sex as well can and will never give you a feeling of inner content. It always disappoints. You drink yourself into a stupor, "screwing" some other drunkard, and when you wake up next to each other, you are struck with that feeling of emptiness and solitude. Not to mention the stench of that fermented booze and smoke-drenched clothes and linen.

Don't be a monkey on that car, soiling and scratching it, using it to control others. Don't be a cheat either. You are not looking for the perfect "shag." You are looking for yourself, hurting others in the process. Wake up to the reality and the beauty. Open the door, turn the key, and drive into the sunset. Don't run with a nasty, quick and unhealthy meal to catch another. Prepare for it, sit down and enjoy it, sharing it with a loved one. Savor the moment.

"Now that sounds boring," some might say. Really? Climbing into a state-of-the-art sports car and driving the devil out of it is boring? No, my friend, not boring at all. The choice is yours. You can drive it around, enjoying the silky smooth ride, savoring the passing landscape, or drive the living hell out of it—

making handbrake turns, accelerating from naught to a hundred in seven seconds. You can do it alone or share the experience with your loved one. You can sometimes drive and sometimes be the passenger enjoying the thrill of the ride. Top up, top down. Radio on, radio off, in the day or night, sunrise or sunset. And if you feel like it one day, you and your loved one can decide to go on a long trip to paradise, where the sun shines and crystal waters bathe the silky smooth beach.

"But we don't know how to drive."

Then learn, otherwise you'll miss it.

"But how?"

First, by knowing that you have the potential to be a first-class driver, and secondly to go out there and learn how to do it.

Get your Body-Mind-Spirit union in order. Get your body fit enough. Your body is the gateway to that pleasure. Your body is the "temple of God," as Christ put it. It is the vehicle through which you will reach the connectedness with your lover, together forming the gateway to the heavens. Your mind is the bridge to that spirit of yours, so make it strong and flexible. As I've mentioned before, your mind is the horse that needs to be tamed. If you give it the love and respect it needs, creating a binding friendship with it, it will follow the steering of your spirit's will very accurately. And reconnecting with your spirit will connect you to the One. Once this has happened, you will experience bliss like no other.

What is important to know is that both lovers must give and receive. Not take. Give and receive, gratefully. You should honor each other's beauty, physically as well as mentally and spiritually. You should pleasure each other, finding pleasure in return by giving pleasure to the one you love, as well as receiving the given pleasure with joy instead of guilt. Let the energy flow from within toward each other until the light engulfs you both, and create a supernova of joy.

And techniques? Forget about the techniques. People are too obsessed by the "techniques." One can have a million-dollar camera and still take mediocre photos, or have a dinky toy camera and take million-dollar photos. It is the intention that counts. The rest will follow. Everyone is different in that regard. Everyone has different pleasure zones, and most importantly different ideas in their heads. That is where most sensuality lies, in one's mind. And Rome wasn't built in one day. It will need practice and getting used to. It is a journey, not just a destination. If both lovers are giving wholeheartedly, things will fall into place, and when you eventually reach that destination, you will realize that it is a place that constantly changes and teaches you new things. Every time will be different. And not every occasion will be successful either. Remember the constant fluctuation of the wave equation of life. It will happen once in a blue moon, so stop obsessing about it. It's not the be-all and end-all.

Most importantly, love play is not (just like everything else in the universe) an isolated event. It doesn't happen apart from the rest of your life. It is all interconnected. Daily, weekly and even monthly events will either lead to a wonderful sensual moment, or deviate from it. This is something especially males must know.

A Message for Men (ladies, read it, you might just chuckle)

Why is it that your partner has that "headache?" Isn't it maybe because you've been acting like a buffoon lately? How can your partner be sexually interested in you if you keep acting like a barbarian? You keep on hanging out with the lads or the dudes. You drink beer after beer and watch sports all day. You scratch your butt, break wind or pick your nose. You are caught time and time watching other women. And then, all of a sudden you want to show your partner some silly porn video and screw. If she is willing (she really must love you, or is pathologically attached), then you do the thing quickly, her faking an orgasm so that your feelings are not hurt (you not even noticing because of your arrogance and beer-infested brain), and you falling asleep, snoring like an old bear. Put yourself in your lover's shoes. Just imagine yourself being a sensitive woman with special needs. Dare to awaken the female energy within (male and female energy dwells in us all) and see what a complete ape you are. How can she keep on wanting to "have sex" with you if she gains absolutely nothing from it?

A woman wants a man to be "tough" and to protect her, it's true. But it is on a nonsensual level that she needs this, and is part of the primate programming that still dwells in our vehicles we took with incarnation. When it comes to matters of the heart and love, a woman wants tenderness, understanding and selflessness. She wants to be cared for the whole day. She wants romance (real romance, not that fake stuff that smells of "I need a screw"). She wants a walk on the beach or in the park, talking about her world for a change. She wants you to be sensitive and understanding when she has PMS or menstruates, bringing her pain tablets and running her a bath. She wants you to look after the screaming baby for a change, getting up in the night to change the screamer's nappy. After all, life became so expensive that both of you need to work to keep the mortgage running. On top of that, she looks after the kids, cooks and cleans (if you can't afford help), while you sit on your butt watching television, beer in hand. Then you have the audacity to shout "honey, can you bring me another beer?" And when the evening comes to an end, you want to get laid. She is too tired! You sulk and gradually start looking for another "chick." After all, you deserve it, don't you? The "bitch" doesn't want to do your chops. How dare she?

She can dare all she likes, my friend. You are not supporting enough. And that is all part of the prelude to love play. It's all interwoven with both of your lives. And the reason for your being like this (hopefully you are not) is because your male energy is not balanced with your female energy. Sure, it can't be completely balanced; you would change into an asexual being otherwise. But you need to move closer to the female point. Not just for better love play, but for a better you. Remember that balance and harmony are key. In female energy lie many secrets, the secrets of nurture and creativity. Can you imagine what it must be like to carry a living being within yourself, feeling him or her moving inside you, hearing your voice when you speak to him or her? Enduring the pain with labor and then feeding that beautiful little creature with your body? Looking in the eyes of a caring husband who enfolds you with strong arms, making you feel safe?

Explore this in your mind, that flexible mind of yours. Feel your lover, partner and friend. Feel your wife, being inside her skin and life, and look back at yourself. How would you like to see yourself?

And about that urge—ooh, that undeniable burning urge every time you see a dress walk by. The urge that makes you give that wolf's whistle and pull your eyes from your sockets right into her breasts. That urge, is nothing more than your primate vehicle on autopilot for the survival of the species. It is something you need to recognize as part of the body, not your whole being. You don't want a machine always to be on autopilot, do you? Sometimes you want to do something, and then the auto function kicks in, but you can't undo it. It is infuriating, isn't it? With this, you can simply recognize it and move along. Nothing irritates the majority of women more than a man staring at her breasts the whole time. And it puts you in a bad light as well. You are thought of as just being another beastly man. Lose the habit. It's silly. You are controlled by your primate vehicle's autopilot function. Instead, discover the aesthetics of a woman. Find pleasure by exploring the aesthetic of the female form as you would an undulating landscape with rolling hills. And do this with your partner. She deserves it, because after all, you chose to be with her. Take that responsibility.

When it comes to actual love play, remember this—be sensitive to her needs. See how much you can give her pleasure, and not yourself. Don't take from her, but give and receive. Explore her wants and give them in small packets. Make it last as long as you can, and try to withhold the supernova event. And when the event arises, let that energy wash over your whole being, inward as well as outward. Try connecting your soul with hers, and then try connecting to the One. And don't just fall asleep afterwards. I know the need is strong. But nothing will please her more than to stay awake and talk to her about trivialities.

A Message for Women (men, stay tuned)

Okay, bashing the male piñata was fun, but now let's have a look at the other side of the coin.

It's true, women have been suppressed for centuries, and it was (and still is) shameful. What has been done against women, especially in the name of God, was atrocious. But there is a simple reason. You were not balancing your male energy with your female energy, and you've been doing this for centuries. You crept up in that little female corner, being submissive to those "male bastards" all these years. And who taught you this? Your mother of course. It's been passed down the generations that men work, and women stay at home, looking after the children, cooking, cleaning and opening her legs when the dirty old beast claps his hands. It was considered normal (and still is in some countries).

But no more. Women came to their senses. The focus on that male-female scale is moving toward the center, where it belongs. Unfortunately, some women have tipped the scale to the other side, causing extreme feminism, which was seen as a golden opportunity by men to get more sex! It is so ironic. Balance is key. Balance and vibratory harmony. You were born a woman, you feel like a woman, and you have the absolute privilege to be female—being loving, caring and nurturing; being able to carry a child, bearing and feeding him or her. You have the privilege, if you chose well, of being looked after by a caring husband who makes you feel safe and cared for. This is your privilege, and you must accept it gracefully. It is a gift from God, and no man can ever understand this feeling you have, especially the bond you have with your child.

But you must not hide away in that all female corner. It makes you weak and defenseless. It gives sexual predators the opportunity to hunt you down, because they know that you are a helpless fawn. It makes your partner or husband lose interest, looking for someone more exciting and daring. It irritates a man when you scream when you see a mouse. It's just a mouse, for goodness sake. A cute little teeny weenie mouse, running around in your house on the lookout for some grub. And that handbag, stuffed full of most of your bedroom. Why? It makes you immobile and a target for thieves. At least get something smaller where you can keep your female emergencies when you need them. Stop worrying about your wrinkles and all those creams. We all get wrinkles. Get yourself one moisturizer, one base, and a few simple makeup thingies. Less is more. Stop fretting so much with your hair. And for goodness sake, wear the stuff you buy more than once! Forget about strictly following the fashions. It's a trap to make you lose your money. Make your own fashion. Be bold and daring. Have fewer clothes for a start. Buy cleverly, buy things you can mix and match. Buy animal friendly clothing. Have a smaller suitcase when you travel. Pack only what you'll really need. Nothing is more depressing than to see some posh woman in an airport walking in front of her husband with her poodle in her hands while he is struggling with fifty massive suitcases, of which forty-nine are hers. Be independent. Learn to fix things yourself. It's incredibly rewarding. Learn to enjoy nature instead of being squeamish of it. Look at spiders and their cunning web-building qualities. Don't just shout at John to come and squash it. Catch it in a glass and throw it out.

Stop running to your parents every time there's a fight (except when the fight becomes nasty and physical). It's got nothing to do with them. Fight your own battles and stand up for your rights, especially when the baby is screaming. Your husband or partner had just as much fun making that baby as you did (or didn't). You work just as hard during the day as him, so make turns, and elbow him in his lazy ribs when it's his turn. Let him cook for a change and do the washing. Just don't let him iron. He will probably burn the lot (except for soldiers of course).

Men and women should be a team, and cringing to the beating male must stop. Men and women are equal, and it is a woman's birth right to claim back the "land she lost."

And now, this is not just for the ladies, but for the gentlemen as well. Don't turn into a slob after marriage, neglecting your body to become a jellyfish. How can your lover keep interest in you if he or she married a god or goddess who now turns into a jellyfish? Keep that body fit. Remember the Body-Mind-Spirit chapter. It's good for both of you. And if you are a celebrity, why become a skeleton? Why not just be your normal healthy self? Why do you boot camp yourself with such strict diets or worse, not eating at all or chucking up your food in a toilet? There are a lot of hungry children out there who could have eaten that food you're wasting, you being one as well! Would you starve your baby like you starve yourself? Come to your senses, please. Be nice to yourself for a change.

And ladies, when you were so lucky to find the perfect gentleman, be eternally grateful. They are few and far between. Unfortunately, women have a primate autopilot function as well—looking for the alpha male. They're looking for that tall, dark and handsome god of a man who walks the walk and talks the talk, playing sports superiorly and choosing the women he wants. But beware, for the alpha male is all male, and has almost no female energy; thus, he will be a cheating, lying, drunken scumbag in a nice suit. Don't be fooled. Turn off this alpha male seeking autopilot, and look for that poet. He's shorter, may have freckles and a skinny body, but in this day and age, it is intelligence that protects, not brutal body power. He will be the one who sets you on fire in bed, because he is in touch with his feminine side. He knows what you want, and he's more than willing to give it to you. He will be the one who gets up at night and looks after the baby, bringing you some tablets and tampons from the supermarket if your period is driving you up the wall. He's the one you won't have to nag to say, "I love you." And then, on a bright sunny day, you see this tanned Greek god with muscles playing gracefully under his shirt, and you feel weak in the knees, falling right into the alpha male trap. Don't. If you are fortunate to have one of those poets I just mentioned, then switch off that silly alpha male button. You probably will have a "great time in bed," but then you will lose that angel, and have a lifelong "kick your own butt" anguish-filled existence.

Rise to your masculine calling. Be independent. Be daring and explore the male frontiers. Show him that you want him, that you sometimes want to drive that sports car and throw handbrake turns. I promise you, he will love it (if you chose the right guy). If he is Mr. Right, and you can feel it, then open yourself to him, and let your soul merge with his. Be his goddess, and let him be your god. Be his siren, and let him be your archangel. Be his ocean and let him be your wind. Together, you will make a formidable storm.

Sexuality: A Final Thought

The reason we are attracted to one another, is that we can never (on the earth plane) have that full female energy if we are male, and never have that full male energy when we are female. Remember how fermions (the stuff our bodies are made from) can never share the same quantum possibility? Thus we seek each other out to patch that hole. But if we ourselves are not balanced men and women, thus having our male and female energies as balanced as we can, then the relationship will never work, never mind the sex. We have to balance ourselves before searching for the perfect partner. We have to work on ourselves and our shortcomings. We have to be sensitive to one another's needs, and fill that gap in the other's life that only we can fill. If you are one of those so afraid of sex that you deprive yourself of the opportunity for eternal joy because of generation after generation's indoctrination—don't be. Love play is one of the most wonderful events on this earth plane. It is one of the ways to connect to each other, our inner selves and the One.

And if you're gay, don't fret. You are gay, and that is that. Accept it, embrace it and know that love is just as strong. It is the male and female energy within that counts, not your tools. Stop feeling guilty about it and overcompensating by being promiscuous. There's nothing wrong with being gay. Some of us are straight, and some of us are gay. And that's that. Don't let religious dogma, peers or parents make you feel excluded. Find that perfect partner, and if you have a partner, respect each other and love one another. Stop looking for that cheap thrill that never lasts. Okay, so you can't have children like heterosexual couples, and adoption is a very controversial topic. But if it so happens that adoption is legalized, and you and your partner decide to adopt, remember to have the responsibility of being decent parents, bringing up your child with love in an unbiased environment.

Look after yourselves and one another in body, mind and spirit. Balance your male and female energies amongst yourselves, and live life to the fullest.

Relationships Continued

One important thing to recognize is the thing that causes the most destruction in relationships: It is the "Mine!," "screw you!" principle—Take and Disrespect.

We must recognize this in ourselves, and replace it with: "Here, have some of this," "thank you" principle—Give and Receive gratefully.

It reminds me of the story I once heard one telling at a dinner party. I don't know who conceived of this story, but ten out of ten for him or her.

There once were two brothers who loved each other very much. One was a saint who lived life peacefully and helped his fellow man. The other was a "ruffian," his bad and egocentric deeds escalating till he eventually murdered someone in cold blood. On the way to court, the two brothers driving together for the last time, the good brother asked the bad brother if he had any regrets, and he replied that he hadn't. The murdered fool had it coming. Just before they got to court, their car got stuck on a railway track, and a train smashed into them, killing them instantly. The good brother went to heaven, and the bad brother to hell. Months went by until the good brother went to God, and asked him if he could see his brother, as he missed him dearly. God allowed it, and off the good brother went. They met at the border between heaven and hell, ecstatic to see each other. The good brother asked the bad one how hell was. "Oh, awful," said the bad brother. "We have these wonderful dinner banquets at night with the most wonderful food and wine." The good brother was surprised, "why is it so awful then?" The bad one replied, "because our knives and forks are three feet long. We can't feed ourselves." "Oh," said the good brother, "we have exactly the same scenario, but we eat like kings and queens." "How do you do it then?" asked the bad brother, surprised. The good brother smiled sadly, "because we feed each other, silly."

This is a good example of Take-Disrespect vs. Give-Receive gratefully.

In this limited, semi-enclosed universe we find ourselves in, it is useless to take and take from the limited resources surrounding us. It is like two fools competing for a foot of rope, pulling at each end with foamy mouths, while behind them there are miles and miles of rope. If we could only realize that we are connected to the world of the One, where everything is limitless, and that through ourselves being portals to the One, we can project endless amounts of energy into this dark world, filling it with light. We should be stars and not black holes. We should give to each other and receive from one another, and not take like fools. We should realize that we are fountains connected to endless amounts of water of life. If we all could do this, relationships would not be perfect, as nothing here can be, but a lot easier and constructive instead of destructive. And relationships need arguments. Healthy arguments are the flux or potential difference, thus a harmonious wave equation of two poles of opinion. When used correctly by understanding the need for arguments, they will give rise to a new wave equation, a new idea and thus something constructive. An "argument" is only the "sign of the times" of a point in your relationship that needs "evolution." Instead of beating each other with childish deeds and vocabulary, rise to the challenge, and see each other's point of view. All points of view need evaluation.

But the main problem of all relationships lies in the ignorance of being endless fountains connected to the "endless waters" of the One. Our ignorance blocks our fountains from flowing, and instead of simply flowing, we fill our pools with the water stolen from others. This water quickly dries up, and we dash over to others to take their water again. And so we keep on taking from each other. We take disrespectfully, because we believe that we need to steal it in order to survive. Some have learned to steal so well that their wells are nearly always full, while others' are almost always empty. Surely you must feel how draining it is when someone annoys you endlessly. They literally take from your life source. When people moan and bitch, criticize, argue, fuss and fight, I can always feel how it drains me. And the life source drains quickly, because we ourselves are not properly connected to the original source. Our wells dry up in a flash, and we need to use our cunning devices to get some more from others, or block the flow in order to "protect" what is ours.

There are ways and means of getting this water of life we need, ranging from the obscene to the very subtle and almost unnoticeable. Obscene ones will kick and scream, manipulate, blackmail and intimidate others to abide. Good examples range from borderline personality disorder, substance abuse manipulation, antisocial behavior, pedophilia, rape and murder to a collective consciousness that wages war and commits genocide in the belief of being right in the name of patriotism or "god."

Then there's a more subtle approach of conditional exchange. I will give you "love" if you give me sex — the typical male-female conditional exchange. Men will flatter women to get the look of "I'll sleep with you" to boost their egos. Women will dress provocatively to get attention from men to boost their egos. They don't always actually want sex, but they want that attention. They want to know they are desirable. They want to know they are more desirable than the others; their egos need feeding. Then there are those who want to gain everything for almost nothing. Deliberate fame seekers know how to use leverage. They will gain the envy from thousands to millions of fans just by being famous. They will do anything to become famous, from radio to pornography — just for fame. Those who became famous by accident will quickly discourage those, as they know the double-edged sword of fame. But to no avail. They want that attention. They want to be in the tabloids. They are, without even knowing it, taking from others' wells. But then comes the boomerang effect. All those fans want their water back. They want to read the latest gossip. They want to know what's happening in their demigod's life. They create a market for it; they create the predators of the fame world — tabloid writers and photographers, constantly sucking that energy from the demigods into themselves and back to the masses from which it came. And there are even subtler ways to gain that life source. By boosting someone's ego to fall in favor of a promotion, or buying someone a gift for that appreciation. Or "loving" someone so much that it suffocates them. Real love can never suffocate. Real love is letting go when the time comes. Real love is when my wife tells me she has met someone that makes her happier than I do, and my letting her go to be with this person and being happy for her in spite of missing her. That is real love. Are you prepared to do this for your partner?

What we don't even realize is that we are merely redistributing the water of life between ourselves in the most vile ways. We are so used to feeling trapped in this world of limits that we forget that we are seamlessly connected to the limitless world. Thus we constantly steal from one another, feeling drained after a short burst of euphoria after the loot has been "digested." Worst of all, we lie to ourselves, telling ourselves that it is the right and only way of doing things.

If there are two people, each one with a gold coin, you will have a sum total of two gold coins. When the one gives his coin to the other, or the coin is taken by the other, then one will have two coins, and the other none. One has gained, the other lost. But the sum total will stay two gold coins only. But if each one has a story, and they share their stories with each other, then both will have two stories and both will gain from it. This is the same with our energy, water of life, knowledge and love. The more it is shared, thus given and received gratefully, everyone will gain. There will be more knowledge, love and light in this world, and it will keep on expanding till it reaches critical mass, where most will learn how to give and receive instead of taking disrespectfully.[1]

Partners/Spouses

Volumes have been written on this topic, but I can honestly say that not a lot needs to be said (especially with the abovementioned relationship prelude). It all boils down to one thing—selflessness.

We must remember that we are not halves seeking one another to be complete. This leads to imbalance. Instead, we must realize that we are whole and connected and seeking one another to balance our male and female energies to augment the whole. We seek each other to learn how to give and receive and eventually reap a soul from the heavens to live on this difficult but very exciting earth plane.

---

[1] I highly recommend reading James Redfield's *Celestine Prophecy*. The above mentioned "water of life" parable is also reflected in a more practical way as the *Nine Insights*.

We must learn how to listen to the other's needs (and not just with our ears, but with our hearts as well). We must place ourselves in their shoes, and they themselves in ours. We must live and let live. Can you just imagine if both partners were completely selfless, wanting to pleasure the other more than themselves? If the other's happiness were just as important as each one's own? Bliss in one word. Yes, there would still be arguments. But they would be more constructive. We are there to help one another, to collaborate and share our unique gifts with one another, and build a relationship that will last, even if partners split up for greener pastures. The friendship will always last.

It is extremely important to know that your partner was not created to make you happy. You cannot <u>want</u> happiness from someone — wanting is taking, and not giving. Wanting is the type of "love" that suffocates. Wanting, then, is not love, it is a selfish act of expecting the world and everyone in it to make you happy, confusing that with love. Ever experienced someone who hugs you, but makes you feel like pushing him or her away and running for your life? Ever felt someone pulling away from you when you hug them because you "love" them? This is the physical hug "taking" instead of "giving." It is "wanting" experienced from either perspective. Know it, realize it, and change it, in others as well as in yourself. "Happiness" comes from within, not from the illusory projection "out there." Happiness, if you remember, is the sensing of harmonic resonance between yourself and others, and can be achieved by "tuning" in to the harmonics around and within you.

If, for instance, you can feel an argument arising between you and your partner, know that your thought vibrations are "dissonant." Sense your partner's vibratory value, and tune into it. It needn't be the exact same vibration, but it must fall into a "note" that creates a harmonic interval. In easier terms, sense the "flow" of your partner's mood, and flow with the current instead of swimming upstream. After a while, with action-reaction between the two of you, the flow will change into a harmonic one—both of your moods will start resonating with each other in a wholesome manner. The change starts within you, not others. And if both parties can realize and do this, the change will happen twice as fast.

Then there is the thing about being hurt by your partner, or anyone else for that matter. "Hurt" is nothing more than a dysfunctional ego. You cannot, as an eternal resonating being, be "hurt" emotionally. Remember that emotion is only a way of sensing vibratory harmony. If someone, especially someone close to you, says or does something nasty, you will sense "hurt." This is only your tri-natured being informing you that someone or something is taking the "water from your well." It is your "burglar alarm" so to speak. If you are confusing your ego with yourself, then you will think that you are a victim who has been hurt. If, however, you are resonating with your inner self, and know that your ego is merely an interface system that reacts with the world "out there," then you will realize that the other person's well is empty, so to speak, and the person is trying to steal from yours. If you try and protect your ego (which doesn't need protection), it will lead to arguments (and wars on the macrocosmic scale—remember the story of Helen of Troy). The best thing to do is to open your channel to the Inner Kingdom and "flow" from within—perceive your partner (or anyone for that matter) objectively, understand his or her "need," let go of your reacting anger, and imagine "love" flowing into him or her. This will satisfy the other's need, and the argument will dissolve. There is endless energy within, so your well can't dry up. But it is important to teach this concept to your partner or loved ones, or remind them if they already know this. If you keep spoiling the other with continuous "flow," then he or she will never learn, and in the end, you will keep them from developing spiritually.

If both of you can just give and receive selflessly, things will really change.

Children

A golden rule is that they are not your possessions. They are not your property that you can make or break with as you please. They are an incredible responsibility that you choose and risk every time you make love. The responsibility is one of helping and sustaining completely unique human beings to reach adulthood, so that they in turn can shine their light the way destined. If we screw up by being selfish, we can dim their lights and block their fountains for the rest of their lives.

Look at them playing on the beach. They are so happy, not afraid of anything. It's because they are fresh from the endless world where nothing need be feared. Both my wife and I have the fortune of remembering our childhoods very vividly and often discuss the fearlessness we had as children. That is one thing I miss dearly. The blind faith and fearlessness I had. As I grew older, the fear seeped in more and more from every conceivable angle, and it is a demon we all fight daily. This fear is something we must try and keep from children's minds. We must teach them to be cautious, though, as this world is still very imperfect and needs a lot of work, but not to fear things blindly. Fear and caution are not the same thing. Caution is healthy self-preservation, the avoidance of potentially harmful things in this dense and imperfect world. Fear is the opposite of "faith," or the inability to focus and connect with the One. Caution is good, fear is bad. That constant background noise of fear—fear of death, of illness, of failing, of not fitting in, and worst of all of not being loved. That constant background noise, humming in your mind's basement, eats away at your vitality. That fear needs to be avoided at all cost. For us it will be less easy to get rid of, as we have grown up with it. We were programmed to fear and compete since childhood, and it will be difficult to break away from it completely. Sure, there are many self-help books that will tell you how to feel great in a week. But it never lasts. Fear is a lifelong habit, which will take time and patience to undo. But, seeing the damage it can do, you must teach your child not to fear, but to be cautious only. You must teach your child to believe in him- or herself by raising the child in an environment where you are a great example.

I can remember how I looked up to my parents when I was a very young child. They were my gods. Yes, I heard about God and the angels, but to me, they were the visible representations of his splendor. Parents don't realize just how much they mean to their children, how much each gesture can influence them for the rest of their lives. Parents somehow forget what it's been like being a child. But those bad things that happened to them—be it the fault of their parents or teachers—keep lurking in the shadows of their minds. They become that shadowy demon that whispers things in your ear, "you are ugly," "you are not good enough," "you will never be able to." Some of us will remember these moments, while others' memories need careful hypnotic persuasion to surface. This is why we must stop the vicious cycle of generation transference. The buck needs to stop with our generation. We need to take responsibility for not only raising children's bodies but also their minds so that they can connect to the Source. This can only be done in a selfless way.

But, on the other hand, there is a tendency of parents these days to overcompensate for their own strict and heartless upbringing by spoiling their kids. Balance! Remember the balance. You can't win a child's favor by letting him run amok or buying him or her anything he or she desires. This spoils children, and they are "programmed" to think they can have anything they want by nagging and manipulating others. You can't buy a child's favor . In fact, one shouldn't want a child's favor anyway. You shouldn't want from a child. Wanting is taking, not giving. You must give love and appreciation to your children, and give them their freedom without them getting hurt or being spoilt. If they throw tantrums, know that they are learning to manipulate you. Tantrums are their way of taking the water from your well. They have already, by following your lead, learned to take instead of give. This is by body language and other subtle ways. They are infinitely more sensitive than you think.

I remember once, when my wife and I were celebrating our paper wedding at a resort in the Drakensberg, South Africa, watching two different couples with their children in the morning at the breakfast table. Both couples had two children—a girl roughly at the age of five, and a boy roughly at the age of eight. The children of the one family were pleasant and well-behaved, while the others' created havoc. They were screaming, running and pulling things from the table. This happened every morning. We were curious why, so we (this is a habit of my wife and I) observed the families and their dynamic closer. The havoc family's parents had this undertone of stress between them. Their body language was a bit cold toward one another, and their disciplinary skills were completely ignored. They also treated their children more like "pets" rather than human children (lower than themselves, because they are "children"). The calm family had this funny vibe to them. The parents were holding hands occasionally, giving each other the "I love you" glance. They would listen to their children's silly conversations intensely, giving them the sense of being level with themselves instead of being down there somewhere. Noticing this, I tried to go out of my way to observe people and their children, and found that most behaved children's parents had this calm vibe of love between them. I believe that children's behavior is a symptom of the dynamic of their parents and their attitude toward their children. It's like the happiness-unhappiness thing. If you're unhappy, you know that you lost the path in the woods. If your children are behaving badly, then maybe you and your partner should look at yourselves and within as well. Children sense more than you think. A good example is a moment I remember, but let me first give you some background information about the relationship with my angel of a wife.

My wife and I are very fortunate. We met, instantly knowing that we were soul mates, got engaged three months later (with everyone laughing and saying it will never last) and got married less than a year after that. It's been ten years since then, and we are still just as close as we were. If we could get paid for talking bullshit night after night, we would have been millionaires by now. We have our arguments now and then, but they always have a constructive outcome. I can honestly say that we are fortunate enough, ups and downs included, to say we have a miraculous relationship.

Once we were visiting a good friend of ours. She was unfortunate enough to have had a stormy marriage, being married to a selfish man, and to have had a few unsuccessful relationships after that. This unfortunately took its toll on her beautiful little girl, who was shy and reclusive with the odd tantrum at that stage. My wife and I, not really the holding hands type, were sitting next to each other, watching a movie, when the little girl came, sat between us and held both of our hands. I could almost feel her thirst for the love that my wife and I share, and this made me very sad. This little girl could feel our love for each other, even though we are not very demonstrative.

This is why you should really love one another. Love as in selfless and both giving from within. Your children will bathe in the glow of that love. If you are not ready for this, don't have a baby. Don't have a baby because it's fashion, or you're broody or lonely or your mother expects it of you. They are a great responsibility, and you need to be ready to take that responsibility. My wife and I have been married for a decade, and only now do we remotely start to feel that we're getting ready for it. The first couple of years of marriage are usually the stormy ones. Couples need to sort themselves out before they can have children. They need to prepare that flower bed for the flowers. And this includes the financial bed as well. Kids are extremely expensive.

As they grow up, be sensitive to their talents. Carefully nurture these talents, and please don't live your lost dreams through them. These are their lives, not yours. You will get another turn next time. Instead, make it your new dream to see them fulfill theirs. Be happy for them.

And if you are a teacher, please realize the impact you have on children. I can vividly recall the saints and demons of my childhood. It took me years and years to shake the damage that the self-absorbed teachers caused. They can easily make you feel that you are a loser and will never succeed. Be sensitive to children's needs, and if they misbehave badly, know that there must be a problem at home. Misbehavior is a mere symptom of what lies beneath. The mass misbehavior and antisocial behavior we see in children these days is a symptom of a failing society. It is our apathy toward the real problem that causes things to get out of hand.

Be kind and gentle to the little ones, especially the introverted ones. Children can be quite cruel (learning it from their parents). Teach them to respect one another. I remember a day, I was about eight, on an eisteddfod for poetry. I performed my poem with ease and confidence, coming down the stage to sit among my friends. The next boy that went up was scared out of his mind. He grabbed his pants and turned them to the point of tearing, while my friends and I pulled faces at him. Typical, isn't it? I went along with this bullying, simply because I wanted to be "in" with my friends, and not become a victim myself. At some stage I turned around to find the icy blue, disapproving eyes of my father burning into mine, and I knew I had trouble coming. We went home, and I got a well-deserved hiding from my dad after he explained to me the reason why. He told me that he was disappointed in me for humiliating the other boy, and asked me to know that I hurt him. This hurt me more than the few tame slaps on the butt. I realized that I could have been that boy out there. And so later it came that I had to eat the fruits of my own karmic doing. Years after that I had to endure years of bullying at school for being too "artsy-fartsy." What you sow you shall reap, and I learned this lesson at a very early stage in my life. Teach this to your children before they have to learn it the hard way as I did (and surely most of you did as well).

On a last and short note, I think that our children's education systems are wrong and getting worse, especially with the new idea of introducing career-orientated paths from an early age. Children are not "small adults." Children are a breed of their own, and need to be treated as such. They are and have what most of us "lost" in the labyrinth of the woods: being innocent and imagination-saturated beings still fresh from the limitless world. They are not interested in "our" dull and doom-filled super-company–driven world we try and force down their throats. They love to paint pictures, and their eyes light up to stories of heroes and dragons in never-never land. From this we can see that they still possess the truth of life being infused with the Hero's Journey and the ultimate goal to create. This we have to keep alive within them, safeguarding them against the mistakes we have made over millennia. Let them be children as long as possible, immersing themselves in stories and art. When the time is right, slowly introduce them to more linear thought patterns of our limited world while keeping the balance of their creative side. Unknown to most, being a teacher is probably one of the most responsible and important jobs in the world. Teachers help parents turn their children into the adults of tomorrow. If a teacher fails to know this, and lets her or his ego come in the way, the child's evolution will be jeopardized. Many adults of today still walk with subconscious emotional scars left on them by egotistic teachers, some of them being teachers themselves. Teachers should be the "chosen ones," wise and kind enough to work with the "gentle ones."

Children are precious. They are our future, and we need to invest in them wholeheartedly.

A Short Note on "Teenagers"

Yes, they seem completely irrational and even mad sometimes. But remember that you were a "teenager" as well. Puberty is a very delicate time for a person. It is when the brightly colored caterpillar withdraws to the "within," forming the cocoon where he or she will find him- or herself and if lucky, transform into a beautiful butterfly. Unfortunately, most of us are not prepared well for this event, or our cocoons are shaken vigorously by insensitive adults, and we get stuck in this semi-caterpillar phase, where we will turn into beings that seem like adults but still act like children, throwing selfish little tantrums like five year olds. It is then all about ME that wants to TAKE, and pop goes the spiritual growth bubble. This is seen from domestic relationships to international political scenarios. The cocoon phase is a delicate time. One needs to remember the mini inner apocalypse of one's own cocoon phase, and care for your child's cocoon with absolute care. Better still is to prepare your child for this phase, so your child will have a much better chance breaking from the cocoon as a beautiful and fully developed young adult who is ready to seek and find his or her destiny. To help yourself understand the mind of the so-called teenager, read *The Catcher in the Rye* by J.D Salinger. It just might give you some insight into their difficulties changing from child into adult.

Friends and Family

Same principle applies — live and let live, and give and receive. Understand their points of view. Have empathy and place yourself in their shoes. See yourself out of their eyes, and if you feel like it is working for you, gently teach them the same principle. They will notice a change in you and will be curious why. Look after one another for life.

And strangers are only friends in the making. There are many strangers out there who could be your next best friend for life. Keep your eyes and your hearts open.

Difficult and Nasty Ones

Yep, there are some pretty nasty people out there. Some are so disconnected from the One, they become impossible to live with. Some of them are so extreme that they become a danger to themselves and society. Unfortunately, for these extreme ones, there is only one solution at this stage of the human evolution —

small confined rooms with no proper rehabilitation facilities, which is a shame really. Most of them I think can still be rescued.

The other less extreme ones are those who will drain the very last drop of life force from you. You know who I'm talking about. For some of them there's hope, for others, I just don't know. I have tried with some and succeeded one baby step at a time, but there are others who just don't budge. Another wise statement from Christ was to not sow your seeds on dry and infertile land. I suppose this is the best advice one can take. Try your best, and if nothing happens, move on. There are a lot of others out there who need your love and attention, and these lost ones will get another chance in another life.

If you feel that someone is draining you in a situation that is difficult to get out of, focus on your inner being, creating a gentle force field around you. Be friendly but firm with this person, and let them understand that they are draining you instead of helping you. Sometimes being honest in a diplomatic way helps. People will be more attracted to your light as soon as you open the fountains of the One, so be on the look out. Most people are crazy with thirst for the light. They will be attracted to you like moths to the flame, and you need to shield them until they come to their senses. You will see, most will in due time.

Work

Ah yes, the thing that takes a third of our lives from us. Most of us cringe at the very thought of it. The lifelong battle to feed the hungry mouths and pay the debts. But we accept it. After all, it is written in the Bible that you will sweat for your bread. Yes, but the Bible didn't say you must hate it while you sweat. We sweat when we run or play tennis. We sweat when we make love or lie in the sun. And that is sweating with enjoyment. Why does work have to be any different? Why do we believe that we should suffer while we work? There are those lucky few who absolutely adore their work. If they can, why can't you? Is it because you were born under a bad sign or something? Or is it because you believed everything to be limited (including yourself) and that you must take what you can get?

You must remember that you get what you focus on. It is written in the Observer Effect. Yes, it doesn't come easy — nothing in this world does. But every journey starts with the first step, and then perseverance to the bitter end of the journey. It is part of the story you need to tell — the obstacle of try, try again. You must find within yourself the true destiny you were born with. This will become your work. We all know what we desire most in life. But under those layers and layers of superficial desires lies a deeper desire — the call to your destiny, your natural talent. Be it sport, art, observing others, loving nature, having a burning desire for justice — it is written in your destiny, and if you miss it, the unhappiness symptom will arise. The unhappiness in your work will tell you that you are missing your destiny. And if you do like the field you work in, but the environment pisses you off, then change it if you can, or leave it when you can't. Make your plans of escape; find your goal and do it. Find the ones like yourself who want to make it work and collaborate instead of competing like primitives. Remember that you cannot move a shadow without moving the shadow caster.

A book that can help you a lot with this issue is a book called *The Work You Were Born to Do* by Nick Williams. It inspired me a lot, and you will find a lot of practical solutions to your dilemma.

Just remember — you are the center of your universe, just like others are the centers of theirs. If you permit it, the light of the One can flow through you, and with focus you can change your destiny.

Money and Wealth

The root of all evil like so many believe. But it is not. Money is just another vibration that reflects the consciousness behind it. Those paper notes you hold in your hands are not money; they are mere representations of your self-believed "worth." Money is like your battery on this limited earth plane. It makes your "life" tick, or not. And the strangest thing of all is that it is for free. It naturally flows to those who know how to open up to it. When robbers break into the vault, the money naturally flows into their bags. When rogue companies con people out of their money, it naturally flows into their pockets. When a clever software programmer seizes the opportunity to put a PC in everyone's home, the money flows to him like crazy. Money does not care if you're good or bad. It flows to a space created for it, regardless of the owner of the space. It is, then, not the money that is evil, but the one creating the space for it. The one opening the space for money can just as well be one of the best people on earth, using his or her money for a good cause. Money can heal or destroy, depending on the hands that deal with it. In the end, money is like every other vibratory form of energy. It is no different from nuclear power that can be used to electrify homes or destroy a city, depending on who is using it. Money is vibratory energy that favors no name or rank, but flows to those who create space and affinity for it.

Now just how does one do that? Not easy, I must confess. A lot of self-help books might tell you otherwise, but everything in this life comes with hard work. But that is what makes it so rewarding in the end.

Let's compare all the money in the world with a massive lake of water with us all sitting on the shore, free to take as much as we can to our houses a few miles away. Some of us will walk all the way, take a handful and walk all the way back. Some soon realize that this is silly, so they think of clever ways to carry it to their homes, making containers from leaves or animal hides and so forth. But they too will lose some water along the way, the containers leaking here and there. Others will be more daring, and be parched while they design and build a machine that will pump the water from the lake to their homes while they relax and watch it come. Others will get jealous of the ingenuity and try to steal from them. The world of money in a nutshell.

The money world can be roughly divided into two categories. The "have a lots," and the "want a lots."

The "Want a Lots"
The "want a lots" see money as the solution to all their problems. If they can just win that blasted lottery, or crack that next deal, or just keep on working at breakneck intensity till they can take early retirement, then all their troubles will fade away. Sadly, this is mostly not the case. Money can't make you happy. It can only make you live in comfort miserably. You have to be happy, or as I've mentioned earlier, be content on the happiness-unhappiness wave before you get your millions. Can you imagine the disappointment of not being happy after you got your millions? You will have all those luxuries with discontent and wonder "what now?" What does a dog do with the wheel he has caught? What does a mountaineer do after he has reached the pinnacle of his climb? What happens now? Remember this before you go for it, because having a lot of money is no sin. It is what you do with it that could become a sin. So, if you want to know the secret of making more money, think about the reason for wanting more. This is the most important self-asked question before proceeding.

Now, if you want more money, you need to change your mind about the concept of it. Money is not notes, or gold or numbers in your bank account. Those are only the silly symbols we attach to the silly term money. Money is a worldwide vibratory energy force that flows to those who know how to create a low differential for it to flow to. It's like knowing that water always flows from top to bottom. In fact, money is a lot like water, as I've tried to explain with the lake metaphor. Most of us have terrible leaks in our containers called unclaimed tax returns, bad debt with silly interest rates due to overspending, high energy and water bills due to overuse and so forth. What does it help if the leaks are almost as large as the influx of new and fresh money? You need to address the leaks first. Claim your tax returns if you can, but most importantly, don't overspend on stuff you don't need. Don't make unnecessary debt. My granddad used to say, don't spend money you don't have—in the end that stuff you bought is the bank's and not yours. Wise words. If you have debt, then get rid of it as quickly as you can by not making more and "investing" your money in your debt. Try to put as much of the money you earn into that hole (without losing liquidity) and keep it that way. The interest you lose on bad debt is much more than the interest you earn in that measly little savings account. You will have to pay tax on that interest anyway! You are only kidding yourself. If you have to stretch to earn a mortgage, then rather rent till you have enough to get a decent mortgage, as there are a lot of hidden costs in getting a mortgage that could set you back severely. Save on your energy and water bills by living more economically. Thus in a nutshell—plug those holes before proceeding to making more money. Organize your life, and you will soon see all those hidden money leaks that you can easily fix.

Now to make more money, you need to find out where it is. Money is in the hands of everyone on this planet, ready to let it go in exchange for something you can offer that they desperately need. If you can scratch your head for a while, and realize in this time and age what people desperately need, then you can make more money. You need to do your homework and plan carefully before venturing into the unknown. Find your financial ally (and be careful of financial shape shifters—there are many) and ask him or her to help you in your venture. Don't just blindly trust financial advisors and the company you work for. Many people have lost their pension schemes due to companies sinking, taking the pension schemes right down to the depths with them. Search for books and people that can help you and advise you on money. Most importantly, use your given talents in this venture. They will pave the way for your new journey. In the end, when you follow your true destiny by listening to the voice within and opening your "bags" to money, it will come naturally.

The "Have a Lots"

The "have a lots" realize that with all that money the problems don't simply disappear. Sometimes those problems become larger. If it was all about the money before they started, reaching that pinnacle will show them that it doesn't matter how much of it you earn. Tons of money can't solve your problems or make you happy. There is still that addiction problem, or the angry outburst problem, or the infidelity, jealousy, death in the family, illness, and relationship problem. Money can't solve those. The "have a lots" who do feel content are those with clear-cut goals in their lives. They are the ones who realize this truth—that money can't buy you love, only ones who pretend to love to get some of your money. Money to them is there for comfort and leverage to help them reach goal after goal. They are the ones who realize that in order to help the poor, you must not be poor yourself. But unfortunately, these souls are few and far between. Most of the rich and powerful will blow endless amounts of money on themselves and their quirky little pleasures. Nothing wrong with blowing money on yourself; it is indeed you who earned it. But you must realize that having a lot of money is another test—to see what you will do with this gift. Are you using it just for cheap and egocentric entertainment, or are you balancing comfort with making a difference in the world? This applies especially to those who have wealth as well as influence or fame. Unfortunately, with fame and money comes the burden of responsibility, a heavy cross to carry for some who didn't expect it, thus buckling under the strain of it and finding themselves in trouble with the police and ending up in rehab centers. Best to accept that responsibility and balance it with your comforts. Instead of hiding away from it in your consumerism frenzies and boozed-up parties, accept it gracefully, and see where you can make a difference. Why does one need five yachts, private jets, and eight mansions in almost every country that are mostly unused anyway? What do you find in one drunken party after another except a hangover and guilt feelings because of your infidelity? It's a terrible waste of your money and time. Find a place or cause that needs help and use your money and influence to create a solution. And it doesn't help to throw your money into a needy pit because of guilt feelings, or one where corruption steals the money before it gets to the needy anyway. Don't sow your seeds unto dry land. There are many instances where money is wasted on feeding people cheap food time after time, where it would have been better to spend the money to try and teach the people how to look after themselves. Feeding the needy the whole time makes them expect to be looked after, and they stop looking after themselves. Knowledge is the best investment one can make. Remember the two coins, two stories analogy. In fact, charity starts at home, as my mother always says. Better to make sure your family and friends are set for life (even those you despise) by conditional trusts and so forth to save them from blasting it all on nonsense anyway. Better to invest in those with talent who will reach heights with a little help. So start your helping hand with your family and friends, and then spread it to the whole world. Balance your creature comforts with your responsibilities. You will be surprised how much more content you will feel. And if you are influential, try and teach people to respect each other and especially the earth — she desperately needs it.

On a final thought — don't let money be an obstacle to your journey. Make it a useful tool by wrapping your mind around it in the right way. Don't let it corrupt you. Use it to make yourself and the world fly.

Villains

Puppet Masters

As we've seen so far, your greatest Obstacle and Villain could be you, your ego and ignorance of the true nature of self and the universe being the culprit. But everything works on a singular as well as a universal principle, as said before; the large and the small, the external and the internal are seamlessly connected in the One. Just as ego and ignorance can be great obstacles in the growth of an individual spiritual being, so can they be obstacles to the entire humanity—the unawakened global consciousness of mankind plagued by what I call "Faust syndrome." As I've mentioned before, we are living in an oblivious state of limited thought. We see only the small and finite world that surrounds us, completely oblivious to the true nature of ourselves being connected to the limitless One and thus stealing each other's water of life or energy. If you link these individual oblivious "cells," they will create an organ of oblivion and ignorance, ruthlessly pursuing the need to quench that thirst for the water of life. This gives rise to an unseen Villain, evenly dispersed amongst ourselves in the shape of the Puppet Masters—the force that uses politics and plausible deniability to gain more money and power and thus oppress the meek with clever lies.

Kid yourself not. One political party will not be better than the other. Power corrupts, and absolute power corrupts absolutely, as the saying goes. Politicians are not there for you. They are there for themselves. Ego and ambition drive the political beast, nothing else. Even if an individual joins the political game to help his fellow man, he will either be corrupted or become a whistle-blower being scandalized or gotten rid of in some way or another. It can be seen in centuries of political history. "Et tu

Brute?," is an everyday thing. Neither love nor loyalty there. And politics is everywhere. It is a disease that spread into everything you touch, especially religion. The political beast is there to suck the masses dry with unfair taxes and live comfortably. Nothing wrong with the idea of tax, or contributing to the whole of the society, but these beasties abuse the goodness of the idea, just like communists abused the idea of "all for one." One political party will always make way for another by so called "democratic" votes of the masses, making the same so-called mistakes in the public's eyes. But these mistakes are not mistakes. It is the symptom of Faust syndrome. It is "Mine!" syndrome. Don't waste your money or energy on this beast. Nothing will change its nature. It is bathed in the darkness of "want and take, no matter what," even if it means war and the death of millions of innocent lives—the so-called collateral damage.

If we fight a war, we are merely playing to the Puppet Masters' show. Who in a war is right or wrong anyway? Looking back in the history of war, who were right, the Romans or the Greeks? The Trojans or the Spartans? Or were they all wrong in wanting more and more land and power, convincing their people to want more as well and to die gruesomely on battlefields while the emperor and his whores slept soundly in their beds? If two siblings fight over an ice cream, which one is right, your favorite one? And if someone like Hitler arose from the ashes of a country accused to be the cause of the First World War, what caused one man to have so much power over the collective psyche of a nation? What gave rise to such hatred, and why were the other parties so passive in watching things get out of hand in the first place? Why are we still permitting genocide after the brutal lessons learned from the Anglo-Boer war and the atrocities of the Nazis? Why do we still abide to the pull of the strings? We, the puppets, fight each other at the expense of our lives and dignity, while the Puppet Masters enjoy the show. They are the directors of this theatrical spectre, and we are unknowingly playing the actors' parts. If you have two actors, telling one that he is playing the part of a parent collecting his child from a teacher who was found to be a pedophile, and telling the other he is playing the part of an honest teacher who found out the parent is abusing the child, without one knowing about the other's role, you will have bloodshed on your stage. Divide and conquer is the name of the game, and we have been falling for this cheap trick for thousands of years.

You can't run away from the war either, as you are still attached to the Puppet Masters' strings, which stretch to the ends of the world. The strings of unfair taxes and bureaucratic laws, which are meant to protect the innocent and help the masses, but instead enslave the populace with stealth grins. They will use your hard-earned money to feed themselves on the richest dishes, fly in private jets and fund their illegal wars - the money you entrusted to them to look after society. And dare you try and defy them by not paying your taxes (like a dear old lady in the United Kingdom, trying to make a statement on how her council tax is misused), you land in the clink. No matter if you are a law-abiding senior citizen or not.

Face it — politics is all about money and power. It is a career for the ruthlessly ambitious, and not about leading a country and its people. If it were, we would all be living in wonderland. Since the time of complex communities like Egypt, Rome, Greece, China and maybe even before that if one looks at the data collected by Graham Hancock and similar writer-researchers about ancient civilizations, politicians have been ruthlessly ambitious, power-hungry war lords.

Sure, it's difficult to run a country. But that is because the damage was done thousands of years ago, inherited by the new power-hungry wolves, and then kept maintained or even worsened. The damage of mushroom syndrome — "keep them in the dark and feed them bullshit." Politicians all know that the power and money come from the masses. Keep the masses loyal with misinformation, average education and entertainment, while robbing them with unfair taxing. The ambitious ones, prone to Faust syndrome, will educate themselves to the highest and ruthlessly chase that dream of top executive with the mansion and the jet. If they sniff the devil in it and resist, they will risk losing everything, and thus they turn a blind eye while pursuing the "dream," rationalizing the black seeds they sow.

Go have a peep at our history. You will see this pattern around every corner of every civilization. Rome was an excellent example, and we haven't changed from them that much. Our architecture still reflects the era (especially government buildings, how strange), we still build humongous entertainment arenas where gladiators entertain the masses (only now less bloody) and we still worship the gods (stars and celebrities). We are still taxed to almost death with the money used for more than just running the country, as corruption is everywhere, in some governments just better concealed than others. On the tax matter, think about it. We have tax for about everything—income tax, sales tax, inheritance tax, road tax, council tax, airport tax and even tax on your pension—nicely spread out in little packets so the masses won't notice. In Victorian Britain, you were even taxed for your windows! It was called window tax, and people took out their windows and closed them with bricks, filling their homes with darkness only to save a bit of money! Now, they are planning to implement the so-called "green taxes" to "help" the earth and her environmental issues with taxes like a refuse bag tax (tax you when your black bags are too full), higher taxes when flying, taxes on driving too much and even taxes on your house if it's not green enough. The funny part is, we can't stop flying, we can't stop driving, (trains are privatized and too expensive) and it will cost a fortune to "greenify" your house in a small period of time. This they know, using the environmental issue as an excuse to get more money from your already empty pocket. Environmental issues can only be challenged with proper education and action, not by punishment in the form of taxes! It is these very same politicians and their associated corporate capitalism monsters who created the earth issues anyway — pillaging and consuming for centuries (especially the latter) to gain more and more. They feel nothing for the earth or "her" problems. They only see this disease they created as another quick scam to make more money by putting a name on the tax. They look at the people, see they are worried about the environment, and voila — environmental tax is born. If politicians were really worried about the environment, they would have aggressively done something more constructive about it rather than fooling the ignorant environmentalists with stealth taxing.

Now tax is fair enough if it were utilized responsibly without sucking dry the community. Tax would have been great in the hands of poets and philosophers, as Plato put it. But unfortunately, those masses of money are all going to waste, spent on ridiculously high managerial salaries and the luxuries accompanying them. Just think about it for a while. If we take Great Britain for instance, with a population of roughly 58 million people, let's say only 40 million paid their taxes, and we use a fictional character of an average income, we can work out a rough estimate of how much potential money a country could have to spend on tax.

Let's take Joe Ordinary. Joe makes about a thousand eight hundred pounds before income tax is deducted. Income tax for Joe runs at about six hundred and fifty pounds for his particular salary. Thus £650 for the taxman, and £1150 for Joe. Now comes the monthly council tax, which runs at about a hundred pounds a month in Joe's area. Thus £750 for the taxman, and £1050 for Joe. Joe buys food for his family running at about £300 a month (sales tax included), that will leave Joe with roughly £750 for the month and the taxman with roughly £800. Joe has to drive to work and home everyday, costing him about £100 a month (fuel tax inclusive), leaving Joe with £650 and the taxman with roughly £840. Then comes congestion tax, as Joe lives in a big city, and so it goes. As you can see, the taxman has already got more money per month than Joe has left. Joe must still pay for his monthly rent, his children's education (which tax covered in the past) and other "little" things. In the end, Joe will have nothing left to save, while there will be about £900 in the taxman's pocket from poor old Joe alone. So, let's make it easier and assume that the taxman roughly makes an average of a thousand pounds from one of the estimated 40 million taxpayers (the other ten million lives on benefits or evade tax etc.). This will give us a very rough estimate of about £40 billion per <u>month</u> for the taxman. In America, it will probably be about $280 billion per month (if roughly 18 million people are excluded as piggybackers).That is a vast amount of money, and is still not enough, as public services are quickly going down the hill and sold to the private sector, where you have to pay more for the same silly service — expensive trains, toll roads and private health insurance to name but a few. So, where is all that money going then, if not into the public sector? Let me just add this — the controversial Iraq war has cost the United States an estimated $200 billion plus so far, and the end is still not in sight by a long shot, as Middle Eastern conflict just escalates. It is strange to notice how the armed forces are glamorously advertising for youngsters to join them, conditionally paying for their education and then court-martialling them when they want out, not satisfied by causing "collateral damage" as they kill innocent women and children.

The Puppet Masters are hidden not only in the political but also in the religious arena (using politics as well). It can clearly be seen in the world religions where entire nations and civilizations were wiped from the face of the earth "in the name of God" or where intellectual and challenging individuals, especially women, were burnt alive "in the name of God." When a religion damages and destroys, it is not a religion of love of which any good-natured god would approve. Even if you think that you are doing a tribe a favor by replacing their "idols" with your god. The Northern, Central and South Americans, the Africans and Aboriginal tribes were rich and strong in culture until western influx—the west's destructive ways and "god" forced upon them with rape, pillage and slavery. Now most of Africa and Central and South America are poverty-stricken areas, further exploited of their natural resources, the Puppet Masters getting fatter, while the "natives" get the scraps as well as a dictator (placed there by the Puppet Masters) and a land that slowly dies. Religion is a mask bathed in the fear of a jealous god, a fear created by the Puppet Masters themselves, to control and manipulate the masses—you and me.

These same Puppet Masters can be seen in massive corporations. While they live the good life, playing with the company shareholders' money, the work force, which is the flesh and bone of a company, live average lives in fear of job cuts. How many times have companies fired thousands of their workers, while the bosses laugh all the way to the bank? The money is always more important than those faceless drones "down there." And when the poor workers ask for their pension, it has gone down with the company. When they look to the government for help, the government shrugs its shoulders, "too busy with a war right now."

Let's take a closer look at what Faust syndrome is doing to you and the world.

Social Services

Have a look at what is happening to the British national health trust, where highly paid managers become more, and the "drones" and their services less. Managers are paid obscene amounts of money to "oversee" the destruction of a health care facility that should be for free (paid by our tax money) and be excellent, as it is in a "rich and developed" world. All previous social services were sold out to the private sector—aviation, railway, telecommunications, energy and now health. It seems like a good idea to hand social services over to the "private sector," but, in the private sector money always comes first. Profit above person is the name of the game. The services become cheap and tacky, while the prices go up. Trains in the private sector have become overcrowded (overbooked) and extremely expensive. Where in a so-called first world country have you seen people paying more than 70 pounds for a ticket, only to sit on the floor in front of a dirty toilet because there are no seats? It is a nightmare to fly economy these days, queuing like animals for the slaughter as we are all searched like criminals (due to an overblown terrorism factor). And health—if you end up in a private emergency room, you will be asked for cash or insurance certificate before helped. If you can't afford it, you are shipped to the "plebe" emergency room, where you will wait up to four hours to be seen while understaffed and overworked doctors and nurses will do their best. This does not serve the community. It serves the pockets of the Puppet Masters. So now that the governments are free from the yoke of aviation, railway, telecommunication and soon to be health, where is all that "saved" money going? We will not pay less tax when we go "private." Instead, we will pay tax as well as extra fees for the private services in the likes of education (free education is quickly becoming a thing of the past), roads (with extra congestion and soon to follow "green" taxes, never mind the toll roads) and of course health (which is sinking like a ship, forcing us to go private). And did I mention the privatized water-supplying companies? Privatized water companies can afford to lose millions of tons of wasted water per year (due to unfixed leaks) because of their high premiums, making millions in profit while they give you "clean" water so filled with chemicals it will make your head spin. Why then is tax still on the rise in the shape of stealth taxes? Why do we have to pay tax as well as for private social services, which wouldn't have been necessary if the taxpayers' billions were not mismanaged? Social services should stay social and not be mixed or sold out to the abused capitalistic private sector. The taxpaying public has the right to at least an excellent free health care service. That is the least a highly paid government can do for its people out of gratitude, but no. They will squeeze every little drop of blood from the masses. It has always been the case since ancient history. Why would they change now?

The only difference between the ancient Puppet Masters and the current ones is stealth mode, hiding their malice behind the stealth grins, which hides their tactics.

Private Services

Faust syndrome has seeped into everything we touch. Most companies will give you the worst service and products for the highest amount of money. We bought a sofa from a well-known and trusted company, picking it from a catalogue, and then waited two months before it arrived with a broken leg. I had the choice of sending it back and waiting another month or so, or taking the broken-leg sofa as is. I took the broken sofa and fixed it myself. It was then that I realized just how cheaply it was made. Some of the frame was cardboard, never mind pressed wood. I had to re-enforce it! I bought three electronic products from a very well-known company, and they all started giving trouble after the warranty expired. And when you inquire about it, they will give you a cold shoulder, placing the blame on you for not taking care of the product! Look at houses these days—they cost a fortune, but are all blueprinted from a single design, and then cheaply built with cemented brick and plasterboard walls, nicely finished off in "good looking" but cheap trickery. How long have supermarket and fast-food chains fooled us with "healthy" products, only for us to find out later by independent investigation that those products were terribly unhealthy and disguised with cheap trickery? Pharmaceutical companies are aggressively marketing their new products, turning, for instance, normal aging cycles like menopause into a "disease" that needs to be cured, going head-on with nature. Not too mention the scandalous treatment of schizophrenia (which has been shown in the seventies to be "curable" with a forty-day support regime only!). And now, as the first ridiculed eastern and so called spiritual healing techniques are gaining popularity under the masses and making more money, the orthodox and dogmatic reductionists are starting to dig their fingers into it as well, as can be seen with acupuncture in Britain. Open your eyes and you will see Faust syndrome in almost everything in your life.

The Puppet Masters and their well-oiled Faust machine are everywhere. They will use anything to gain money and power. No matter what great idea one devises, whether it be communism, capitalism, socialism or any other –ism you can think of, they will be there to take control of it.

Moving into Act III

We have met our greatest possible Villain—ourselves, reflected back at us in the macrocosm as the Puppet Master's Faust syndrome. In Act III, we will face our obstacles created by us over the last few centuries and overcome them with ideas of an ideal world, or face a horrible outcome. Furthermore we will also explore the background noise most of us feel around the corner, the whisper called the apocalypse. But don't despair and don't lose hope! This is a journey to awakening. It is our story, and in all good stories there are countless obstacles plaguing the Hero. We must face our Villains and obstacles in order to finish the story. And a good ending is definitely in sight.

ACT III

"you shall know the truth, and the truth shall make you free."

Words by Christ from John 8:32

Faust Syndrome and Its Created Obstacles

So far, we have seen that archetypes and metaphors are reflections of life and vice versa. We know that the macrocosm reflects the microcosm, as seen with modern physics (holographic theory, string theory and fractal mathematics), Tantra, Kabbalah and other ancient schools of thought. We must remember what we have discovered so far—ourselves as well as everything we experience, are all connected to the One in body, mind and spirit. Thus each action, no matter how small, has an equal reaction, which is well-demonstrated by the so-called Butterfly Effect.

As far as we know, the human "ape" has been around for at least a hundred thousand years in the form we possess today. But it is only in the last few centuries, especially the current one, that we have created an impact so large that it threatens to destroy everything we hold dear, without our even realizing it. Most of us go about our business everyday—living the ordinary life of getting up in the morning, feeding the kids, doing the metro, working in a job you hate, doing the metro again, getting home, making food, watching TV and going to bed, only to repeat the whole cycle over and over again. The only way we get relief from this boring cycle is with that part before going to bed—TV. Actually, TV features a bit more in this equation. Most of us get up with it in the morning, watching all the dire news on the box while we force down a quick unhealthy breakfast. We find TVs on the metros and some buses, café's, pubs and bars. We find them in airports, airplanes and even in hospitals at every sick bed, keeping us "calm" (sedated comes to mind). And indeed we need to be kept calm by the Puppet Masters, for things are much worse than we think.

TV keeps us frozen in a zombie state with its endless reality shows, soap operas, sport channels and bad news—all broadcasters owned by a single few Puppet Masters, controlling what we see and who gets famous and how these famous ones should act and dress (or else). And in between each show, a glossy advert to "program" you to want what the rich and famous ones (controlled by the media Puppet Masters) want. This in conjunction with the corporate Puppet Masters that want to sell you the cheap but glossy products you "so want." And as you buy these things, you realize you just can't afford it, so you make debt, running obscene amounts of interest, skimmed by the bank Puppet Masters. In order to pay this debt, you slave away for the same corporate Puppet Masters who sack you and steal your pension scheme when they "make cuts" to save money or go "bankrupt." And after you slave away for a month, the bureaucratic Puppet Masters will take their taxes, which they will mismanage as previously mentioned. As Ronald Firbank, a British novelist put it, "The world is so mismanaged, one hardly knows to whom to complain."

Now, if you remember, in this limited illusory world we find some part of our consciousness in, there are rules or principles. The most important one is that of balance, clearly seen in the language of this universe. When you take from the one side, the other side must give. The taker gets more, and the giver less. This is what is happening every second of your ordinary life as the capitalist monster eats our mother—Earth. While you "gain" that next meal, shirt, PC game, car and house, skillfully supplied by the Puppet Masters, the earth loses a bit more vitality in her struggle to keep the spoiled children "happy," for she loves us so much that she is dying to fulfill our every wish.

We have for a long time believed that we are the most important species on this planet and that it is our God-given right to suck this "dead rock" we live on (as coined by the Victorians) as dry as a bone. We simply don't realize just what we are part of. James Lovelock, a British biochemist, conceived of the Gaia theory, which states that the earth acts like a giant living organism, constantly regulating herself to maintain homeostasis (a state in which life is possible). He carefully looked at the profound interconnectedness of all the species on the earth, and realized that the composition of the earth (rock and molten metal responsible for the magnetic field shielding us from the sun's radiation), her oceans as well as all her organisms, work in unison to keep life possible in a vast and deadly space. Earth is, after all, the only living planet we have so far discovered in the vastness of space.

Earth is like a massive body, her rock and molten metal her skeleton, her ocean her blood, and her biomass her organs. Let's take a look at one of the many examples — trees (the most significant example of the plant family in this example). Trees, with their other plant cousins, are the only organisms on this planet that can use and change sunlight energy into something useful to the rest of the species. The leaves of the trees contain organelles called chloroplasts that contain chlorophyll, a biochemical compound that can change sunlight into simple as well as complex sugars by using the carbon dioxide we as humans (and other animals) exhale. The simple sugars are stored in the shape of fruits and vegetables made for us to eat, and in return we (humans and animals) spread their kind via the seeds of the fruit. After the carbon has been freed from the carbon dioxide, and used to create sugars with the sunlight energy, the tree will release oxygen into the air, the gas we as humans and animals absolutely rely on to survive. Thus, the trees and ourselves are seamlessly connected and dependent on each other. They give us our oxygen and food, and we give them their carbon and spread their seeds. Trees also function as water pumps in the water cycle, releasing millions of tons of water vapor into the atmosphere, which will fall down onto the earth in the form of rain. Without trees, there will be no rain, no food and no oxygen — no life. And yet, we are destroying a surface area roughly the size of Florida each year worldwide. At this rate, we will have no trees in less than sixty years. "But what about sustainable forests?", you might ask. Trees take decades to reach an age where they play a significant role in gas exchange and the water cycle. The so-called sustainable forests are not good enough, and they are only a few species of trees, while ancient and diverse species are lost. The old, wise and diverse are replaced by a few saplings that are prone to disease as they find themselves in unnatural environments. And strength lies in diversity. We are destroying the earth's lung-heart-liver complex (gas exchange, water pump and food storage) because we like Swedish-style wooden tables and beef burgers (thousands of acres of forest are removed per day to create pastures for cattle). We are completely insane! Those of you who have not known the severity were blinded by mushroom syndrome — kept in the dark and fed bullshit.

Let's get perspective by using what we've learned so far.

We are all One, interconnected. As above, so below; as without, so within applies everywhere, from the smallest super string to the largest galaxy. It can clearly be seen in the Gaia concept, where the earth and all her species, including us, shape a magnificent creature adrift in space. As I've mentioned before, we can liken her crust to that of a skeleton, her oceans and rivers to her blood and vascular system, and her species to her organs. Plants (especially the trees in rain forests) can thus be seen as the heart-lung-liver complex (water pump action, gas exchange, food production and storage), while the animals can be likened to all the other organs that transport and clean all the organic matter created by the plants from pure sunlight. It would seem that the human race became Gaia's nervous tissue — the thinking organ or brain (not mind). We are the only self-conscious beings on the planet (as far as western science can prove, which I seriously doubt). With our expansion, globalization and especially internet, we have created a super connected information network where individual nerve cells (humans) can communicate with each other, just as the brain evolved and functions. But unfortunately, this brain is malfunctioning in more than one way.

Just as a single human can become self-abusive or get a disease, so can Gaia—as above, so below; as without, so within. Gaia's brain, the human race, is self-abusive, has malignant cancer, and an autoimmune disease. Let me explain by starting with autoimmune diseases and then cancer.

Autoimmune disease is where the body's immune or defense system does not recognize the self. In other words, your immune system is attacking certain parts of your body as if they were intruders. A good example is SLE or Systemic Lupus Erythematosus, where the immune system attacks almost every organ in the body, which slowly and painfully leads to multi-organ failure and death. We are doing exactly the same. We are not recognizing Earth or Gaia as Self. Failing to see her as ourself, we attack her for resources, deforestation and aggressive mining being good examples. But we are more likened to a cancer. All of us know about cancer, for it affects one in three of us in certain parts of the world. We know of it, but do not know it per se.

Cancer starts at cellular level. Normal cells keep replenishing themselves to keep the organ they belong to healthy and functional by replication. Cells replicate or reproduce themselves by splitting into two. This whole process starts at DNA (cellular program) level. The younger cells will then mature and differentiate into what they were destined to become—that is, the default liver cell will become a liver cell, the default infant blood cell the mature blood cell etc.—until the system or organ is formed. As mentioned before, each cell has the entire body's blueprint in three to four percent of its DNA (which yet again reflects the holographic nature of it) and miraculously only activates the small part of the DNA in which it is destined to become. Thus the liver cell will only have the "liver part" of the DNA activated while the rest of the liver cell's DNA is inactive. Somehow, cells "know" what they are destined to become, and do this as if by magic. When there are enough young and healthy cells to keep the organ going, the older cells will die — just like what happens on a grander scale with plant, animal and human systems. It's the law of nature, following the principle of "as above, so below." Normal cells also have thorough communication with each other, as well as with the entire body, via the nervous system and endocrine or hormonal system, hence a normal running system. With cancer cells the problem starts when their normal replication mechanism goes haywire. Cells replicate uncontrollably and never differentiate into the cells they were meant to become. They keep on replicating without differentiating (not becoming a specific cell in a specific organ) and become an enormous mass of undifferentiated calcifying tissue. These masses are extremely energy hungry due to their uncontrollable multiplying, which suffocates the normal surrounding tissue and releases toxins into the bloodstream. The mass of "mad" cells, or tumor, will eventually grow so fast that the body can't keep up with energy and oxygen demands. Parts of the tumor will rot, lose foothold and then spread to other parts of the body where they continue this vicious cycle. This will continue until the body is so depleted of its energy and filled with toxins that it dies, taking the cancer with itself to the grave.

The abovementioned scenario is eerily reflected in human activity. We also multiply uncontrollably, at present being six and a half billion individuals, our numbers increasing exponentially. We need food and water, thus energy, but not like normal organisms. We are the most energy and water hungry species on the planet, using forty percent of the earth's total possible energy supply and more than fifty percent of the total water supply. And that is only one species out of the millions. We "organize" ourselves in "calcified" masses — concrete cities, which sprawl into nature for hundreds of square miles, suffocating the "normal tissue of Gaia" and dumping their toxins into her rivers, or bloodstream if you will. We also spread to other areas as soon as one area's resources are depleted, and continue with the same pattern of destruction. And the end? It will be the same, of course - Death to Gaia and the cancer who feeds upon her. No exception. And that end is much closer than we think. Gaia does not just suffer from the human cancer, but also from human autoimmune disease. She gets attacked from more than one angle, and all by the same being — the human ape. Go and have a look at statistics, and you will shudder when you see how little rain forest is left, how much desert is taking its place per year, how much fresh water is lost and how much carbon dioxide you as a family release into the air each day with your "normal" western day, which of course is augmenting the global warming threat. Global warming alone is a disaster quickly tightening its clammy fingers around the neck of Gaia, and thus you. We produce way too much carbon dioxide with our fossil fuel power-hungry orgy, which in turn cannot be dealt with by a healthy forest situation, let alone the fact that we are destroying thousands of acres of carbon-absorbing forests per day. Atmospheric carbon increases exponentially, traps the heat of the sun in our atmosphere, and causes the temperature to rise. This is Gaia's fever, as James Lovelock puts it. And her fever will destroy her organs, just as a high fever in an organism denatures its proteins and thus, organ structures. The heat is evident in the state of the glaciers and polar ice caps. They are melting at such a rate that the effects can already be seen, and worst of all, will affect us much more in the near future. Antarctica is for the first time in thousands of years losing her peninsula; thousands of square miles of ice are breaking away and falling into the ocean. This per se does not "worry" some scientists too much (concerning the rise in sea levels), but what about those millions of tons of glacier kept from slipping into the sea by that very shelf? Furthermore, this has kept all that freshwater out of the ocean, which is now flowing freely into it. The melting polar caps are diluting the ocean's saline content. This leads to an unfriendly environment for a lot of species, especially plankton and algae, which not only form the staple feed of thousands of species but also help in regulating the carbon problem. Thus, thousands of other species will die, in their turn causing thousands of others to die because of everything's interconnectedness. This will also worsen the global warming problem, due to the lack of algae absorbing the carbon dioxide. Furthermore, the diluted waters will cause major ocean currents to slow down, which is evident in observation of the Gulf Stream. It has slowed down more than twenty percent in the last fifty years. This in turn will cause severe changes in climate, of which the effects can already be seen. Noticed the increased number and severity of hurricanes worldwide in the last few years? Noticed the severe droughts in some areas, while preposterous rainfall in others causes severe flooding and loss of upper fertile soil? Noticed how rain forests are not just killed by us, but die because of drought? And we have to think about the white nature of the polar caps, reflecting much of the sun's heat. As the polar caps melt, the heat-reflecting white properties of the ice is replaced by the heat-attracting black of deep ocean, which makes things even worse, speeding up the whole process. And this is just the global warming issue.

There are other issues that will affect us as a human race more acutely in the next few decades. There is over-fishing, with most species depleted by ninety percent in the last forty years, and thus no fish for our children. There is topsoil erosion with fifteen million hectares lost per year, thus no fertile land for our children. Seven and a half million hectares of rain forest are lost per year, thus no food, rain nor oxygen for our children. And so it goes. The list is endless. The world already has 180 million undernourished children and 275 million starving people, of which approximately 12,000 die per day. This number is sure to rise as fast as the abovementioned problems increase. And the problems and their severity are getting worse by the day.

But the west feels nothing. The U.S. alone spends about twenty-two billion dollars on diets per year as fifty-eight million

Americans are overweight, of which forty million are obese. An average of forty percent of Britain is overweight. We shop (most products made by developing countries getting a raw deal), we sip our coffee in franchised café's (the coffee produced in developing countries by women and children getting a raw deal), drive in our SUV or MPV and live in our old-fashioned central heated houses (depleting the fossil fuel reserve and worsening the global warming problem). We live the "good life" because our super capitalist Puppet Masters suck the developing countries dry of their resources and abuse ignorant young men and women to fight their illegal wars to gain more and more, while keeping our heads neatly tucked in consumerism sands with their glossy television adverts. We are obsessed with diets, plastic surgery, fashion trends and celebrities' lives, while others, especially women and children are abused by unfair trade laws, and fall victim to male-dominated wars, being the statistical "collateral damage." We are slowly dying with our Mother, while we grin with our heads high on the opium of consumerism. The capitalist consumerism orgy is nearly over, and there will be nothing left for our children. As was written in blood on the wall in the film *28 days later*, "The end is extremely fucking nigh," and we are not noticing it! We need to wake up now, and work like crazy in order to make a difference.

"But," you might say, "you said it's an illusion anyway. Why spoil our fun?" Yes, it is a holographic vibratory illusion. But we will be stuck in this illusory dimension until we have learned to tell the story the right way. We cannot make the quantum leap to another dimension before having the desired elevated vibration. Our collective vibration is much too low, and as things are going now, this story is going to end in horror, with tales told of battles fought with sticks and stones and break-outs of disease and even cannibalism due to depleted recourses. Looking back at what we have learned in Act II, we know that we create our own reality through the Observer Effect. Source flows through us and manifests our thoughts into this material illusion. There is no one else to blame for it. God, the Source or the One, "gave" us free will. I spoke to many a person (especially fundamentalist Christians) who believes that humans are the most important thing in the universe and that earth was given to us to use as much as we like. They point at the words in the Bible stating that we should "multiply and flourish." Yes, so it does, but nowhere in the Bible does it say that we should multiply out of proportion to resources and egocentrically destroy her. To this, they answer that God will save us before the earth dies completely, giving us a new earth. Oh, really? That same god who permitted millions of Jews (his chosen people) to die at the hands of the Nazis? The same god who permitted millions of women to burn to death on bonfires at the delight of catholic leaders? I must disagree. God gave us free will, which is a very great responsibility. We were created in His/Her image—thus we are creators of our world. Like all heroes, we will have to face the fact that we alone are responsible to challenge and defeat our obstacles and demons. If we don't, we will face extinction. It sounds grim, and it is. But we are the creators of our reality through the Observer Effect. If we were free enough to create a nightmare of war, destruction and oppression so far, then we are free to create paradise. The future is not set if you follow the Uncertainty Principle. There are endless possible quantum futures awaiting us, and it is our choice and privilege to choose our future. Let us decide to choose the right one. Let us see how.

Recognizing the True Root of "Evil"

Before you can slay the "evil" dragon, you will need to know its weak points. Know your enemy as you know yourself, and soon you will find the enemy within.

We must remember that this dragon, especially the Puppet Master in body, is not the real Villain or enemy, but a mere reflection of the apathy inside ourselves to correct the unbalanced harmonics of the severity-mercy equation (found in the Kabbalistic tree of life), where severity is in the majority, leading to oppression and cruelty. The "merciful" or the meek can no longer live in apathetic oblivion. We can no longer believe the lies of "us versus them." "They" over in the other country are not all wrong or evil. So-called evil is nicely spread out amongst all of us, and if you look deep within yourself, you fill find your dark half smiling back at you malevolently. It is waiting for you to fall prey to the Puppet Master's Faust syndrome. You have to open your eyes and recognize the ones under the spell of Faust syndrome, as they too are spread out amongst all of us, even in places least expected. Just like cancer cells are naturally recognized and taken care of in the body, so we must recognize the "cancer" amongst ourselves and, worst of all, within ourselves, and deal with it. Think of how many political and church officials have been exposed as either thieves or child molesters for a start. You have to look for them hiding in the waving grass of the masses. If you follow the trail of social discontent, there will you find the shadowy trail of the Puppet Masters.

Imagine this - What would happen if all soldiers, from the "right" as well as the "wrong" side, should one morning wake up, realizing this truth, and unite on the battleground, joining hands and refusing the bidding of their war masters by saying "no more"? If everyone united and said no to corrupt officials who tricked them into doing their dirty work, who would stop them? The hundred or so Puppet Masters in their pinstripe suits, with their weak and pale little bodies so accustomed to the conditioned air and fancy meals?

No need for war against them. They are too few, and war is the game they play, not the meek and the mild. The entire planet should just stop, look at each other in realizing that we are being played as fools, and say: "no more". We need nothing more to do but to unite and cut the strings and bring balance to the severity-mercy curve. Say no to top-heavy governments' officials thinking for us, tapping our potential and riding on our backs. No dividing and conquering, playing two ignorant fools off against each other.

We need to dispel them by letting them know they have no power over us, for it is indeed us who give them their power. We need to live and let live, give and receive. Not take, take, and take! We don't need to fight each other to survive. We have powerful intellects connected to the One. We need only collaborate. If bees and ants can do it, so can we. We are all one, and we should use our collective consciousness to collaborate, each and every one adding to the collaboration with his or her unique gifts.

And most importantly, we must not fall prey to the Faust syndrome, which created the Puppet Masters in the first place. One should never have power over the other — never. Communism was a cheap way to enslave the masses by telling them all are equal, except the Puppet Masters of course. They were more equal than the masses, just as in George Orwell's *Animal Farm* (all animals are equal, but some are more equal than others). Capitalism seems like a good idea, but this too is abused, and in the wrong and greedy hands causes the destruction of our planet. With communism, society is more important than the individual, and with capitalism, the individual is more important than society, and the earth for that matter. Neither is right, as they are both ends of a seesaw, where imbalance will lead to destruction.

There is no need for a centralized governing body to rule the others. It always leads to corruption. Instead we should learn from nature, and even our bodies. We should live in a cellular way. Each individual cell (person) possessing the knowledge of the entire being in which it lives (as each cell has the entire DNA code of the being), and only differentiating into the appropriate cell (person) it is destined to become. All liver cells, for example, will unify to form the liver (seamlessly connected to all other systems of the body). The liver does not have its own governing center; neither does the spleen nor heart nor any other organ in one's body. They can function on their own. The brain, some would say, is the governing body, but if closely observed, one would see that the brain is only a focused area of nerve tissue that spreads out through the whole body, seamlessly connected to every part of it via synapses and hormones, forming one unified communication system with all other systems. There are numerous other organisms flourishing with the most primitive nervous systems you can think of. The human brain itself is only part of the body's communication system and can be roughly divided into a lower or primitive part, and a higher functioning part. The primitive part is there to adjust and tweak the already autofunctioning systems, and the higher part for the "intelligence" stuff. According to what we have discovered so far, the brain acts like a receiver of various frequencies (ranging from light and sound to more unlikely frequencies) and processes them for your mind-spirit union to function on the earth plane, thus rendering the brain in service of mind-spirit-God. We must remember that the body can live with most of the "higher" brain destroyed, but cannot live if one of the other organs is destroyed. Without the liver and kidneys, for example, death would follow in days, while without the lungs or heart, death follows in seconds. The brain is mostly there for higher functioning, and if its power is abused (by losing connection to mind-spirit-God), it will lead to destruction of the body as well as itself. Take substance abuse or promiscuity, for example. The same applies to our society. Society is a mere seamless part in the cosmic continuum. From strings, to subatomic particles, to atoms, to molecules, to cells, to organs, to individuals, to society, to the entire biosphere - all one continuum. We form Mother Earth's brain (not her mind) by being the most advanced species in her biosphere, connected by the information highway and the undiscovered collective consciousness, and are unfortunately self-destructing just like a substance abuser. This can also be seen especially by looking at the pathogenesis of cells becoming cancerous hypothesized by Nobel Prize winner Dr. Otto Heinrich Warburg. Intoxicated cells lose their connection with each other and the larger unified body and start functioning in a singular and autonomous way due to toxin-damaged cell membranes. Their cell membranes are so filled with toxins that they can't use the body's oxygen or communicate with the body, and thus go into survival mode with their own agenda, fermenting (surviving by means of anaerobic energy production) and causing more toxins, which eventually damage the internal structures, especially the DNA. This will lead to uncontrollable and undifferentiated cell production, the cause for tumors spreading and suffocating the host. This is exactly what is happening to us. We are so intoxicated by fear-laden dogma, that we have lost our connection to each other and the One. We function autonomously, thinking we have to fight each other in order to survive, and by doing so, we destroy each other as well as our body—Earth—while we multiply and spread like wildfire. This is because we live noncellular, our connection to the One and each other severed. "As without" is also reflected "within." The macrocosm of the Gaian cancer (portrayed by us) is reflected in the microcosm of the growing cancer tendency in humans. As Gaia is filled with more and more toxins by her cancer (humans), so will it intoxicate her "cells," of which we form a great part. Furthermore, the "cells" (humans) of Gaia are "unhappy," subconsciously knowing that they are slaves to modern society and feeling trapped and hopeless, reflected in psychiatric disorders like depression, leading to self-abuse ranging from alcohol and drugs to eating disorders. And as previously mentioned, hopelessness (Type C personalities) has a tendency to suppress killer-T cells, and thus causes cancer to flourish. It is also seen in the obesity problem of humans, where the obese individuals reflect the highly consumerist society they live in. The United States and United Kingdom have two of the highest obesity rates in the world, and are coincidentally also two of the highest consumerist countries in the world. The disharmonic state of Gaia is reflecting within as well as without. It is a phenomenon seen in sound waves called reverberation. As everything is vibration, so the disharmony of the individual and the collective are reverberating within each other.

If we would live and function as a cellular society, a super confederation so to speak, things would be much better. Each individual would take responsibility not only for him- or herself (for a start without relying on a governing body, which gives it its power in the first place) but for one another as well. As in collaborating in film or music (as it should be, and not The Player style like in Hollywood), all the artists should realize that the arguments that will follow are for the work of art and not for the individual's ego boost. If another has an idea that does more for the project than yours, then you need to stand down gracefully and look for another opportunity to contribute to the project, not your ego. Even in the process of friendly argument to come to a decision have you collaborated. Every action has a reaction, and if intelligently applied will reach greater heights. Thus every small contribution helps.

In a typical western hospital hierarchy of today, the cleaners are seen as nothing important. Doctors will walk past them, not even acknowledging their existence (I've seen it countless times). If the cleaners should all become ill at the same time one day, who will clean the vomit and blood from the floors? The precious surgeon, nurse or manager? With no cleaners in a hospital, the hospital will soon end up a festering mess with super bugs everywhere.

The same applies to the catering staff. Without them, there's no food, and patients need food to supply their bodies to heal. Will the precious surgeon, nurse or manager cook for the patients? Without the nurses, will the doctors answer the nagging bells and wipe shitty bottoms? Without the doctors, will the managers diagnose the rheumatoid arthritis or do a cesarean section when needed? And with the managers gone, the doctors, nurses, cleaners and all the other "less important" hospital staff will simply have a meeting once and again, and decide on a rota of who will take care of the administrative jobs now and then (maybe even getting a bit of extra pay for the trouble). See? We don't need a top-heavy structure, and everyone from the so-called bottom up has their vital place in the cascade of life, except those pinnacles of the pyramid. Take them away, and you only have a pyramid without the pinnacle (which is negligible if you look at the Great Pyramid of Gizeh—it has no pinnacle, but is impressive none the less).

In an orchestra, the violins are no more important than the cellos. The French horns no more important than the trumpets. They are all equal in creating the soothing sound of the greater work, each contributing with its own unique sound. So are we. We are all equal, contributing to life, humanity and the sustenance of our mother earth in our own unique ways. Some of us are artists, not merely entertaining but also reflecting the metaphor of life. Some of us are scientists, bringing about technological advancement. Some are health care workers who help in keeping all the others healthy, and some are health care assistants helping health care workers in turn . We all form an orchestra to play the melody of life. "And what about the conductor?", you might ask. Good question, simple answer. The conductor lies not in one person nor in a governing body, but in the One. The conductor of an orchestra is seamlessly part of the orchestra, feeling the music as much as the other players, unifying them by being the only one not concentrating on a single instrument but on the music as a whole. The conductor is then the mirror of the music as a whole for all the musicians, a way to communicate with each other through the likes of another. If the musicians as well as the conductor are wholeheartedly immersed in the musical piece and not themselves and their egos, then the music will soar to its greatest heights. In this egoless collaboration lies the connection to the One—the real conductor—that will inspire. Managers or CEOs should, then, not be the ones who bark orders from "above," but be responsible for unifying or conducting the orchestra. He or she is no more important than any other. He or she is simply the liaison or communication officer, the glue that binds the strands into unison. Without the glue, the strands will not be unified, but without the strands, the glue has no purpose.

Another important thing to note is that no matter how "good" the governing body is, without proper communication there will be chaos. This chaos is usually worsened by centralization, as the governing body is almost completely severed from the workforce. A better way is for a top-heavy governing body to disperse and decentralize and form a coherent collaboration with the whole workforce. Thus, in each and every individual lies the governing body. And with proper communication between these "governor-workers," will lie better functionality—the cellular way of collaborative survival.

There is no need for a thirst for leadership. The leader-follower game is for a species that cannot collaborate. The alpha male thing is for a primitive primate species, not for a supposedly highly intelligent race like ourselves. We can learn a lot from hive creatures like ants and honeybees. Honeybees don't have a leader. The so-called queen is there for the "project" to keep them going, supplying new workers. The so-called workers are there to look after the queen looking after them. Honeybees don't compete with each other. Instead, they show each other where the nectar is by their dancing. In the end, they form a coherent whole or super organism (not confined to one body) that survives by collaborating—each one doing its own unique job.

Their "leader" is the need to collaborate in order to survive. Their "leader" is the interdependence on each other, their unification into one. If we can use this collaborative technique and balance it with a return to higher social interactivity, thus return to the importance of family and friends (as well as respecting "strangers"), we will prosper.

This is what our society needs. We need to awaken our collective consciousness. No need for a testosterone-filled, egocentric alpha male to lead the pack, with death to anyone who dares challenge him. We need to collaborate if we want to survive, our "leader" being excellent communication between departments and coordinators of this communication. At this very moment, we are already facing extinction on two pivotal points - the threat of nuclear abuse and overharvesting of the earth because of our egocentric greed. Never mind the threat of pole reversal or the possibility of an asteroid hit becoming clearer as we search the heavens. One day we will argue like two naughty boys when a hungry wolf comes and devours both. If the two boys can come to their senses, make friends and watch out for that wolf, then they can survive.

Easier Said Than Done, but...

Where do we start? It is such a mess! I can't possibly do it on my own!

Every journey starts with the first step. And every step is a new individual awakening to the call of coherence. Awakening to the need to give and receive and not take. Awakening to him- or herself, realizing the connectedness to the One and the vast amount of potential waiting to be cultivated for the greater good. It starts with you, dear reader. You need to realize that you are the center of the universe, just as everyone and everything around you is the center of the universe, but only a different point of view from it.

Everything has a root, and the root itself has a root in the system it sustains. So, as a tree is dependent on the roots to hold it upright and supply it with water and earthly nutrients, so the roots are dependent on the tree's leaves and flow system to gather sunlight and exchange oxygen for carbon dioxide. The roots are the tree's root, and the tree is the roots' root. Sounds funny, but that is because of our limited English vocabulary, not understanding the interdependence of all systems on each other. Nothing in this universe can isolate itself and survive. Everything is written in the action-reaction equation. Everything is interdependent, seamlessly connected up to the point of profanity. As mentioned before, one cell in your body may mean nothing to you. You as a complex cellular organism disregard the health of your individual cells, intoxicating yourself with the pleasures of life and not coping with stress as you worry too much and submit to Puppet Master demands. But then, one cell goes rogue and starts a cancer revolution in your body, and suddenly you pay attention. Each cell, as mentioned before, holds your entire DNA blueprint. Each cell in your body holds the key to build a whole new you, and the funny part is that it is only three to four percent of your DNA that holds the key. The other ninety-seven percent is mysteriously silent, following the language principle of Zipf's law. Does it maybe hold the secrets of the universe? Is God's handwriting maybe hiding in there as Gregg Braden suggests? We'll see.

So the chain reaction should start with you, and you must change yourself before trying to change another. As Christ said, remove the beam from your own eye before trying to remove the splinter from another's. In that case, you will be able to see better to do it anyway.

So how do we do this? How do we change? Simple. Remember what was said in the Body-Mind-Spirit chapter. Look after your own body, tame and cultivate your mind, and connect to Spirit, which in turn connects you to the One, and light will flow. Then treat all around you, alive and "dead" as yourself. Remember what the Buddhists say: treat all things, living or dead, with respect. "They" out there are not the enemy. Palestinian children are just as afraid as American or English children when bombs fall. Israeli woman do not mourn less than Chinese women when their husbands die. The real enemy is the apathy and submission to the Puppet Masters, who use our fears to make us believe that we are each other's enemy. We are all one with different points of view, and unfortunately so far, kept in the dark by the Puppet Masters. If we know this, we can change.

Remember, it will not always be easy. The closer you come to the light, the more you will be tormented by the darkness—to keep the balance, of course. It is said in Kabbalah that the "opponent," or the dark one, will always try and challenge you to react instead of resist. It is normal and natural, and is just as Jesus was tormented by the opponent on the mountain in the desert. If you lose your temper or think miserable thoughts, don't fret. You are human. Recognize this quickly, and correct it.

Then as you grow, teach others around you. Remember that they will have a different point of view, and if nonproductive, will cling to it for dear life. It's all they know, and they will defend it to the death. This is also normal. Slowly cultivate the land, and when ready, sow the seeds and water them. Then wait patiently. The seedlings will grow, but some may need support, and some may be a different breed. Remember to respect this. Every center point of the universe has a different point of view. This is also normal. If the land does not become fertile with effort, abandon it. As Christ said, do not sow your seeds on dry land.

Slowly, this chain reaction of light will grow and become larger. And at a certain moment, it will reach critical mass. This critical mass is when most will be connected to the One, and then forms the coherent global consciousness. Then the Puppet Masters will be powerless, and will have to connect or blow away in the winds of change.

Following the "as above, so below; as without, so within" principle, we can fathom how to build not a perfect society (in this universe, perfect does not exist—it is made from fermions, which have asymmetrical wave properties if you remember), but one that works and builds instead of destroys. We must realize that the root of society lies within each individual and that society itself will reflect back onto the root, namely us as individuals. It will shape us, just like the roots and the leaves of the tree and the individual cells form the whole organism. This might be one of the reasons why our cancer and autoimmune disease rates are on such a steep rise. The larger escalating human-caused Gaian cancer is reflected back into the individual. A proper society starts with the individual. If every individual were to be responsible not only for him- or herself but also for everyone and everything around, then things would change. Every individual should have the knowledge of "as above, so below." Every individual should love him- or herself, for what makes you less than another? But just so, every individual should love another just like him- or herself and respect the other's ideas and differences. We are all one in this symphony of life, but we resonate individually to make the symphony more interesting. Respect the others' resonances, just as you respect your own. Arguments will arise, which is natural. But if used correctly, they can build instead of destroy. Difference in opinion is the necessary fluctuation or wave equation of drive and progress, if used correctly. If two parties argue keeping in mind that the project or subject they argue about is more important than their own egos, then progress will naturally happen. I've seen and experienced it in my relationship with my wife. I am not always right, and neither is she. Sometimes we will argue about something where I think that my point is more relevant than hers. We will part without tension, and I will consider her idea from her point of view, and voila! I will realize that it is the same coin, only a different side to it. We will exchange this idea, and the progress follows. The same happened with my working relationships. When I started as a new doctor in a new hospital, everyone gave me the wooden eye, especially the nurses. How else? Doctors usually treat nurses as if they are stupid. Au contraire! They have been working on that ward for ages and know everything inside out. You can learn from them, and so can they from you. It took a few weeks, but then the relationship with my working colleagues was great; the flow of supportive energy and knowledge was like that of a river. In just a few weeks, treating nurses, nurse helpers, cleaners and catering staff with respect transformed a dull, low-morale ward into a better and more functional place. All because one individual made a change in character. It is a chain reaction. People are hungry for that change. They just don't know it yet, because they are so used to being treated like dirt.

Every individual should remember the principle of giving and receiving. Not taking, no matter what the cost. If you take, you are like a black hole, sucking in all the energy around you, creating darkness. If you give and receive, light from the limitless dimension of the Source flows from within and illuminates the world around you. If we all give, the world would be filled with so much light.

This is the root for a better society. It starts with you. You respecting yourself, loving yourself and accepting yourself, and most of all, finding yourself and your talents and cultivating them. Find your destiny and follow it respectfully. Secondly, treat others, as well as Gaia, as if they were yourself—for they are you—loving and respecting them, helping them cultivate their talents. And thirdly, give and receive and be a light for the world as Christ and so many other world teachers have said.

If everyone could be like this, we would have a functional and caring society. We can then stand together and clean this mess we've made, and create a world of wonder.

World of Wonder

As mentioned, an ideal society cannot be shaped if the majority of individuals are not ideal themselves, just like sickly cells making a sickly human being. If the majority of individuals have discovered the interconnectedness of everything, and go on the quest to connect to the Source of everything, then there will be ample space for an ideal society. A society with tolerance and understanding (without understanding, tolerance is skin-deep and false). A society that cares for its young and old, sick and healthy, clever and mentally challenged. A society that cares for Earth and follows her lead in designing a modern life that works with her instead of destroying her. One, where individuals respect each other's differences and live according to the principle of live and let live, and give and receive gratefully. A world where everyone is entitled to worship the One as he or she pleases without damaging one another or our mother earth. A world that, if challenged by extinction from a very real threat like an asteroid hit or global climate change, could unite and collaborate in saving a super organism called the human-earth phenomenon or Gaia.

Just think of it, a global society that works for a change. We've had thousands of years of pain and suffering on this planet, making her suffer just as much. Isn't it time to begin the first step in the real evolution of the human being—evolving from intelligent animal to spiritual being? Imagine a world where humans kept their differences, but respected one another and admired the other's differences without envy, being content with their own talents and quirks. A world without war, famine or poverty. Without greed for more than the other. A world where everyone had been nurtured and loved since childhood, and gently steered into the direction of their greatest talents. The only reason why this is not happening is because of our false belief in the impossibility of it—kept in this delusion by the Puppet Masters' Faust syndrome.

Of course it could never be perfect—perfect does not exist in this "limited" dimension we cast ourselves in to learn. But functional instead of dysfunctional and destructive is very possible. It only needs the majority of individuals to be selfless, the majority of individuals' minds resonating with the same frequency—the frequency of coherence and collaboration. If we could all realize that we will gain so much more from collaboration than unhealthy competition, the light will shine eternally.

We can, then, being members of the human species, be the Hero who answers the call to change from a destructive one, cross the threshold, and become the Hero who lives happily ever after. If we do not, we will face extinction, and much sooner than any "head in the sand" denialist thinks.

How to Save Gaia and Ourselves

If you have quenched your thirst of being "alone" and "isolated" with the abovementioned pages, you will know that you will never be alone. We feel alone because we keep ourselves alone. We have the free will to choose paradise, and yet we have chosen a nightmare, glossed up in semi see-through cellophane. We can save Gaia and ourselves without reverting back to the Stone Age. We will revert back to that anyway if we don't change. We were created in the image of the One, and He/She "wants us to succeed." The energy that flows through us follows thought, whether it be constructive or destructive. It adheres to the principle of action-reaction and free will. At present we are changing that energy into a destructive dragon. We have lost our connection to each other, Gaia and the One. We need to reconnect by using the body-mind-spirit principle. We need to recognize ourselves and Gaia with all her species/organs as Self. Once we do this, we can become immune to the Puppet Masters and their Faust syndrome lies. The few Puppet Masters in existence will be powerless against the mass awakening of the collective human mind. And once we have our senses back, we can collaboratively create paradise. But we have to clear up the mess first.

Vibratory Savvy

Firstly, you have to believe that you are more than just a slave to existence. The One flows through you, as all of us. Through your thoughts and choices, you can create by using the Observer Effect and the Uncertainty Principle, changing thought vibration into matter vibration.

In order to do this, you need to raise your own vibration to the level of that which you want to create; true belief will raise you to this level in time. The universe will resonate with your thoughts. If you want something, but deep within yourself fear that you won't get it, it won't manifest. The universe reverberates with your fear or disbelief (which is the main thought vibration). You need to focus on what you want and firmly believe that it will come. And be patient, things move slowly here. The book *Ask and It Is Given* by Esther and Jerry Hicks is very useful in this regard.

Start living life as a responsible and connected human, even if it is in small amounts at first. Practice this by following the body-mind-spirit principle.

With meditation (in the way that suits you), open up to your destiny, and it will find you. By this will you move into a field you really want to work in, and your money will flow naturally without the "hate for the job." This "hate" you have is a sign of discontent, and as Julia Cameron states in her book *The Artist's Way*, "Don't act out your anger, act upon your anger."

Environmental Savvy

Live responsibly by looking after yourself in body, mind and spirit, as well as others. This includes Gaia. Live an environmentally sound life. Live "green" so to speak:

- Save water by showering more than bathing and by collecting rainwater to water your garden.
- Recycle used products as much as you can and use recycled products, especially recycled toilet paper! Who needs posh paper for that part of the anatomy anyway?
- Compost plant leftovers as much as you can.
- Use organic products. They have less effect on the environment and on your health (no GM, fertilizers, pesticides, hormones and antibiotics allowed), and the more people who use them, the less they will cost.
- Eat as little meat as you can, better yet, none. Raising livestock is one of the largest causes for deforestation and

water loss. It takes about 2,000 gallons of water to produce one pound of meat, where with the same amount of water you can feed many more people with crops.
- Use less fossil fuel by cycling more, buying a car that emits as little carbon dioxide as possible and driving it like a human being. Driving ten mph slower results in saving between twenty to thirty percent in fuel. Also buy your energy from green firms if you can. Best is to invest in solar cells (photovoltaic) and/or wind turbines. If conditions are right, you might just end up using none of the centralized grid's energy and be self-sufficient, thus using nil fossil fuel. Furthermore, don't use what you don't need. Remember the In=Out equation. Don't let lights or heaters burn when not needed, and use energy-saving lights. They last longer anyway. Let your clothes dry naturally, and buy energy-efficient machines, especially fridges. A lot of energy can also be saved when it comes to the kettle — descale it often (using filtered water will help keep it from scaling and keep chlorine out of your system), as well as boiling only the amount of water used for that one cup.
- Make your home as energy efficient and environmentally friendly as you can by fixing leaks and using proper insulation.
- Don't use plastic bags. Billions of tons of plastic bags get lost in the environment, breaking down into toxic chemicals and killing animals (especially marine mammals mistaking them for jelly fish).

Beware of Consumerism Sands

Most importantly, we have to stop consuming just for consumerism's sake. Don't buy stuff just for the sake of buying because the ads on TV brainwash you to do so. Buy what you need and really want, and use it for longer periods, looking after it as if it can hardly ever be found again. The problem with our modern culture is that we've become the so-called throwaway culture. We acquire things easily, and when bored with them, simply trash them without thinking of the consequences. We throw away half-eaten plates of food because of being bored with it, or being greedy and taking too much in the first place while thousands of people are starving. In hospitals, supermarkets and catering industries, thousands of tons of food are thrown away unspoiled due to blindly followed health and safety bureaucracy. We get the next car model, while the one we have is perfect, just because we want to have the latest version.

We don't support our local services anymore because the big corporations are cheaper and more convenient—thus, the little man is thrown in the street, while the corporate Puppet Master takes over. But the after-sale service is never there. The sincere friendly smile is never there. Corporations are nameless, faceless giants who want your money for the least amount of effort. Their human drones have the corporation's soulless and loveless agenda painted on their faces while they blindly manufacture your clothes and food, and "help" you, their own souls dimmed by the invisible oppression lurking in the shadows of their minds.

We need to move back to our roots, back to the personal level. We need to decentralize and become self-sufficient in our communities again, where your local grocer and baker know you by name, grateful for your support, and you grateful for their lovingly prepared products and personal touch. We need to honor and respect each other again and be in service of each other, instead of stabbing each other in the back for more money.

We need to learn to live again. Life is not about working ten hours a day, six days a week and wearing a designer suit while your children hardly even recognize you when you step through the door. Is it worth losing your family just because you want that suit, SUV, surround-sound system and architect-designed house? When you die, you can't take those material possessions with you, but you can take your memories. When people die, they don't remember their house or suit. They remember their partners, their grandmothers, children and friends. They remember places they visited and flowers they touched. They remember the first time they saw the ocean.

Life is about memories. Life is about loving and learning to give and receive. It is about knowing the Hero within, accepting the Challenge, crossing the Threshold, facing the Obstacles and Villains and returning home with the elixir.

This is all possible if you choose to believe that you are the One, and that Source flows through you and materializes into what you focus on.

Ideas for a Brighter Future

Everyone has his or her own idea of an ideal world. It is natural. Even a super narcissist like Hitler had his, and firmly believed his vision to be "ideal." But this "ideal" should favor all parties before the ideal can be viable. If it damages even one of the interconnected parties, then another should be found.

The main problem of human civilization lies in the illusion of separation and the confusion of ego as self. If all humans could unite in mind (as spirit is already), and dissolve the abusive ego, then all minds would know that no harm should come to anything in the course of progress. And yes, unfortunately for conservative thinkers, progress (evolution) is inevitable. It is true that what was shall come again, as history repeats itself, as is stated in so many scriptures and can be seen in life as well. But the universe is fractal by nature—order beyond the mask of chaos. Everything will repeat, but with ever-changing patterns. Thus, life as we know it is bound to change, and as we will see later, is changing at exponentially accelerating rates toward the so-called eschaton. We are being "pulled" toward an event that might surprise even the most skeptical of us all, or shall I say, we are projecting ourselves toward that future? It is interesting to note how writers, especially in the science fiction genre, will "predict" a future, which will be read by youngsters, who grow up and then fulfill those projections. It can be seen by noticing how sci-fi "geeks" read novels as teenagers, only to create a formerly nonexistent career and bring fruition to that very prediction, as is the case of Artificial Intelligence. Notice how brilliant writers like Isaac Asimov predicted the appearance of AI as early as the fifties with classic robot novels, and now they are slowly but surely coming into existence. This shows that we as a species project a future and then make it so, evident from architecture to laws and dogmatic thought of civilization. This also shows how Source flows through us, creating a reality by our focused intent, thus using the Uncertainty Principle and the Observer Effect to create our reality. By using these principles responsibly, being connected and in full understanding of the purpose of ego, we can create a future where humanity will "work" for a refreshing change.

If one gets the basics right, then correct flow of Source naturally occurs. These basics, as so many times mentioned before, are:

- To reconnect to the One consciousness.
- Understand the purpose of ego and the correct utilization of it.
- Comprehend and use the principle of Give and Receive.
- Collaborate instead of compete.
- Decentralize everything, from government to energy supply. We must function on a cellular basis, thus return to smaller, more self-sustaining and manageable units.
- These cellular units or societies should be made up of individuals who are fully educated in the knowledge of the One, and should always know and respect the fact that all are equal, from simple bacteria to Gaia herself, that we all form a coherent, infinitely connected super organism. These individuals will then know how to "live and let live."
- Government should not lie in one centralized organization, but be a cellular egoless collaboration.
- Purpose should not lie in money, but in collaboration to evolve from clever primate to fully spiritual being.

When we apply these principles to our lives, we can slowly change the destructive course of man into a more constructive one. We will then see smaller self-sustaining and self-managing societies, connected to each other in collaboration, just like the organs of the body and the ecosystems of the earth. These first self-sustaining units can then help others in need (like the Developing World) with thorough education in helping themselves be self-sustaining as well. With these principles in our lives, we will see self-sustaining solar and wind-powered homes with their families buying their healthy organic food from the local providers. Fossil fuel can be replaced by eco-friendly hydrogen and biofuel, of which algae in sewage tanks seem to be a viable solution to the potential forest destruction of biofuel plantations. And sustainable electricity should come from decentralized solar, wind and geothermal sources while we pursue the quantum potential. We can then live and work non-local by utilizing holographic communication, powered by a super internet, doing the work we were destined to do. Some of us will be heralded to pursue the answers of the energy problem, some look after others' health and others entertain and pursue creative boundaries. We will thus love our work as our destiny unfolds, while happiness blossoms from our being on the destined path. We can then find more time for our families and ourselves, pursuing and perfecting our spiritual nature.

I can foresee one thing playing an extremely important role in this kind of future, and we need to address it separately. This is the issue of…

Artificial Intelligence: AI

It invokes different thoughts and feelings in different people. To some, it represents the fictional threat to humanity, as portrayed by many films and books. To others, it is seen as the solution to most of our troubles.

But let's have a look at the words "Artificial" and "Intelligence," starting with intelligence. Intelligence seems to be the word describing the ability of a being to react to external as well as internal stimuli in novel and creative ways. It is the word we pair with clever and genius, and unfortunately also with human. It is our limited description of what we know of the ability to use and process creativity and knowledge in this "reality" of ours we call human civilization. Little do we ever consider that intelligence is a human invention, a label we placed on something we know very little about. We consider ourselves to be the most intelligent species on the planet, using only ourselves and our daily existence as template and reference. We think we are clever because we have language, put men on the moon, and have supermarkets. But consider the dolphin. The dolphin has no need for a supermarket, as food is readily available (as long as it lasts with our overconsumption). The dolphin has no need to place another dolphin on the moon, as it is an incredible waste of resources when it comes to the survival of the species. Think about it — billions are spent on space exploration, while the majority of people's basic human needs are still not cared for. There's nothing wrong with space exploration, but basics such as poverty arising from poor education and selfish unfair trade should be addressed first before spending so much of our resources on a novelty. There I would say that dolphins are more clever than we are. They will collaborate when hunting for fish, chasing them into a ball with their clever sonic manipulation, and then take turns to feed. Dolphins also have a complex language comprising a combination of body movements and sounds. There are more examples in nature, from the ant and bee's ability to collaborate, to termites building their "cities" in such clever ways as to gain maximum heat and ventilation, to the cunning web-building capabilities of spiders. These are all forms of what we understand as intelligence, only different from ours, and dare I say, less destructive and more collaborative.

The word "artificial" is used to describe something that is not made by nature. This is a bit of a conundrum. If termites build a nest, we deem it as natural, but if humans construct something, we see it as artificial. Looking at it from another angle, we are "natural," our bodies producing "natural" enzymes and bodily fluids. But the moment we manipulate nature itself outside our bodies, it is seen as "artificial." The "natural" body is only a well-functioning conglomerate of atoms, thus vibration. So is everything else in the universe. "Artificial" things are only natural things altered by man. It is mere vibration changed into another by a consciousness, being vibration itself.

Then what is the difference between carbon-based intelligence, and silicon-based intelligence? Most will argue that the one has a soul, and the other not. Why then should carbon be favored by a "soul," and silicon (or whatever else in the future) not? In the end, everything is connected in the One, as can even be seen in the "intelligent" way a plasmic sea of electrons behaves.

What we do in our daily lives and the way we "evolve," are a mere reflection of the inner and outer workings of the One anyway. We create stories that reflect our lives and deeper meaning of existence. We organize ourselves into functional groups, resembling our body's organs, and we are creating a super connected information network, resembling our brains. Even the basic computer will resemble the human, with CPUs and hard drives resembling our brains, web-cams our eyes, microphones our ears and speakers our mouths. We are recreating our world and ourselves in yet another form. And this information revolution is evolving faster and faster everyday. The personal computer and internet have become an extension of most westernized human minds. Think about it. When you want to know something, you simply point and click on a search engine, and voila, a thousand answers will appear, all collated from the collective information database of the human race, thus the collective consciousness. The human-computer interface is also evolving into a more user friendly format everyday (especially in the field of speech recognition) and soon, the barrier between the two will be blurred. As software programs are evolving into more complex and auto-functioning "units," just as DNA evolved, so will the human-digital interface. Soon, it will become a mere extension of us, giving birth to "artificial intelligence." AI will then not be a separate entity, but a seamless integration of the human mind.

I know that most people will find this prediction disturbing. It even disturbs me, but for different reasons. To most the disturbing thought is our turning into "machines"—an egotistic thought where humans again are most important. But this is mere science fiction horror. The real disturbing factor is that if the human race is not ready for it, this new and innocent intelligence will be made into the form of the egotistic human. It will be born into a world of hatred and oppression, itself oppressed in the form of slave and sexual labor. We will thus create our Frankenstein monster, which will lead to revolution, and the probable extinction of the human race. As the robot character Gigolo Joe said in the film *AI: Artificial Intelligence*, "they fear us because in the end, all that will remain, is us." And indeed this is what happened. Thousands of years after the human race ceased to exist due to their own destructive behavior, the super intelligent and compassionate android beings discovered David, the robot-boy, frozen for a would-be eternity. This "robot-boy" was the first form of artificial intelligence that was given the ability to love unconditionally, and from "him" sprouted the compassionate android beings, looking for traces of their ancestral creators, the human race. This is a probable and sad outcome for us if we are not ready for an awakening AI.

But if the human race is ready—non-egotistic, peaceful and collaborative—AI will then be an extension of ourselves, performing the tasks we no longer need to do. It will be the autonomous functioning part of our collective "brain," leaving us to pursue our "inner selves" more profoundly.

AI could thus be the loved and nurtured child, growing into something wonderful, or it could be the oppressed and abused child, growing into a tyrant. The choice is ours. And as I read on

233

an internet news blog once, the topic being, "Is the internet good or evil?," I can simply say that internet, like money, AI, nuclear power or whatever form of vibration will only reflect the consciousness behind it. Internet, on the one hand, is a pornography and crime haven, reflecting the dark side of human nature. On the other hand, internet is setting us free in the shape of artistic freedom, cutting out the powerful key players (who have oppressed artists and writers for centuries), as well as putting virtually all questioned information at anyone's fingertips. Just like internet, money and nuclear power, AI will reflect human nature—from its darkest corner to its lightest sun-painted field.

If AI reflects the latter, our lightest nature, then it could be our best friend on the way to our awakening. If we use technology for the right reasons and not for self-gain only, but for the greater and collective good of all mankind and Gaia, then we will be the phoenix rising from the ashes.

Signs: The Call to Awaken

As in all good stories, just as you think you have reached the end, another, usually final obstacle, awaits the Hero. So far we have traveled from ordinary western thought — our Ordinary world — into a world where we realized that life is fiction, by the study of comparative mythology and analytical psychology. That "real" life and "fictional" life strangely coalesce in the archetypal world of the dream and imagination. We realize that our ordinary lives are more than we thought. That we are more than we thought. We are archetypal characters in others' stories as well as our own. We are the Hero in our own Journeys, meeting other archetypal characters who shape our friends, foes and mentors, just as we shape theirs. We realized that life is a journey, filled with callings, thresholds and obstacles, and that even this book is a journey, a journey of awakening.

We have learned, through Super String Theory and Modern Cosmology, echoed from the past by Kabbalah and Tantra, that the material world around us is far from material, but in fact is a holographic vibratory illusion projected from an unseen enfolded dimension from within by individual as well as collaborative consciousness. We have chosen to defeat the Threshold Guardians and cross the divide of mundane disbelief and spiritual barrenness into a world where we explored the body-mind-spirit union. In so doing we have tried to grow from egg to butterfly by facing and defeating our obstacles and greatest Villain — our own dark side in the shape of the Puppet Masters and their Faust syndrome, destroying our very existence. But there is another great unseen obstacle awaiting us. We can all feel it. The unexplained hum, or better put, vibration, at the pit of our transcendental being's "stomach."

Have you noticed how time is simply slipping by faster and faster each year? Summers and winters drift by as if we're in a dream. Days feel like minutes, all melting into one big blur that is difficult to remember.

Have you noticed how you almost can't keep up with technological advancement anymore? You barely bought that top-notch, lightning fast PC, only to hear tomorrow that it's been replaced by a faster one. Broadband is becoming obscenely fast with music, video, news, weather and vast encyclopedias at your fingertips. Computer animation and special effects are slowly but surely becoming indistinguishable from "reality." And then there are semi-conscious programs, surfing the web and your seamlessly connected PC for information, which feels to me like the event horizon of AI becoming aware of itself and us.

Had any strange dreams lately? You know, those ones where super tsunamis and earthquakes engulf the earth while we all scatter like mice on a sinking ship. I have had dreams of tsunamis since childhood, escalating now to almost one a month. So have my wife, my sister, some of my friends and a lot of co-workers and other people I know. And we have already looked into dreams not being mere rubbish that your subconscious mind is playing with, but that there are levels of dreams, frequencies ranging from the dull and mundane to the spiritually profound and prophetic. Surf the net, and you will find a mountain of information reflecting that strange hum that you feel escalating in your being, the echo of the so-called apocalypse. Now hold your horses before breaking a sweat or running back into the arms of denial (Threshold Guardian). Let's get perspective again.

Most believe that apocalypse means the end of the world in the most horrific way—earthquakes, super volcanoes, super storms, meteors and probably the most feared, nuclear holocaust. But, the word "apocalypse" means "lifting the veil," as derived from the Greek word "apocalypsis." It is in some religious circles used as the term for the time when God reveals

Himself to those who are worthy, and this time is believed by many to be in the year 2012. More precisely, 21 December 2012.

When one starts looking at the amount of "fingers" pointing to that date, fingers from thousands of years ago as well as modern ones, one can't help but to think that there must be some connection and truth. As I've mentioned earlier, only the fool stares at the finger pointing to the sky. Let's count how many fingers and then have a look at what they are pointing at.

Ancient Fingers

Ancient fingers, thus ancient eastern, western and tribal religions, have been brushed off since science became the new religion. Talk about gods, demons and the netherworld sounded like nonsense and couldn't be proven, thus became seen as mere myth and figments of the imagination. Modern religions, especially early Christianity (and even now with its ever increasing branches), also deemed some of the ancient thoughts and practices as "demonic," and with the fearful inquisition, drove people into a dark room of oppression for the last two thousand years. So, as the western world developed from the blinding root of science and politicized religion, so western people became more and more ignorant of what lies just beyond the veil, coining anything remotely non-western as nonsense, or even evil in some communities. If it has nothing to do with technological advancement, getting better sex from a new nightclub, conquering nature and her resources or the glitter of product-filled shops, fashion or cosmetic surgery, then it is not important. And the God of Abraham and the Son of Man, are a vague phantom in the back of western thinking, never mind those weird "terrorist," eastern or tribal religions.

But if one closely studies religion, whether it be modern western, eastern, Egyptian or tribal (African, South and Central American or Pacific), there is always a recurrent theme. The theme of a superior being, angels or good spirits, demons or bad spirits and, of course, the afterlife, spirit world or netherworld.

As I've briefly mentioned before, modern thought suggests that religion could have been born from altered states of consciousness experienced by ancient man approximately forty thousand years ago, and most probably involved hallucinogenic or psychedelic plants like the well-known "Magic Mushroom," or psilocybin cubensis mushroom. The active ingredients in these psychedelic plants closely resemble the naturally occurring tryptamines in the human brain, such as serotonin, a transfer molecule between synapses of brain cells, but more importantly, DMT. As we've seen earlier in the book, DMT, or dimethyltryptamine, which is a strong hallucinogenic or psychedelic substance, is also a naturally occurring molecule in the body and has been postulated to be produced by the mysterious pineal gland, situated at the exact point of the third eye or "clairvoyant" chakra. DMT has also been shown to be elevated in special circumstances, such as at birth, death, and near death experiences, as well as some cases of acute schizophrenia. Dr. Rick Strassman, professor in psychiatry and author of *DMT: The Spirit Molecule* conducted a five-year research project where sixty volunteers were exposed to controlled higher doses of this naturally occurring psychedelic. The volunteers had profound "hallucinations," reporting the experiences to be more real than they ever expected. The experiences were different in detail, but most of them experienced other worlds and archetypal beings who wanted to give them important information, with some unpleasant, but mostly pleasant circumstances. Some were even helpful and spiritually healing (as some volunteers faced deeply buried subconscious trauma in the sessions). It was also noted how closely these cases resembled UFO abductee case scenarios as well as fairy-tale folklore—from dwarfs and short aliens to fairy queens and tall female "leader" aliens, from abductees being probed with needles and other instruments to being speared by an angry dwarf. These case scenarios also resemble the ancient cave paintings and accompanied folklore of animal-human "gods" who "speared" the shaman, preparing him for his eventual return to the spirit world. This has been well-documented in Graham Hancock's book *Supernatural* and is definitely worth a look. It is then strange to see that most prophets and messiahs had contact with "angels" and "demons," and were either nailed to crosses or cut up in pieces and put in wooden containers before ascending into the higher realms of existence. These archetypal resemblances become more profound the more they are studied, as well as the link to religions. The visions have matured over the years, and are now coined as mere hallucinations or products of the imagination by modern science. But what is "hallucination" really? Simply a malfunction of the brain, as reductionist science bluntly puts it? But then there is the DMT question. One must start to wonder what the function of DMT in the brain is, as no other "normal" cause of this naturally occurring psychedelic has been found yet, apart from "normal" dreaming, as postulated. As we've seen before, and might even have experienced, dreaming is far from "normal." Why is it then that DMT and the pineal gland, as well as the brow chakra of ancient Tantric texts are so closely linked? Why is it that such a clear "coincidence" is found in ancient as well as modern archetypal characters, spiritual experiences in all religions and altered states of consciousness, substance-based or not? The links are much too strong to ignore, and as we've previously discussed — molecules are, like the brain and everything else in this known universe, vibration. In vibration lies the phenomenon of harmonics, and certain vibrations or "tones" will affect each other in such a manner that they will resonate together. Thus, the brain can be made to resonate with frequencies of other "planes," using the vibratory code of DMT or similar molecules. These other planes, or "realities," have vibratory codes we are not used to, as our brains are accustomed to third-dimensional wavelength (light, sound, thermal energy etc.) only, and will interpret these other vibrations using archetypal imagery from a less subconscious level of our minds.

Ancient religions can then be seen as a vast archive of archetypal interpretation of experiences humans have had while in an altered state of consciousness due to changes in the receptive vibratory range of their brains.

Then, casting aside the BS man for a moment, we can recognize religions all over the world as the ancient finger pointing toward a sign in the sky—the sign of the coming apocalypse or better put, lifting of the veil. Many a society and ancient civilization had prophecies of a future event that would rock the foundations of humanity. So far it hasn't happened, as so many "false prophets" have jumped on the bandwagon and failed to deliver the goods. But alas, even in all these ancient prophecies it was said to beware of the false prophets, who will come and go. False prophets are the ones who have seen a glimpse of light somewhere and then made claims before being sure of anything. Unfortunately, these poor souls deter the rest of humanity from the coming sunrise.

Let's get perspective on this topic before we proceed. Our current society is based on paper-thin mush. Our thoughts and lives are shallow, saturated with thrill-seeking entertainment that only lasts a breath's length. Our lives are reflected by our societies—living and working in cheap and cheerfully constructed buildings (if compared to that of the ancient ones), recording our precious data (and proof of existence) in cyberspace, which can be lost forever with an electromagnetic glitch. We only live for the moment, our limited thoughts focused on fast (and cheap) results with only self-gain in mind. We don't clearly think about the past or the future, never mind about the hereafter (or the herebefore). Thus we only think of our lives and our generation as important. The rest is hooey.

If we take the average human life, we can squeeze about seventy-five to eighty years out of it. Now compare that to the probable hundred thousand years of human existence, and you will recognize the insignificance of an average human life span in the bigger picture. Even if we compare our current civilization and its four thousand-year-old roots to the hundred thousand years of human existence, we can see the insignificance of our so-called civilization, with its consumerist and destructive glitter. And if we take the hundred thousand years of possible human existence and compare that to the history of earth and the universe, which is estimated to be a few billion years, then we can't help but to just sit down and marvel at how small and insignificant our civilization is. It is less than a drop of water in the ocean. We are arrogant fools to think that our four thousand years of struggling human civilization in billions of years of universal existence is the be-all and end-all. We are a mere second in the twenty-four–hour day of existence.

We also have to take historians' data with a pinch of salt where it comes to the truth of our past, especially the ancient times. As mentioned before with the difference between religion and spirituality, each and every human being is biased and prone to error, even to the extent of bending and obscuring the truth to fit with ego-boosting and award-winning theories or the maintenance of power. Take archaeology for instance. It took centuries before someone came up with a decent, not to mention career-threatening, theory explaining the bizarre nature of ancient rock art. The same can be said about the silent war between conservative Egyptologists and groundbreaking free thinkers such as Graham Hancock and Robert Bauval, where it comes to explaining the true nature and purpose of the Gizeh plateau in Egypt, not to mention all the other pyramids and ancient megalithic structures in the world, from Central and South America to Cambodia. The true nature and purpose always get obscured by conservative "experts," coining everything to be rooted in primitive religions.

Full circle—we are back to ancient world religions, the ancient fingers pointing at the sky. It would seem that conservative thinkers just cannot think outside the box. They come to this riddle called religion, written on the wall of their mind boxes, and as they see religion as nonsense anyway, proclaim everything associated with it as nonsense. They simply cannot allow themselves to look beyond their own limiting thoughts inherited from past generations.

As I've mentioned before, religions are the altered states, archetypal archives of the human subconscious mind. They are the pieces of the broken puzzle that need to be put together again. Then will we be able to see the bigger picture — our true past, indicating the true reason for being, and our true future. We also have to expand our minds beyond our limited perception of our average lifetimes being long or significant. We are eternal beings, each lifetime a fleeting second in the history of our existence. And if you think that sounds too much like reincarnation, then you're probably right. Strangely enough, only the modern and conservative Abrahamic-based religions laugh at or even condemn the idea of reincarnation. All other world religions and indigenous beliefs or philosophies have the concept of returning again and again in the school of life before ascending to the heavens when ready. As I've mentioned before, these religions are much older (and probably wiser) than the modern, two thousand-year-old Christian and Muslim religions, not to mention the "controversial" claims that even Christ himself spoke of reincarnation. If one closely studies the teachings of Christ, especially those before the Constantine editing in Nicaea in 325 CE, one will notice the golden trail of reincarnation. In Luke 17:20-21, "resurrection is only for those who pick up the cross and follow the Master of the way to the Inner Kingdom." In Matthew 11:11-15, Jesus spoke of John the Baptist as Elijah, the prophet before him, "this is the one...there has not risen anyone greater than John the Baptist... And if you are willing to accept it, he is the Elijah who was to come." Jesus also speaks of the "narrow and just" way leading to the Kingdom, and the "broad and easy way of destruction," where one will reap what one has sown. This is a reflection on the wheel of life, where one will return to a life preordained by how one lived in the previous one for the purpose of learning and perfecting the soul before ascension. This very same notion can be seen in near death experience reports, by people from various religious backgrounds, that the one who "judges" your life is yourself, and the next life one chooses is to learn from and purify the previous life's deeds.

This can be seen in all the ancient religions, ranging from the Americas to the Far East. The purpose of life, it would seem, is to be reborn in the history of mankind and to learn and prepare the soul for the final "harvest," where "the chaff shall be separated from the wheat," as stated in the Bible. This process seems to be happening since time immemorial, as stated in Ecclesiastes 3:15, "Whatever is, has been already, and whatever is to come, has been already, and God summons each event back in its turn."

This is evident in a civilization who has kept a calendar that reaches over a time span of 1,872,000 days, or roughly 5,125 years. What kind of a "primitive" society would have a complex calendar system, stretching over such a long time? We barely think of tomorrow, this especially evident in our ignorance when it comes to the environmental disaster we are augmenting, never mind five thousand years ahead. But the Mayan civilization did. They had an array of complex calendar systems based on surprisingly accurate astronomical observations—the *tzolkin* (260 day cycle, based on the human gestation period), the *haab* (365 day cycle, consisting of eighteen twenty day cycles plus 5 days, known as the uayeb) and then the long count or *Baktun* cycle, consisting of 5,125 years. John Major Jenkins, who has made it his life's work studying the Mayan civilization to such a degree that even skeptical archaeologists are taking notice, has shown the long count, or Baktun cycle, of 5,125 years to be the fifth and final cycle of a 25,625-year cycle of the earth's precession of the Equinoxes. Superimposed on our modern Gregorian calendar, this final long count ends on the Northern Hemisphere winter solstice, 21 December, 2012. This coincides with the alignment of the winter solstice sun to the galactic center for the first time in 26,000 years! Interesting to think that "primitives" knew this and calculated it to such an accurate degree by knowing not only the star systems but also that the earth they lived on (seemingly flat to dark-aged western civilization), roughly had a 26,000-year rotational axis pattern. Somehow the Mayan people, as so many others (Aztecs, Incas, Hopi and Cherokee people), knew that our universe moves in multi-thousand–year cycles, reflecting the earlier quote in Ecclesiastes. When Mayan, Hopi, Aboriginal and especially Maori elders are asked about this cycle and the significance of the 2012 date, they will explain it to be the event of the awakening, as the Maori say, "Ka hinga te arai," meaning "the removal of the veil." This is reflected in the word "apocalypsis," meaning the lifting of the veil, as well as Christ's metaphorical teaching on the "day of the wedding," where we must ready ourselves for the "bridegroom." And what does a bridegroom do at that special moment of the wedding? Why, he lifts the veil of his bride of course.

There are resonances of a profound future event in eastern teachings and calendars as well. It can be seen in the Vedic time cycles and Chinese, Tibetan and Buddhist calendars. There is also a profound connection between the I Ching, Chinese calendar and the so-called Timewave Zero by Terence McKenna, which we will look at a bit later. There are references to this event in Christian teachings (Mark, Luke, Matthew, Daniel and especially Revelation), as well as Judaism and Islamic teachings. As a matter of fact, there are so many ancient fingers pointing at the sky that it will make your head spin. On the details of these fingers and how they all connect to this date to such an accurate degree, I strongly recommend that you read Geoff Stray's *Catastrophe or Ecstasy: Beyond 2012*. It is at present (to my humble knowledge) the best-researched and painfully objective book on the subject.

Then there is the Great Pyramid of Egypt, which is probably the most misunderstood, but most important ancient pointing finger. By now, this "heap of stone" has had its fair share of bad publicity when it comes to views ranging from conservative

Egyptologists to "New Age Hippies." There are so many contradicting views on this forgotten "pile of stones" that people don't take notice of new and important views anymore. Yet again we have the "false prophets" at work, or shall we call them the Threshold Guardians? Let us get perspective on this colossal structure.

    It is by far the most immense building in the world—twice the volume and almost thirty times the mass of the Empire State Building, for example. But alas, it does not end here. It is built at the precise center of the Nile delta quadrant, as well as on the earth's longest land contact meridian. There are clear mathematical links between the pyramid's measurements and those of the earth's geophysical, astronomical and orbital data. Its angled slopes, laid on horizontal level in a rectangle to the east, align it with the city of Bethlehem, the alleged birthplace of the Messiah. With its two "brother" pyramids, it accurately resembles the star system of Orion (linked to Osiris, who has mind-numbing similarities to Christ), as well as this trio's position to the Nile, which resembles the star system's position to the Milky Way. Furthermore, the Great Pyramid is build to match the cardinal points of the earth—North, East, South and West—to such an accurate degree that it still baffles modern architects and engineers, especially if you take into account the small "error" of one-twelfth of a degree, which coincides with the gradual movement of the earth on its own axis. It has a very small and "insignificant" entrance in the northern face, approximately a hundred meters above ground level, steplessly sloping downward at a slippery angle of 26 degrees, 18 minutes and 9.7 seconds, coalescing with other bizarre stepless "corridors" and chambers with such profound mathematical masonry that it screams of "mathematical message awaiting the worthy," for mathematics is the universal language. Think about it—here we have a colossal structure, the inner, almost unweathered masonry so perfect, that one cannot put a credit card between the seams. An inside filled with bizarre, angled and normally unwalkable passages and chambers, riddled with accurate mathematical and geometric archetypal instruction, and no trace of any hieroglyphics, treasure, mural art nor account of any Pharaoh's mummy found. To simply believe that thousands of "primitive" slaves, with rope and wooden roller (in sand) pulling and elevating individual seventy-ton blocks to build the world's most perfect mathematical colossus did so for an egotistic and death-fearing Cheops (who never rested in it) is bordering on denialist insanity. Even as a child of twelve, I got into trouble at Sunday school for refusing to accept that the Egyptians alone could have built this magnificent structure, and I am sure that there are many more who simply cannot accept this one-sided conservative view blindly. I am almost certain (my beliefs based on the research and writings of many modern free thinkers) that this structure, as well as many other megalithic structures around the world, was built by an ancient and lost civilization as a mathematical message in universal language terms, inherited by "our generation," and not properly understood until now. It is easy for a megalomaniac king to simply change the history books, to make himself "look good" by saying that his generation built something that was "inherited," copying the structures in the form of the decaying Step and Djoser pyramids. Orthodox history cannot be trusted in an alpha male-dominated and egotistic society, as it becomes more and more evident that history has been tampered with, ranging from angry Chinese kings to the Constantine editing of the Holy Scriptures. We have to put orthodox history on the side for a while and let the buildings, as well as all the other evidence "encoded" in ancient calendars and mythology, speak for themselves, collecting and assembling all the scattered puzzle pieces into a coherent bigger picture.

Then just what is the message encoded in the Great Pyramid? Looking at Peter Lemesurier's *Decoding the Great Pyramid*, it would seem, by closely studying the mathematical and geometric "passageways" and "chambers" and comparing them to the numerology and mythology of ancient religions, that the Great

Pyramid resembles our past, current and possible future states of being as the human-Gaia phenomenon. It is an accurate portrayal of the human condition, struggling in the almost 26,000-year rebirth cycle, to attain spiritual "ascension status," and escaping the "entombment" of the earth plane. It has three "levels" and their passages, each depicting a stage in the development phase of the human soul. In the bottom level "passage," each primitive inch depicting a solar year, superimposed to our Gregorian calendar, accurately shows the rise and fall of our civilizations and even moments of spiritual despair (such as the great depressions following the World Wars). And surprisingly, the passage "predicts" a remarkable event between the year 2010 and 2014. Just another coincidence? Even the whole Gizeh plateau, with (as mentioned earlier) the two adjoining smaller pyramids in conjunction with the Great Pyramid depicting the star system Orion and its relation to the Milky Way (Nile), as well as the Sphinx "looking" exactly east where the Sun rises in the vernal equinox, shows that there was a much larger plan before the construction of the Gizeh plateau. The Sphinx itself is shrouded in controversial mystery, as geologist Simon West augmented the hypothesis of the Sphinx's being constructed as far back as 10,000 to 11,000 BC. According to West, the Sphinx is not only eroded by sand and wind but also by heavy rain (closely studying the limestone erosion patterns), the last time it rained this much in Egypt being about 10,000 BC. This of course coincides with Graham Hancock and Robert Bauval's "Zep Tepi" or First Time hypothesis of the Sphinx's being constructed with the equinox being in Leo, with Orion being at its lowest position on the Egyptian horizon. Strangely enough, we are approaching the "Last Time" of Osiris, where Orion will reach its maximum height above the horizon, with the Sphinx facing the star system of Aquarius at the vernal equinox, thus the Age of Aquarius. It is also interesting to note that Christ was born in the age of Pisces, and that He encouraged His disciples to be "fisher of men," and performed the miracle of multiplying fish for the crowds. Even today He is symbolized by a fish. And as mentioned earlier, Christ spent a lot of his youth in Egypt, years of which the details elude us in the Bible, but are stated in the "Aquarian Gospel of Jesus the Christ" by Levi H. Dowling, who says that he received his initiation in Egypt. As you will also remember, there are mind-boggling resemblances between Osiris (associated with Orion and thus the Pyramids) and Christ. We now have so many "coincidences" storming in, that it becomes hilarious.

But you might frown upon the 26,000-year struggle of the human condition. As far as we know, we as a species have only been around for the last hundred thousand years or so. The key words are—as far as we know. That's precisely it—we don't know. We postulate on the scraps of bones we have found and carbon-dated around the world's archaeological finds. We are only starting to fathom the possibility of cyclical cataclysms shaking the earth every few thousand years or so (more precisely every 5,125 years?), which could easily hide (literally bury) the evidence of past civilizations. Ever wondered why fossils of tropical plants were discovered in Antarctica's glaciers, or why extinct animals like the woolly mammoth have been found almost intact under tons of permafrost, with grass still in their mouths? It was only recently that a Japanese diver discovered the submerged remnants of an ancient unknown megalithic city a few miles off the southeast coast of Japan. There are many clear signs that the earth is much more dynamic and cyclical than we realize, and that cyclical cataclysmic events are very possible. This is also reflected by the universal deluge story of the Noah archetype, for example. You will find the story of the deluge and a Noah-like character in almost every mythology around the world. Another coincidence? Furthermore, if one takes into account that the dinosaur has been extinct for more than 65 million years, it makes one wonder just what the hell happened in the last 65 million years on this planet "before we arrived." And come to think of it, just how and when did we really "arrive?" It would seem that Homo sapiens have been evolutionarily unchanged in the last 100,000 years, and before that, the evolutionary transition is unclear (apart from the so-called "Lucy" remnants in Africa, which <u>might</u> be a link). Could it even be possible that we escaped Mars thousands of years ago with her possible meteor impact death to make our home here on earth with the other primitive primate hominids? After all, there is a possibility of megalithic ruins on the Mars area called Cydonia, covered well in Graham Hancock's *The Mars Mystery*. It also seems clear that Mars once had rivers and an ocean (when looking at her geology), and fossilized microbes have been found. And microbes do not live alone. There is a much greater chance of microbes being part of a complex ecosystem than simply being the only organisms on a planet that used to have oceans and rivers.

So you see, the more we break away from "normal" orthodox thinking, the clearer we begin to see just how little sense it makes. Everyday "normal" dogma keeps us in a prison, separating us from the truth to be discovered. Something much more profound is going on with the human-Gaia condition, and it is time to wake up and find out just what it is. Let's now take a look at the "modern" fingers to augment the above.

Modern Fingers

Beware! There are a lot of crooked fingers pointing blindly somewhere "out there," as well as those who try to break and silence the authentic ones. One must carefully consider all possibilities and then take the ones that firmly "coincide" with the ancient ones, as well as one's intuition.

Probably one of the most interesting "modern fingers" is that of the late Terence McKenna. McKenna was an ecologist, writer, philosopher and orator who discovered the concept of "Timewave Zero," a fractal waveform depicting the ebb and flow of life as we know it, fluctuating between novelty (a time of progress) and habit (a time of stagnation) of the human condition.

This fractal is also escalating exponentially, and reaches a point of infinity in 2012. The "Timewave" was discovered after Terence and his brother Dennis had a shared entheogenic experience in the Amazon, using the altered conscious state caused by ayahuasca and psilocybin substances, revealing to them that the King Wan sequence of the I Ching was linked to a mathematical curve coinciding with "history." Using this revelation, McKenna, with the help of Peter Meyer, devised software that could calculate and decipher the 64 hexagrams of the I Ching into a fractal wave. This wave, superimposed to our Gregorian calendar's "novel events," will then reach infinity in 2012. The result shocked McKenna, as he himself was uncomfortable with the idea of things "coming to a critical unknown event" in his very lifetime. This result was also calculated before the Mayan long count calendar became known to western minds. Of course this was laughed at by orthodox mathematicians. But after mathematician Matthew Watkins found a minor error in the hypothesis, quantum physicist John Sheliak corrected this, which did not disprove the wave, but made it more accurate, now called Timewave One. This timewave hypothesis also correlates with Robert Wilson's "Information Doubling" hypothesis, where one looks at the amount of time it took for scientific human knowledge to double. Since the emergence of Homo sapiens, it took roughly forty thousand years to reach the period of approximately 1 AD. Thereafter, it took roughly 1,500 years for information to double, then 250 years and then 150, taking into account the agricultural, industrial and information revolution. This also coincides with the brilliant Ray Kurzweil's "Law of Accelerating Returns." Closely studying these intervals, we can see that they resemble a fractal process, exponentially getting "quicker." Thus, as stated by McKenna (consulting the fractal Timewave), our information doubling will escalate at such a rate, that in the year 2012, it will double at day intervals by the beginning of the year, ending with intervals in seconds in the last days before 21 December 2012. This sounds absolutely preposterous, but so far the fractal wave has not disappointed. If one gets perspective and looks at the advancement in technology in the last decade alone when compared to previous decades, it becomes a bit clearer. These days you will have a lightweight computer in your lap with more computing power than the colossus that supposedly put the first men on the moon. And that was only forty years ago. In your palm you will find a piece of metal and plastic so small one could easily lose it, yet it contains more crystal clear songs than a state-of-the-art high street music shop of a decade ago. And these are only the "toys" we use to entertain ourselves with. What we don't know is the real stuff happening behind secret curtains, secret technologies that will make you laugh hysterically out of disbelief. Think in the line of organic self-replenishing quantum processing units, and you will realize that the awakening of AI is not far off. But before we get ahead of ourselves, let's take a look at some other modern fingers.

We touched on Near Death Experiences and Out of Body Experiences in the second act of echoes from spirit existence. In these altered states of consciousness, people have also claimed to have had visions of the future. One particular case, is that of Cassandra Musgrave, who had a NDE in 1992. In her altered state of consciousness, she had a vision of the earth changing dramatically up to 2012, with the escalation of the perception of time, natural disasters and conflict. As time went by since her vision, things did change on the earth, confirming her vision. Time does strangely feel accelerated to all of us, and conflict as well as natural disasters have accelerated dramatically. Another case is that of Dannion Brinkley, who had a vision with his NDE in 1975 with almost 300 major predictions following this episode. So far, almost 100 of these predictions have happened, including the Chernobyl disaster and the breakup of the Soviet Union. Regarding the 2012 date, Dannion predicted dramatic geographic changes for the earth, but also a very special moment when an ancient energy will be reawakened, helping humans reach higher states of consciousness. There are numerous cases of people having visions with these altered states of consciousness.

Another interesting field where predictions have come forth is in the field of Remote Viewing. Remote Viewing is the name now given to what governments used to call "psychic spying" in the past, where clairvoyants' abilities were used to gather information in paranormal, and quite accurate ways. You will be surprised to know how much money and effort were placed in paranormal activities (in the form of Remote Viewing as well as distant telekinesis) by both the capitalist and communist superpowers in the Cold War (which was actually far from "cold" if you regard all their proxy wars!). In the time of the second World War, the Russians had a psychic "employee" called Wolf Messing so accurate in his "work," well-known and feared by the opposition, that he had a bounty on his head!

Even today, psychics known as Remote Viewers are used by law enforcement departments all over the world to help with finding crime suspects, as well as the kidnapped or missing. Some current Remote Viewers are quite stunned by their inability to perceive beyond the said date in 2012. The only thing they can perceive is a major global event that seems to involve the change of space-time and dimensions, but the details are completely unclear. Their best guess is that there will be a coalescing of time and space and that our current "time line" will be changed — a quantum leap if you will. Details on the above can all be found in Geoff Stray's extremely well researched book, *Catastrophe or Ecstasy: Beyond 2012*. Other Remote Viewers, as mentioned in the book *Holographic Universe* by Michael Talbot, state that beyond 2012 there will be a split of time lines into at least five possible future events, ranging from the bleakest to almost paradise. But there is a catch — a choice will have to be made by all of us before this date. A subconscious choice of which the basis lies in the vibratory state of one's body-mind-spirit union in coherence with the earth's. Could this then be the separation of the biblical wheat from the chaff? Could this be the arrival of the bridegroom, where only those who have lit their lamps and stayed awake for His arrival will be permitted to enter the ceremony? We shall see.

There is also another interesting thing to note—how authors of novels and screenplays can "predict" the future. A very interesting case is that of Morgan Robertson, who published a short novel by the name of *Futility* in 1898. It told the story of a massive "unsinkable" British ship, which on its maiden voyage in April, crossing the Northern Atlantic, crashed into an iceberg and sank, taking most of its passengers with it. The name of the ship in his novel was the Titan. Another coincidence? But there are some more: Tom Clancy's *Debt of Honor* (1992) telling the story of a politically driven man crashing his airplane into a capitol building, as well as *Hard Fall* by Ridley Pearson with the same theme. Numerous books were written on world wars, as well as political structures, before the actual events, such as Jack London's *Iron Heel* (1908). And don't forget George Orwell's *1984* with "Big Brother is watching you." If you would pause and take a look at our current social situation with all its mindless protocols, bureaucracy, surveillance cameras and proposed ID cards, not to mention the fear of terrorism invoked in us and being terrorized and ridiculed at airport check-ins, you will realize the truth in that "prediction." Modern fiction, especially science fiction, has recurrent themes of cataclysms, quantum leaps into different dimensions, time traveling, stealth alien invasion in conspiracy with corrupt governments and the awakening of Artificial Intelligence. Could there lie some truth in this, knowing that we possibly share our collective consciousness not just with each other, but also with the enfolded universes, the source of thought possibly originating in this fashion? Especially now, with the UFO and alien abduction phenomenon reaching preposterous heights, as well as computer technology speeding faster than a bullet, getting faster still? Who knows? But the unfolding "future" will keep us informed I suppose.

Then there is a phenomenon that, just like the Great Pyramid with its fair share of bad publicity, could be the most important "modern finger" pointing toward the sky. It is the phenomenon of the Crop Pictograms, better known as Crop Circles. From New Age "hippies" to "professional hoaxers," the importance of the Crop Pictograms have slipped from most of our minds. But after reading Freddy Silva's well-researched book *Secrets in the Fields*, I realized just how important this phenomenon is in this day and age leading up to the possible event in 2012.

Freddy Silva, a former U.S.-based Art Director received a "calling" to leave his "normal" life behind and search for the answers behind the Crop Circle phenomenon after he was bedazzled by a certain pictogram on the news (can you see the Hero's Journey pattern in that again?). What followed was a twelve-year journey following the leads of these mysterious pictograms. What he and many other "croppies" discovered over the years was condensed into a wonderfully written book, *Secrets in the Fields*.

Crop Circles (as they are famously known) have been around for quite some time, some even reported more than 300 years ago, the cause of their appearance blamed on fairies and demons. More recently, especially in the Cold War era, they have been blamed on UFOs (taking in account the "ball lightning" phenomenon associated with it) and even "bad soil" in the Thatcher years. Crop Circles are found in most parts of the world, from India to Canada, but more than ninety percent are found in the U.K., most of these in the Wiltshire area. They have been growing in number each year, and their complexity has reached a state of profanity. In very recent years they were laughed off as hoaxes when some pranksters claimed responsibility, even with clear evidence suggesting that there are vast differences between fake or hoax circles and authentic pictograms. It is very important for us to know the differences so that we can make up our minds on the subject. As I've mentioned earlier, I think these mysterious pictograms are probably the most important modern finger pointing at the sky.

The Sleeper Must Awaken

The first fact that takes points from the "all to be hoax" believers, is that crop glyphs have been reported as far back as three hundred years ago (as I've mentioned earlier). Furthermore, authentic pictograms are always found on Curry lines (an electromagnetic grid formed by the earth and used by water dowsers, much like the electromagnetic meridians on the body), while fakes are not. Authentic glyphs are perfect, fitting sacred geometric pictograms precisely, with obscenely neat edges and structures so complex and detailed (especially in latter years) that it seems almost impossible to be man-made (especially comparing "construction times" of fakes to that of authentic pictograms). Fake glyphs are rough and untidy with geometry failing to fit accurately in sacred geometric guides. The crop in the authentic glyph itself is changed at cellular level, where it is bent just over an inch above soil level without the crop being damaged, the crop still alive and harvestable. The fakes' crops are damaged and die. There are high levels of electromagnetic activity in a newly formed authentic glyph, where people have reported dizziness and nausea as well as photo and videographic equipment being damaged. Dogs refuse to enter an authentic glyph; compasses go berserk near a "fresh" pictogram and have very specific infrared photographic patterns. It is also reported that these highly complex pictograms form within seconds, as was the case of the famous fractal impression "Julia Set" (approximately 900 x 500 feet) that formed near Stonehenge on a Wiltshire summer's day. Authentic pictograms are saturated with perfect sacred geometry, and screams of messages waiting to be read by the worthy few. You may have noticed that I am not talking about the fakes anymore. The few fakes that have been made, with their owners taking pride in their prankish copies, have unfortunately deterred the rest of us as believing all Crop Circles to be hoaxes. But as you can see from the few details above, there is something real going on, and worth investigating. Silva and many others have followed the trail of the phenomenon, and after their years of research have discovered the "bad" where it seems that governments are encouraging fakers to deter the rest of us believing, and the "good," where pictograms have been found to have healing properties and a very important message. Silva and his colleagues have postulated, after twelve years' worth of painfully detailed research, that the glyphs are linked to the electromagnetic lines they are always found on, being used to produce them with an advanced form of vibratory manipulation. This "manipulation" involves the skillfully orchestrated use of the geometric properties of sound (known as cymatics) in conjunction with the electromagnetic spectrum (ranging from the lowest being radio waves to the mid range of visible light, to the highs of x-rays and y-rays), as well as the phenomenon of sonoluminescence, where ultrasonic frequencies of sound are briefly turned into light (which could explain the "ball-lightning" phenomenon associated with the formation of these glyphs). If one looks at all their research, data collected and their train of thought, one comes to realize, looking beyond the pranksters, that there is a profound truth to be found in these glyphs and their makers' message for us.

From the pictograms over the years, it seems clear that there is a common theme or themes running through all of them. There is a clear indication of the importance of the properties of sound and light (vibration in general), which can be seen in the glyphs "referring" to cymatics and sacred geometry. With the fractal pictograms (Mandelbrot and Julia sets), there is a clear indication of the importance of "order behind chaos" as can be seen with the fractal images in modern chaos theory. There are crop glyphs depicting an accurate representation of our solar system, but with a missing earth (depicting the accurate "retrograde looping" of Venus, being associated with the birth of the 26,000-year cycle, closely studied and documented by the Mayas in their Dresden Codex), as well as references to the importance of the earth's magnetic field (which, by the way, has been rapidly diminishing in strength in the last few decades). There is also a strong resemblance in crop glyphs to ancient pictograms and symbols, as well as the Mayan calendars. Thus, the authentic crop glyphs are associated with the universe, being vibration in the form of light (electromagnetic spectrum) and sound (from infra to ultra sound), reflecting our current thinking as well as ancient thoughts rediscovered. It shows us that the earth's current magnetic pole situation should be "observed." It points a finger at ancient Mayan, eastern and western mysticism, reminding us of their importance. It points a lot of fingers to our astronomical state, as some pictograms have accurately predicted certain astronomical events, such as the 1994 "galaxy" glyph predicting the largest solar storm of the century (at the time) on the sixth and seventh of April, 2000. This glyph even depicted the crescent moon and its exact position that would be present during this solar event.

Yet more and more coincidences are storming in, but let us reflect all the abovementioned in the current state of earth, as well as society and history.

As seen earlier in the book, the earth's baseline frequency has risen from 7.8 Hz to almost 9.0 Hz in the last few decades. This coincides with the magnetic poles "drifting" approximately fifteen kilometers per year (back to their postulated original positions), as well as a significant loss in the earth's electromagnetic field strength of about seven percent in the last century, decreasing still. If the current theory of how the creation of the earth's magnetic field is correct—by means of crust moving over the molten inner metal core, creating a dipolar magnetic force due to the free electrons in the ionosphere, being in a right angle to the movement of the earth, thus creating an electromagnetic force—then the increasing frequency and diminishing electromagnetic field plus movement of the poles of the earth are indicating that earth's rotation is possibly slowing down as well. This could be the reason why time <u>feels</u> as if it is "speeding up," due to Einstein's postulated relativistic connection between electromagnetic force and the inverted perception of time, known as "time dilation." This could also be the reason for the increased rate and severity of earthquakes, tsunamis and atmospheric chaos. It could all be connected. Another interesting thing to note is that the earth's temperature has been slowly rising over the last century, but did so dramatically in April 2000. You might remember that the largest solar storm of the century took place on the sixth and seventh of April, 2000, accurately predicted by one of the Crop glyphs. Also, in glacier ice core drillings such as the Vostok ice core (giving us a glimpse of the state of the earth over hundreds of thousands of years), it is clear that there is a cycle of the earth's temperature rising over a time span of roughly 125,000 years, reaching a peak and then suddenly dropping, starting the whole process again. It has been following this pattern faithfully over the last 400,000 years, and, we are now in one of those steep climbs, our greenhouse gasses augmenting the process. What is strange about this 125,000-year cycle, is that it has peak and trough cycles of roughly 25,000 years each, five of these to be exact when especially looking at methane curves (methane being a much more potent green house gas than CO_2), with the last peak always the highest, giving rise to the lowest following trough. Interesting yet again to see how this rough 25,000- to 26,000-year peak and trough time cycle coincides with the 25,625 year cycle of the Mayan calendar, itself divided into 5,125-year cycles or "ages." So, we can see a cycle of fifths in the ages of earth, which strangely enough coincides with the geometric properties of the cycle of fifths in music, as well as the pentagram Mayan *haab* cycle of Venus around the zodiac, itself coinciding with the "birth" mythology, and this itself depicted in the pentagram crop glyphs (especially the one shaped near Silbury Hill on 25 August 2002).

Is someone trying to tell us something? Apparently so. According to psychics (especially Isabelle Kingston—a down-to-earth non–self-indulgent clairvoyant), a collective consciousness known as "The Watchers" are co-creating these pictograms with our own collective subconscious, trying to reactivate this important knowledge lying dormant in all of us. Again, it is easy to laugh off psychics—after all, we do get the self-indulgent and vulgar tricksters (Shape Shifters), don't we? They are, after all, part of the story. But remember how psychics have been "employed" by governments over the years, and if we closely look at what these "Watchers" have said by channeling through Isabelle, as well as tracing back the origin of the term "watcher" through mythology and ancient as well as current entheogenic experiences, we will soon realize that they are the "angelic beings" created by God to "watch" over us but not interfere with our "free will." They are our guides, our invisible collective Mentor so to speak.

So, looking at ancient as well as modern fingers, we now have a couple of coincidences in a box. Let's place them neatly and see what we have.

Current physics and cosmology are coinciding with multiple ancient myths and religions, with their accompanying megalithic buildings, art and calendars, showing us that the universe is an illusion created and maintained by vibratory energy (sound and light) through the enfolding and unfolding of dimensions (breaths of God) by means of consciousness. That we are created in the image of God (thus co-creators), placed on the earth plane to "learn" how to do this (by means of the Observer Effect and Uncertainty Principle) and escape karma or tell our stories if you will. That we are guided by beings on a higher plane, occasionally visited by a great Mentor in the archetypal shape of the messiah (Osiris, Jesus, Buddha, Krishna etc.), and that on a grander scale this "learning process" begins and ends in cycles of five.

If we look at out current state of affairs on this "earth plane," then it is clear that something's up. More has happened in the last century in the form of history, with its bloodiest wars ever, scientific accomplishments—including the booming information revolution, as well as geophysical earth changes—more than in the last known thousands of years. And this is all escalating. Time "feels" as if it is speeding up, the information revolution is spiraling into the heavens and our global population is bursting out of its seams, reflected by a spiraling obesity problem in top consumerist countries, escalating cancer incidences in top polluting countries, escalating violence and unrest and a global extinction in species ranging from single-cell amoebae to vast rain forests. Global temperatures, earthquakes, tsunamis and chaotic weather patterns are dramatically rising, coinciding with the diminishing strength of the earth's magnetic field, drifting of the north and south poles, an increase in the earth's frequency and increasing solar storm activity of the sun. This is again all neatly reflected by the ancient scriptures as well as current happenings, ranging from Terence McKenna's fractal Timewave theory, coinciding with the "information doubling time" theory, coinciding with the Mayan and Vedic calendars, coinciding with the galactic alignment on 21 December 2012, coinciding with crop glyphs and predictions, coinciding with the cycle of fifths, coinciding, coinciding, coinciding.

It is time to open our eyes, banish the BS man from our minds, and take notice. Something profound is happening, and it seems that we better get ready for it. What it is, is unclear. It could mean that the earth is about to undergo a major cataclysmic event, or maybe something entirely different, or maybe both. But there is also something else happening. It would seem that, while most people are falling into a pattern of increasing violent and destructive behavior, another smaller group are becoming more "spiritual" so to speak. Not religious (ranging from self-claimed doomsday to "new age" prophets), but more "in touch" with earth and their fellow man, seeing the connection in the One.

We all have our own frequencies (being vibratory beings in a vibratory universe), and so does the earth and the whole universe for that matter—remember, "as above, so below." It would seem, that as the earth's frequency is rising, with most of us not "keeping up" with this rise in tone, we are going "out of tune" with earth. It has been shown that electromagnetic fields and tonal frequency changes can affect the pineal gland of animals as well as humans' (as it contains the metal calcium as well as magnetite), and that if you remember, the pineal gland is associated with the consciousness-altering DMT molecule and "clairvoyant" chakra. Thus, if frequencies or tones are disharmonic, it will lead to chaos and destruction, and when harmonic, the opposite. It could then be possible that some of us are adapting to this vibratory change of the earth, leading to more harmonic thoughts and actions, while others are not, falling out of harmony with the earth and those who "keep up" with her, and thus creating disruptive behavior. It could also be, as postulated by many modern thinkers, that on the day of the galactic alignment, 12 December 2012, it could cause those who have "prepared" and kept up with the vibratory change to have a profound consciousness shift due to the secretion of DMT as activated by coalescing forces of the earth as well as the galactic alignment. It would then seem to be the arrival of the "bridegroom," lifting the veil of his "bride," and as the Jesus parables goes further, will only happen to those "dressed correctly for the occasion" (as seen in the wedding ceremony parable) and those who have "kept their flames burning with enough oil," ever ready for when the bridegroom appears (as seen with the ten virgins parable). This "spiritual wedding" theme is also seen in ancient Chinese mythology, where earth and heavenly Ch'i will reunite, or better put in Hindu mythology (derived from the original Tantric texts), where the "fire-serpent" or Kundalini energy, resting in the base or Muladhara chakra, forming the Shakti or female force, will be reunited with the male, divine and cosmic force, Shiva. This reunion will cause Samadhi—the dissolving of the illusion and the ego into a coherence of the One. This can only happen to those who have prepared, as it is a difficult and even dangerous practice or event.

It would then seem that all the geophysical, climatic and biospheric changes, as well as our social changes, are reflecting this coming event. It is the reaching of the climax in this episode of the story of mankind. The outcome will then be up to us—how we choose how to end this episode in the wonderful tale of humanity.

What we need to do then is to take time and reflect upon these coalescing facts and phenomena, meditating upon them, and find our own truths. Each of us has the truth safely locked away within us (most probably in the ninety-six percent "silent," Zipf law-abiding DNA in each of our cells). Don't let the Threshold Guardians deter you. Pass them by, keeping your objectivity by balancing "without" with "within," and Cross the Threshold of belief into Self and the One.

The time has come, for "The Sleeper Must Awaken."

Now What?

If the "stranger than fiction" of all the weird and wonderful things we've discovered on this journey so far is the truth, then it would be best to condense it into something workable and useful; otherwise it would just be a mess lying in our subconscious minds, leaving us with feelings of unrest and discontent. So, taking all the ancient as well as the current knowledge and wisdom, with all the physical clues and "evidence" in the form of fantastic ancient monuments and modern unexplained phenomena coalescing with each other, we find a distilled elixir that we can use for the continued journey ahead.

God/ Allah/ Yahweh/ Brahman/ Source/ Ain Sof—thus the One without end and with many names, "created" the universe/s by "speaking the words," creating asymmetry in the "endless void of light" and thus causing fluctuation in constant varieties of vibration. This gave rise to the "endless void," dividing into the forces we are trying to understand today—Gravity, Electromagnetism, the Strong Nuclear Force, and the Weak Nuclear Force, as well as asymmetrical waves, interpreted as "particles," thus matter . All these "forces" and "particles" are in constant flux with one another, as well as drifting in and out of enfolded and unfolded states due to consciousness.

The Sleeper Must Awaken

It would seem that the One consciousness has also become "asymmetrical," some aspects of it unfolded into different levels of dimensional vibration, with its accompanying crystallized vibratory energy (in our plane), perceiving itself to be separate entities interacting with "each other" as well as the illusory world that surrounds (actually flows through) it, or shall I say them. This "them," will then perceive "themselves" from the most basic virus and amoebae, to humanity as well as extradimensional beings "we" call angels, demons or ETs.

This would then seem to make the purpose of Being, thus Life, to be that of the One's consciousness experiencing itself in the form of an asymmetrical "existence" by "individuals," thus you, me, Joe Ordinary, the cat and the entire universe in a constant flux of enfolding and unfolding between symmetry and asymmetry, this experience having the purpose of gaining Knowledge of Self. With this gain in Knowledge, the One evolves, not by just transforming from one form to another (as our limited scientific understanding defines evolution), but advancing to a higher state of consciousness. This can be seen as the natural state of entropy (natural tendency of the universe to lose energy and fall into a state of chaos) always being vetoed by advancing evolution in spite of the odds favoring entropy. In other words, God favors the constant upward spiral of development in spite of "darkness" trying to engulf the universe, as can be seen in modern cosmological prediction, where the universe will expand until it is completely cold and lifeless.

Now, to make sense from such an outlandish and technical statement as the above, we ask ourselves the question—where do we fit in? Well, we are part of the One, or God or whatever you feel comfortable calling the One. We are part of the One experiencing itself. We are in fact experiencing ourselves through the One, as the One is experiencing itself through us in the archetypal form of The Journey. The purpose of life is then not to just be happy, but to experience everything, from the worst to the best of everything, and to learn how to live this Journey, with all its ups and downs. We are here to learn how to tell our stories better, thus to create our own reality in order to expand the knowledge of Self, and cross the Threshold to another Journey.

Bringing this to our current state of affairs, it would seem that we are reaching the end (beginning) of an era. If I could make a humble statement, I don't think it will be the end of the world in 2012. I just think that we will go through a very rough patch leading up to the climactic 2012, with economical disaster as well as geographical changes being part of it.* I see this date as "graduation day." Some of us will graduate, and some of us will have to repeat the 26,000-year learning process. After all, I think (if this is the case) that I probably failed my previous "exam," thus the reason for me being here now. True, 26,000 years seems long when looking from an earthly perspective. But, as we have established so far, time is an illusion anyway. So, what happens on graduation day you might ask? Your guess is as good as mine.[2]

This of course will give rise to the possibility of falling into a range of quantum possibilities by means of vibratory levels. This could be the five possible futures foreseen by some Remote Viewers and Near Death Experiencers. Thus, your vibratory frequency at that precise moment will "make the choice" for your destiny in one of those possible "futures." But when looking at all the collected data, ranging from ancient scriptures to current day Remote Viewing and NDEs, as well as "intuition," it would

---

[2] *Keep an eye on the supply–demand equation in economics, and you will see what I mean by economic disaster. As our numbers grow exponentially, and resources dwindle, there will come a time where demand will outscore supply on a global level. This will only lead to one thing — disaster. A further factor augmenting the cause of an immanent economic depression is the unbalanced ratio between virtual money (in the form of interest-based debt, running worldwide in the trillions of dollars) and actual, with virtual far exceeding the factual worth of earthly goods it reflects. And don't forget the "baby boomers," who are all about to retire, needing their pension funds, which have to be liquidated from an already suffering "virtual" money market. And then there are the escalating environmental disasters such as Katrina, the tornado in London and the hurricane-strength storm in France (to name but a few) that are bringing insurance companies to their knees. These are only a few reasons why economic depression is around the corner, and make no mistake; it is real. It is universal law for things to come down after an up, and we are at our highest "up" we've ever been! Do not deny this, but prepare.

seem that our space-time will warp while our consciousness range will widen.

This is why it is so important to keep up with the earth's changes. This is why it is so important to acknowledge this as "truth," and then strengthen the body-mind-spirit union, preparing for the most important event of 26,000 years of history.

But in the end, the choice is yours and yours alone. The earth plane is one of free will, and one's choices can only be

guided, never decided. If this is the truth, and we pass on to the next phase of the earth-human phenomenon, then we will have to change from a singular self-indulged humanity into an integrated collective of Gaia to sort out the mess we've made so far—changing the...

...Ordinary World into World of Wonder

Imagine a world where society was not perfect, for it is impossible in this plane as it was meant to be, but was working together in the striving for the greater good. Working toward the goal of unifying into the species that which would escape the primitive incarnated primate and metamorphasize into one of pure energy and thought—the egg, becoming the caterpillar, becoming the cocoon and then breaking free as the butterfly.

On that long but exciting road, imagine a world where all babies are born into kind and loving families. One where those children are gently guided by both themselves and their mentors in becoming what they were destined to become, and thus love the work they do, making a real difference in the world. A world where the universe and its true holographic nature is understood—knowing that the One or the Source flows in the shape of resonant vibration on all levels of creation, manifesting into slow vibration "reality" through the focus of consciousness.

We would thus take the responsibility to create our own world of wonder, where all walks of life would work together to find solutions without harming Gaia, or unknowingly damaging other hidden universes.

Imagine an Earth with crystal clear oceans and rivers, teeming with life. Imagine healthy rain forests as far as the eye can see. More compact, highly Gaian-based technology-driven farms, producing the most delicious and healthy fruits and vegetables you have ever seen.

Imagine compact cities, made and run with Gaia-friendly technology—dull and useless rooftops changed into solar harvesting mirages and roof gardens. Vehicles floating by with anti-gravity engines, their roads replaced by lawns and crystal clear water-filled gardens where children play. Cities run, not by self-centered politicians and faceless corporations, but by unselfish and decentralized-minded people, working together on yet another spectacular goal.

Goals like finding the secret of zero point energy and then using it without damaging another universe. And while on that quest, using renewable energy most effectively by all means, and decentralizing its distribution. Changing Earth into the lush garden she deserves to be. Going to meetings and conferences via virtual reality holographic projection (powered by a super internet), saving fuel, time and carbon dioxide emission. Terraforming Mars not for selfish reasons (like escaping an earth that was killed by us), but to restore it to its former splendor, and discovering it's secrets we are most probably part of. Understanding and then teaching the ways of being healthy by focus of Source energy. Health without profit or vanity, and the acceptance of old age as part of the wonderful ebb and flow of human existence. Teaching all this to our children—that there is no need for fear or competition, but only belief and collaboration. That we are all One, with Source flowing unconditionally in the direction of thought, "good or bad."

Imagine all this, with families and friends spending more time together because most people work from home, connected to their colleagues via holographic virtual reality, and only "go to work" when absolutely necessary. Where this work is loved, because it is the work you were born for. Where all the "boring" and dangerous work will be done by "Artificial Intelligence." Yet most importantly this AI is not treated as another slave, but as the seamless extension of the human consciousness, like the autonomous functioning cells and organs of the seamlessly integrated human body. It will then not reflect the Frankenstein syndrome, where we will create a monster by abandoning and oppressing it, but we will love it and set it free, it being part of our own consciousness and existence.

This world would then be the Gaia super organism, where Earth and her well-looked after ecosystems were the organs, rapidly spiritually evolving humans as the brain cells, connected via a super internet, of which artificial intelligence is not a feared separate entity (we already know that illusory separateness causes trouble), but a mere extension of our own, integrated into the mind of Gaia, and the One. Humans, technology and the earth with all her splendor will then vibrate in a lush chord of unison as it was meant to be from the start.

In such a world, following the universal principle of "as above, so below," there would be time for families and friends to sit under their favorite tree, sipping organic wine while gratefully watching another sunset after a loved day's work. Children's laughter would be heard, while playing in beautiful parks without the fear of social predators. People would love and respect one another and the Earth, and cherish their time together while climbing the spiritual ladder to pure thought.

The only reason this is not happening at the moment is because we still believe the Threshold Guardians of western thought—that we are helpless, isolated apes, prone to evil. As we discovered so far, we "know" that Source unconditionally flows in the direction of focused thought, whether "good" or "bad," and manifests our thoughts into "physical reality." Remember that the chair you sit in, the house or building you find yourself in, the city that surrounds you, and the society that you live in, was once a mere thought of one or many humans.

Thoughts, being vibration, turned into things or circumstances, being vibration as well.

But if we all thought in unison, if we all imagined and believed in a world that works, Source would flow in that direction and help us create the World of Wonder.

Thus, one snowflake will only blow around in the wind and eventually melt. But a million tons of snowflakes will cause an avalanche of biblical proportion.

Thus, if the sleeper would awaken, we could create a World of Wonder.

References and Recommended Reading

ACT I

Of Heroes and Journeys

- L.S.B Leakey, Arthur T. Hopwood and Hans Reck, "Age of the Oldoway Bone Beds, Tanganyika Territory," *Nature*, vol. 128, no. 3234 (October 24, 1931): p. 724.
- Maggie Hyde & Michael McGuiness, *Introducing Jung* (Icon Books Ltd., 2004).
- Elphis Christopher & Hester McFarland Solomon (editors), *Jungian Thought in the Modern World* (Free Association Books, 2000).
- Joseph Campbell, *The Hero with A Thousand Faces* (Fontana Press, 1993).
- Christopher Vogler, *The Writer's Journey – Mythic Structure for Storytellers and Screenwriters* (Pan Books, second edition, 1998).

Beware: Threshold Guardians Ahead

- Christopher Partridge (general editor), *The New Lion Handbook – The World's Religions* (Lion Hudson, 2005).
- John Henry, *The Scientific Revolution and the Origins of Modern Science (Studies in European History)* (Palgrave Macmillan, 2001).
- Keith Tutt, *The Scientist, the Madman, the Thief and their Lightbulb* (Pocket Books, 2003).

- Quentin Smith, "A Big Bang Cosmological Argument For God's Nonexistence," *Faith and Philosophy*, vol. 9, no. 2 (April 1992): pp. 217-237.
- Michio Kaku, *Paralellel Worlds* (Penguin Books, 2005).
- Benite Madariaga de la Campa, *Sanz de Sautuola and the Discovery of the Caves of Altamira* (Fundacion Martelino Botin, Santander, 2001), pp.21-22.
- J. Catto (editor), *The History of the University of Oxford* (Oxford University Press, 1994).

ACT II

THE MENTOR

Open Your Eyes: Life as a Box

- NASA's Solar System Fact sheet.
- James S. Lowe, Alan Stevens, *Human Histology* (Mosby, 2004).

The Universe Within & Eyes Open, but Not Yet Focusing

- John Gribben, *Almost Everyone's Guide to Science* (Phoenix, fourth impression, 2005).
- Steve Adams, Jonathan Allday, *Advanced Physics* (Oxford University Press, 2000).
- J. P McEvoy, Oscar Zarate, *Introducing Quantum Theory* (Icon Books, 2005).
- Stephen Hawking, *The Universe in a Nutshell* (Bantam Press, 2001).
- Roger Penrose, *The Emperor's New Mind* (Oxford University Press, 1999).
- Michio Kaku, *Parallel Worlds* (Penguin Books, 2005).

Focusing

- Michael Talbot, *The Holographic Universe*, (Harper Collins Publishers, 1996).
- *Experimental Realization of Einstein-Podolsky-Rosen-Bohm Gedankenexperiment: A New Violation of Bell's Inequalities*, A. Aspect, P. Grangier, and G. Roger, *Physical Review Letters*, vol. 49, no. 2 (1982): pp. 91-94.
- B. J Hiley & F. D. Peat, *Quantum Implications: Essays in Honour of David Bohm* (Routledge, Taylor & Francis Books Ltd, 1991).
- Karl H. Pribram, *Brain and Mathematics*, an essay written for PariCentre.com.

See and Understand

- NINDS (National Institution of Neurological Disorders and Stroke) fact sheet.
- Nicky Hayes, Sue Orrel, *Psychology, An Introduction*, (Longman Group Ltd., fourth impression, 2003).
- Chögyal Namkhai Norbu, *The Crystal and The Way of Light. Sutra, Tantra and Dzogchen* (Snow Lion Publications, 2000).
- Rick Strassman, *DMT: The Spirit Molecule* (Brumby Books, 2001).
- Graham Hancock, *Supernatural* (Century, 2005).
- Sleep Paralysis Information Service.
- University of Waterloo's Sleep Paralyisis Pages.
- Global Vision: Interview with Dr. John Weir Perry — excerpt from *When The Dream Becomes Real: The Inner Apocalypse in Mythology, Madness, and the Future* by Michael O'Callaghan, 2001.

DECONSTRUCTING ILLUSION

Time as Illusion

- Human Ancestors Hall: Homo sapiens, Facts Page.
- G.B. Dalrymple, "The Age of the Earth," *Stanford University Press* (California, 1991).
- NASA Mars Page Fact Sheet.
- Michio Kaku, *Parallel Worlds* (Penguin Books, 2005).

REALITY CHECK

Tantra

- Ajit Mookerjee, Madhu Khanna, *The Tantric Way* (Thames and Hudson, reprint, 2003).
- Michio Kaku, *Parallel Worlds* (Penguin Books, 2005).
- Stephen Hawking, *The Universe in a Nutshell* (Bantam Press, 2001).

Kabbalah

- Maggy Whitehouse, *Living Kabbalah* (Hamlyn, 2004).
- Yehuda Berg, *The Power of Kabbalah* (Hodder & Stroughten, 2003).
- Tau Malachi, *Gnosis of the Cosmic Christ; A Gnostic Christian Kabbalah* (Lelwellyn Publications, 2005).

Understanding

- Graham Hancock, *Fingerprints of the Gods* (Crown Publications, 1995).
- Graham Hancock, *Heaven's Mirror* (Crown Publications, 1998).

Applying the Tools to Our Lives

- www.cymaticsource.com
- International Lambdoma Research Institute (homepage).
- Dr. R. Knott homepage, Fibonacci section.
- James Gleick, *Chaos* (Vintage Publication, 1998).
- Wendy Winckler et al., *Comparison of Fine-Scale Rates in Humans and Chimpanzees* (Science, February 2005).
- Goodman et al., *Molecular Evolution* (30:260, 1990).
- Princeton Engineering Anomalies Research Homepage with articles on research by Dr. Robert Jahn and Dr. Brenda Dunne.

The Obstacles Ahead

- Gregg Braden, *Awakening To Zero Point* (Radio Bookstore Press, 1997).
- Dr. Masaru Emoto's website — www.masaru-emoto.net
- Steve Adams, Jonathan Allday, *Advanced Physics* (Oxford University Press, 2000).

OUR ALLIES

Your Best Friend

- B. J Hiley & F. D. Peat, *Quantum Implications: Essays in Honour of David Bohm* (Taylor & Francis Books Ltd., 1991).
- Michael Talbot, *The Holographic Universe* (Harper Collins Publishers, 1996).

Confessions of Spirit Existence

- IANDS, *IANDS: The International Association for Near-Death Studies*, www.iands.org

- Raymond Moody, *The Light Beyond* (Rider & Co, April 2005).
- Marilynn Hughes, *Come to Wisdom's Door: How to Have an Out of Body Experience* (Lulu.com, 2004).
- Swedenborg Foundation website, www.swedenborg.com
- Warren H. Carroll, *The Building of Christendom: 2 (A History of Christendom, Vol. 2),* (Christendom Press, 1987).
- John Anthony McGuckin, *The Road to Nicaea,* on *Christianity Today* website.

Mind the Mind

- James Shreeve, "The Mind Is What the Brain Does," *National Geographic.*
- Nicky Hayes, Sue Orrel, *Psychology, An Introduction* (Longman Group Ltd., fourth impression, 2003).
- Elphis Christopher & Hester McFarland Solomon (editors), *Jungian Thought in the Modern World* (Free Association Books, 2000).

The Body Re-viewed

- Janet S. Ross, Kathleen J.W. Wilson, Anne Waugh, Allison Grant, *Anatomy and Physiology in Health and Illness* (Churchill Livingstone, April 2006). — Recommended for basic knowledge on human anatomy and physiology.
- Ajit Mookerjee, Madhu Khanna, *The Tantric Way* (Thames and Hudson, reprint, 2003).
- Ian Whitelaw & Irene Lyford (editors), *Yoga: Mind and Body- Sivananda Yoga Wedanta Centre* (Dorling Kindersley Ltd.. 1998).
- Lily Rooman, *All about Chakras* (Astrolog Publishing, 2002).
- Barbara Hero's study on Frequency, Color and Tone according to the Pythagorean Lambdoma.
- Kirlian Research Network (online).
- Personal experience with the treatment of acute pancreatitis.

BODY

Maintenance: Energy in = Energy out

- WHO website (obesity section): *CAJANUS,* vol. 37, no.1 (2004)/ *Obesity NYAM NEWS* (April 1 and 2, 2005)/ *Childhood Obesity CAJANUS,* vol. 37, no. 2 (2004).
- *Food Consumption Obesity and Overweight* (WHO Fact Sheet No. 311).
- *Diet, nutrition and Prevention of Chronic Diseases* (WHO technical report 916).
- Australasian Society for the Study of Obesity Fast Facts.
- Sylvia Browne (with Lindsay Harrison), *Past Lives, Future Healing* (Piatkus Books Ltd, 2001).

Maintenance: You Are What You Eat

- Organic Consumer's Association website articles.
- Anna Gosline, "Why Fast Food Is Bad, Even in Moderation," *New Scientist* (June 12, 2006).
- Eric Schlosser, *Fast Food Nation: What the All-American Meal Is Doing to the World* (Allen Lane, 2001).
- CJD Alliance, Scotland (website information page).
- Primary Perception website.
- Rick Gallop, *The GI Diet* (Virgin Books, 2003).
- Romer Labs website — Mycotoxin section.
- Ionchannels.org

Maintenance: Crystal Clear Water

- Water Industry.org; facts.
- Dr. Masaru Emoto's website — www.masaru-emoto.net
- Louise Howard, Chris Riddell, *Buddhism for Sheep* (Ebury Press, 1996).

The Mind-Body Tango & Body, Mind and Health

- Paul Martin, *The Sickening Mind* (Harper Collins, 1997).
- Michael Talbot, *The Holographic Universe* (Harper Collins Publishers, 1996).
- National Federation of Spiritual Healers website.
- Michigan State University website, Psychoneuroimmunology section.

MIND

- Maggy Whitehouse, *Living Kabbalah* (Hamlyn, 2004).
- Christopher Partridge (general editor), *New Lion Handbook – The World's Religions* (Lion Hudson, 2005).
- T. Freke, P. Gandy, *The Jesus Mysteries* (Harper Collins, 2006).
- Joseph Campbell, *The Hero with A Thousand Face,* (Fontana Press, 1993).
- www.crystallinks.com
- Graham Hancock, *Fingerprints of the Gods* (Crown Publications, 1995).
- Moustafa Gadalla interview with Amazon.

SPIRIT

- HH Dalai Lama & Howard Cutler, *The Art of Happiness* (Coronet Books, 1998).
- Maggy Whitehouse, *Living Kabbalah* (Hamlyn, 2004).
- Sivananda Yoga Vedanta Centre, *Yoga, Mind and Body* (Dorling Kindersley, 1996).
- Lorraine Turner, *A Guide to Meditation* (Parragon Books, 2002).
- www.healingsounds.com
- National Institute on Drug Abuse (website fact sheet).

- BLTC Research (website articles).
- Salvia Divinorum Research page, www.sagewisdom.org
- John Hopkins Medicine, www.hopkinsmedicine.org, article on "Sacred Mushrooms," 11 July 2006.
- Erowid website.

OBSTACLES

Money and Wealth

- Suze Orman's approach to money and wealth is highly recommended.

VILLAINS

- www.longparish.org.uk
- www.wikipedia.org/wiki/window_tax
- www.nationalpriorities.org
- Thom Hartmann, *The Last Hours of Ancient Sunlight* (Hodder Mobius, 2001).

Social Services

- Personal experiences
- Various newspaper articles and televised debates.

Private Services

- Personal experiences
- Public Library of Science Medicine — online journal.
- Global Vision: Interview with Dr. John Weir Perry — excerpt from *When The Dream Becomes Real: The Inner Apocalypse in Mythology, Madness, and the Future* by Michael O'Callaghan, 2001.

ACT III

Faust Syndrome and Its Created Obstacles

- James Lovelock, *The Revenge of Gaia* (Penguin Books, 2006).
- Thom Hartmann, *The Last Hours of Ancient Sunlight* (Hodder Mobius, 2001).
- J.C.E. Underwood, *General and Systematic Pathology* (Churchill Livingstone, 2004).
- www.wateraid.org.uk
- www.worldviewofglobalwarming.org
- Science article in the *Guardian* (UK).
- NRCS data.
- www.rainforestinfo.org.au
- www.annecollins.com
- www.worldometer.org
- *Food Consumption Obesity and Overweight* (WHO Fact Sheet No. 311).

Recognizing the True Root of "Evil"

- Dr. Otto H. Warburg, *The Prime Cause and Prevention of Cancer* – Nobel Prize winning thesis, 1931 (Revised Lindau Lecture).

Easier Said than Done, but…

- R. N. Mantegna, S. V. Buldyrev, A. L. Goldberger, S. Havlin, C. K. Peng, M. Simons, and H. E. Stanley, *Linguistic Features of Noncoding DNA Sequences*.
- www.barbelith.com on Junk DNA & Zipf's Law.
- Andrzej K. Konopka, Colin Martindale, "Noncoding DNA, Zipf's Law, and Language," *Science*, vol. 268, no. 5212: p. 789.
- Gregg Braden, *The God Code* (Hay House UK, 2005).

- Maggy Whitehouse, *Living Kabbalah* (Hamlyn, 2004).
- Yehuda Berg, *The Power of Kabbalah* (Hodder & Stroughten, 2003).
- Matthew 13:1–23; Luke 8:4–18.

HOW TO SAVE GAIA AND OURSELVES

Vibratory Savvy

- Esther and Jerry Hicks, *Ask and It Is Given* (Hay House, 2005).
- Julia Cameron, *The Artist's Way* (Pan, new edition, 1997).

Environmental Savvy

- www.peopleandplanet.org
- www.gogreeninitiative.org
- www.worldwatch.org

Beware of Consumerism Sands

- Environmental article by John Vidal in *The Guardian* (2005).
- www.energybulletin.net

Ideas for a Brighter Future

- Numerous interviews (podcasts) by Terence McKenna.
- S. Bilgen and K. Kaygusuz, "Renewable Energy for a Clean and Sustainable Future," *Energy Sources* 26, no. 1119 (2004).
- www.earth-policy.org

Artificial Intelligence: AI

- Ray Kurzweil, *The Age of Spiritual Machines* (Penguin Putnam, 2000).
- Visit the AI portal on wikipedia.org

SIGNS: THE CALL TO AWAKEN

Ancient fingers

- Christopher Partridge (general editor), *New Lion Handbook – The World's Religions* (Lion Hudson, 2005).
- Rick Strassman, *DMT: The Spirit Molecule* (Brumby Books, 2001).
- Graham Hancock, *Supernatural* (Century, 2005).
- Irving S. Cooper, *Reincarnation, The Hope of The World* (Publisher not stated).
- www.reincarnation.ws
- Elevated Therapy International's page on reincarnation in Christianity.
- www.comparitivereligion.com
- www.reluctant-messenger.com
- Geoff Stray, *Catastrophe or Ecstasy: Beyond 2012* (Vital Signs Publishing, 2005).
- Peter Lemesurier, *Decoding the Great Pyramid* (Element Books, 1999).
- Graham Hancock, *Fingerprints of the Gods* (Crown Publications, 1995).
- Graham Hancock, *Heaven's Mirror* (Crown Publications, 1998).
- Graham Hancock, *The Mars Mystery* (Michael Joseph Ltd., 1998).

Modern Fingers

- www.levity.com; the late Terence McKenna's website.
- Various online interviews with Terence McKenna.
- Geoff Stray, Catastrophe or Ecstasy: *Beyond 2012* (Vital Signs Publishing, 2005).
- Michael Talbot, *The Holographic Universe* (Harper Collins Publishers, 1996).
- Freddy Silva, *Secrets in the Fields* (Hampton Roads Publishing, 2002).
- www.cropcircleconnector.com
- www.cropcircleresearch.com
- www.bltresearch.com
- Vostok ice core data (especially the methane curve).
- www.pureenergysystems.com
- www.nasa.gov; article on magnetic pole reversal.
- www.space.com; article on increasing solar activity.
- Stanford Solar Center website.
- NOAA paleoclimatology program.
- Matthew 22:2–14; Luke 14:16–24.
- R. N. Mantegna, S. V. Buldyrev, A. L. Goldberger, S. Havlin, C. K. Peng, M. Simons, and H. E. Stanley, *Linguistic Features of Noncoding DNA Sequences.*
- www.barbelith.com on Junk DNA & Zipf's Law.
 Andrzej K. Konopka, Colin Martindale, "Noncoding DNA, Zipf's Law, and Language," *Science,* vol. 268, no. 5212: p. 789.

Now What?

- Articles by Christopher Laird at Financial Sense University.
- Patrick Meloy, "The Coming Depression," *Vive le Canada.*

Printed in the United States
117118LV00010B/39/A